Rationale Divinorum Officiorum by Guillaume Durandus

Volume Six
A modern translation of Books Seven and Eight

Translated by

Janet Gentles

Paschal Light

Copyright © 2019 Janet Gentles

All rights reserved.

ISBN: 978-1-913017-06-4

Contents

PREFACE TO VOLUME SIX	i
TRANSLATORS INTRODUCTION TO VOLUME SIX	iii
BOOK SEVEN	1
1. PREFACE TO BOOK SEVEN	1
2 SAINTS FABIEN AND SEBASTIAN	29
3 SAINT AGNES	30
4 THE CONVERSION OF SAINT PAUL	31
5 SAINT JULIEN	32
6 THE BLESSED AGATHA	33
7 THE PURIFICATION OF SAINT MARY	34
8 THE CHAIR OF SAINT PETER	44
9 THE ANNUNCIATION OF THE VIRGIN MARY	47
10 SAINTS APOSTLES PHILIP AND JAMES	50
11 THE FINDING OF THE HOLY CROSS	53
12 THE APPARITION OF SAINT MICHAEL	56
13 SAINTS GERVASE AND PROTASE	60
14 SAINT JOHN THE BAPTIST	61
15 SAINTS PETER AND PAUL	67
16 THE SEVEN BROTHERS	71

17 SAINT JAMES	72
18 THE SEVEN SLEEPERS	74
19 THE FEAST OF SAINT PETER'S CHAINS	76
20 THE MACCABEES	78
21 THE FINDING OF SAINT STEPHEN'S RELICS	79
22 THE TRANSFIGURATION OF THE LORD	80
23 SAINT LAWRENCE	82
24 THE ASSUMPTION OF THE GLORIOUS VIRGIN MARY	85
25 SAINT BARTHOLOMEW, APOSTLE	90
26 THE BEHEADING OF SAINT JOHN THE BAPTIST	91
27 SAINTS FELIX AND AUDACTUS	94
28 THE NATIVITY OF BLESSED MARY	95
29 THE EXALTATION OF THE HOLY CROSS	98
30 THE FEAST OF SAINT MATTHEW, APOSTLE AND EVANGELIST	100
31 SAINT MAURICE AND HIS COMPANIONS	101
32 THE FEAST OF SAINT LUKE, EVANGELIST	102
33 THE FEAST OF THE APOSTLES SIMON AND JUDE	103
34 THE FEAST OF ALL SAINTS	105
35 THE OFFICE OF THE DEAD	108
36 THE FOUR-CROWNED, MARTYRS	126
37 THE BLESSED MARTIN, BISHOP AND CONFESSOR	127
38 THE BLESSED ANDREW, APOSTLE	129
39 THE BLESSED NICHOLAS	131
40 THE VENERABLE BEDE, PRIEST	132
41 SAINT THOMAS, APOSTLE	133

42 SAINTS STEPHEN, JOHN THE EVANGELIST, AND THE HOLY INNOCENTS	134
43 THE APOSTLES	142
44 THE EVANGELISTS	146
45 THE MARTYRS	152
46 THE CONFESSORS	158
47 THE VIRGINS	161
48 THE FESTIVAL AND OFFICE OF THE DEDICATION OF A CHURCH	164
BOOK EIGHT	169
1 COMPUTATION, THE CALENDAR, AND WHAT RELATES TO THEM	171
2 PART ONE, THE SOLAR YEAR	173
3 WHAT THE SOLAR YEAR IS	174
4 PART TWO, BEGINNING WITH THE MONTH	185
5 OF THE WEEK	194
6 OF THE DAY	202
7 WHAT THE LUNAR YEAR IS AND THE DAYS IT CONTAINS	205
8 THE REGULAR LUNAR NUMBERS	207
9 THE EPACT	209
10 THE EMBOLISM	212
11 THE GOLDEN NUMBER	217
12 THE EASTER TERM	220
13 THE CYCLE	227
14 THE CONCLUSION OF THE WORK	229
SCRIPTURE INDEX	231
SUBJECT INDEX	240

PREFACE TO VOLUME SIX

This volume contains the translation of the final two books of the *Rationale Divinorum Officiorum* of William Durandus. As Durandus has shown at length in the previous books, the Christian church reflects in its buildings, its leaders, its vestments and furnishings, and above all in its worship life, the glory of God's creation and redemption through Christ. Books Five to Eight continue this project by showing how all time is ordered according to the same spiritual patterns, through the Daily Offices (Book Five), through the liturgical year (Book Six), and now through the celebration of the festivals of saints (Book Seven), and the computation of the calendar (Book Eight).

Those who have read any of the previous books of this work will find that in Book Seven Durandus does not feel much of his usual need to suggest spiritual interpretations. He can simply list the various feast days of apostles, martyrs, confessors, and virgins, giving the reasons for their celebration and some description of how they are observed. Taken as a whole, these festivals serve to give medieval European Christendom a biblical and historical basis for both celebration and moral education. The reader today can approach this book seeking both information and spiritual inspiration.

Book Eight, on computing the year, month, week, and day by the solar year as well as the lunar phases, may seem to readers today to be a historical curiosity. But for Durandus these matters communicate to the people the majesty of God found in the relationship between the heavens and the earth. Further, for him it is obvious that the church is the keeper of time for society, and so accuracy is essential. So we can at least appreciate the reasons for his inclusion of this book on the calendar—nothing else that he describes in the previous books will work properly if time is not regulated according to God's created order.

Janet Gentles has been known to me for many years as a woman with wide-ranging and deep spiritual interests. Her passion for spiritual insight has taken her, not into realms of imaginative speculations or trendy practices, but into an examination of the spiritual depths of the Church's historic liturgy and the ancient traditions of the Jewish and Christian faiths.

When she became aware of the work of Guilluame Durandus, *Rationale Divinorum Officiorum*, she felt that here was a project that needed to be done—translating and publishing this entire work in an accessible format in English. She has translated and edited the entire eight books, organized into six volumes, with copious footnotes giving the biblical references and explanatory and historical information. This is not intended to be a work of historical scholarship, although I suspect that many scholars of liturgy and medieval history will find it useful. Rather, Gentles has produced an accurate and user-friendly English version that serves to introduce this work of Durandus to a wider audience. She believes that it will appeal to anyone who is interested in probing more deeply into the spiritual wisdom and practice of the high medieval flowering of spirituality in Western Christianity.

Rev. Dr. David Kuck
Lecturer in New Testament
United Theological College of the West Indies
Kingston, Jamaica

TRANSLATORS INTRODUCTION TO VOLUME SIX

In this volume we find the last two books of the *Rationale*. Book Seven focuses on some of the many feast days of the Church. The majority of feast days are to commemorate the lives of the saints and it is undoubtedly true that some of the lives of early saints (some of which are given in this book) descended into legend long ago. Nevertheless the saints are mentioned in the Canon of the Mass. Some found in this work are still recalled in Masses today, while others doubtless are those used during the author's time and have been replaced today. Why do we invoke the saints? Durandus answers this in Book Six, in the chapter *The Rogations*: 'It must be noted that we invoke the saints because of our shortfalls, because of their glory and out of respect for God.'

Now there are two points which should be born in mind when reflecting on the lives of saints in general.

The first is that they are put forward as examples of admirable Christian lives which we should aspire towards emulating. To do so specifically would be impossible but in a general sense they can serve as an inspiration to all. They reflect not only a deep commitment to, and also a willingness to sacrifice oneself for, in one way or another, Christ and His Church.

The second regards the origin and purpose of feast days. Origen addresses this in his work 'Against Celsus'. In chapter 22:

> *I have to answer, that to the perfect Christian, who is ever in his thoughts, words, and deeds serving his natural Lord, God the Word, all his days are the Lord's, and he is always keeping the Lord's day.*

> *He also who is unceasingly preparing himself for the true life, and abstaining from the pleasures of this life which lead astray so many,— who is not indulging the lust of the flesh, but 'keeping under his body, and bringing it into subjection,*[1]*—such a one is always keeping Preparation-day.*

In the next chapter he adds:

> *But the majority of those who are accounted believers are not of this advanced class; but from being either unable or unwilling to keep every day in this manner, they require some sensible memorials to prevent spiritual things from passing altogether away from their minds.*

The rigours of embracing a Christian life with intensity are tremendous and feast days can provide a refreshment from this for those who endeavour to tread this way. This applies particularly to those who live a disciplined monastic life. From another perspective these feast days also began to serve as a contrasting activity to the drunken and lascivious nature of pagan festivals. Christian feast days were for feasting on spiritual things as an occasional day of refreshment, in addition to Sundays, in contrast to being extensively engrossed in mundane activities.

Further inspiration and aspiration can be drawn from the saints by turning our eyes and hearts towards heaven and there perceiving those who have run the race before us and gained the prize.[2] Indeed, it is always worth remembering that baptism does not imply immediate salvation. Rather it is a commitment, with the help of Christ, to engage ever more fully with the journey. Among so many others the great St Paul recognized this of himself when he says, 'Not as though I had already attained, either were already perfect'.[3]

Book 8 deals turns its attention to the ecclesiastical year. The Christian calendar, with regards to its contents, dates from the fourth and later centuries. However with regards to its form, it

---

[1] See 1 Corinthians 9:27
[2] See 1 Corinthians 9:24, Hebrews 11:40, Hebrews 12:1
[3] Philippians 3:12

TRANSLATOR'S INTRODUCTION

comes down from classical antiquity, chiefly from the Romans. The Romans had numerous calendars which contained, together with astronomical and astrological notes, tables of civil and religious festivals and public sports. In the final book of the *Rationale* a detailed explanation is provided of the various components which constituted both these annual cycles and how the various days of the Christian calendar could be calculated.

This was doubtless of great importance to the clergy of that time not least of all because of the time taken in travel and the limited means of communication in comparison to today. For us, however, it can largely be seen as a historical relic although it does provide some interesting insights into how the use of simple verses resulted in great accuracy. It may also offer a greater understanding of the structure of the ecclesiastical year.

In the *Rationale* Durandus builds, in great detail, what could be described as a three dimensional spiritual structure. He shows not only how the spiritual journey can be seen as one of ascent but how this is also reflected through time, through the various ages of the world and the ages of man. However he is not entirely comprehensive in his explanations as he purposefully omits much, pointing towards even more profound spiritual truths without entering into them. The same is also to be frequently found in the writings of the Church Fathers and, indeed, in the Bible itself. Sometimes a seemingly nonsensical fact or an apparently totally irrelevant piece of information is added to what is being said. At other times a detailed explanation is begun but never completed. In most instances these are not reflections of the either the authors poor writing style or lack of knowledge. Rather they are pointers to an even more profound teaching, an unwritten *sapientia* or wisdom which has always been there for those who are spiritually prepared, able, and desirous of seeking it out.

Finally I would like to thank Rev. Dr. David Kuck for his encouragement and advice from the beginning of this project, for writing the prefaces of each volume and for his assistance with the ancient Greek. My thanks also to Mary Kuck for her many hours of skilful proofreading.

BOOK SEVEN

1. PREFACE TO BOOK SEVEN

1. Having first spoken of the Divine Offices in general, the Sunday services and the Lord's festivities in particular, it is useful for us to add something about the Offices of the saints' festivities in this seventh book. Certainly, the Church celebrates the feasts of the saints for many reasons. First, so that we may reciprocate; for they themselves celebrate feasts concerning us, since the angels of God and the souls of the saints experience great joy in heaven, 'over one sinner that repenteth.'[4] Secondly, because by honouring them we do our own proper actions, for their feast is ours too, hence the Apostle says, 'all are yours; And ye are Christ's.'[5] Thirdly, that they may intercede in our favour, which comes from reading in the third book of Kings[6] that Beersheba, which by interpretation means, 'the well of satiety,' that is to say, the Church Triumphant, obtained the kingdom for her son. Fourth, so that we may imitate them, for their examples excite us to imitate them. Fifth, to increase our security and raise our hope. For if men, mortals like us, could have been brought up so high by their merits, we could rise in the same way; because, 'the Lord's hand is not shortened.'[7] Sixthly, to honour the divine majesty whom we honour in the saints, when we honour them, and when we proclaim admirable the One who sanctified them. Seventhly, so that at the sight of their beauty and purity man remains

---

[4] Luke 15:7
[5] 1 Corinthians 3:22-23
[6] 1 Kings 1 First and Second Samuel are also called first and second books of Kings, First and second Kings then become third and fourth
[7] Isaiah 59:1

confounded, looking back at his own sins, and disdains the goods of the earth, as they did themselves.

2. The eighth and principal reason is that we recall the memory of the saints on the anniversary of their honour, for our own benefit, because in them we honour God. For, as they are perfectly happy, they do not need our prayers, since they have every wish; moreover, it is an insult to a martyr when one prays for him.

3. St John Damascene[8] provides other reasons why we must honour the saints, and also their bodies or relics. Among the reasons he gives, some relate to the dignity of these saints, others relate to the inestimable price of their bodies themselves. They are worthy of our veneration for four reasons; for they are the friends of God and the children of God, the heirs of God and guides to us. Regarding the first reason St John says, 'I call you not servants, etc.'[9] Regarding the second the same saint says, 'to them gave he power to become the sons of God.'[10] Regarding the third, the Apostle says, 'we are the children of God: And if children, then heirs; etc.'[11] Regarding the fourth, it is said, 'If anyone goes out of his way to find a guide who leads him to some mortal king and pleads his cause before this king, how much more must we not honour the guides of the human race, who intercede for us with God, erecting temples and venerating their memory?' The same John Damascene also gives four reasons for the inestimable price of their bodies. Indeed, the bodies of the saints were the sanctuaries of God, the temple of Christ, vessels containing spiritual fragrance, and springs of living water. St Augustine gives a fifth reason, namely, that they are the organ of the Holy Spirit. On the first quality it is said, 'For they are the sanctuaries of God, the cenacles of the Holy Spirit.' On the second, 'Since, because of understanding the God of Israel dwelt in the bodies of those men, as the Apostle says, "know ye not that your body is the temple of the Holy Ghost, etc."[12] Now, "God is

---

[8] St John of Damascus (Book 4, chap. 7)
[9] John 15:15
[10] John 1:12
[11] Romans 8:16-17
[12] 1 Corinthians 6:19

a spirit,"[13] we must therefore honour the animated temples of God. If man rejoices at the construction of the walls, God, for His part, rejoices at the conversion of the saints, as the psalm says, "Lord, I have loved the habitation of thy house;"[14] that is, what it affords to the diversity is not from the beauty of marbles, but the variety of graces.' On the third he says, 'If the water has escaped from the rock to flow into the desert, if it has sprung from the jaw of a donkey to quell Samson's thirst, it is not incredible that the relics of the martyrs, who were thirsty for the anointing oil of God, emanate a perfume and holy virtue.' On the fourth he says, 'For these saints live in the truth, who stand with the presence of God, and the master Christ has given us the salutary sources of His saints, their relics which, like a brook which fertilizes the earth, fill us with blessings which come in a thousand different forms.' Regarding the fifth St Augustine says, in his book the *City of God*, 'We must not despise, but on the contrary greatly honour the bodies of saints, who the Holy Spirit used as organs to operate uprightly when they were on the earth.' Also as the Apostle says, 'Since ye seek a proof of Christ speaking in me?'[15] For his part, Blessed Ambrose says in *Hexameron*, 'The most precious thing is that man is the organ of the divine voice and the lips of his body express the celestial oracles.'

4. Now, there are, in the New Testament, four different kinds of saints that we honour during the course of the year. Indeed, there are the Apostles, martyrs, confessors and virgins; and they are designated, according to Rabanus, by the four parts of the world. The east marks the Apostles, the south the martyrs, the north the confessors, and the west the virgins.

5. But, although one must celebrate the feasts of the saints and build altars in their memory, yet we must sacrifice to none of them, or even to the angels; we owe sacrifice to God alone. For never does a prelate, in the places where the bodies of the saints are, never does a prelates, standing at the altar, say, 'We offer you this sacrifice Peter, Paul or Cyprian.' Rather, what is offered is offered to God, who crowned the saints, in memory of those

---

[13] John 4:24
[14] Psalm 26:8
[15] 2 Corinthians 13:3

whom He crowned, so that the affection which they had has the effect of increasing, to our benefit, both the charity of the saints which we want to imitate and love for the one whom we can help. For neither the saints nor the angels want us to worship them in latria,[16] which they know to be due only to God alone. That is why Paul and Barnabus, seeing that some people, impressed by the miracles they were doing, wanted to offer them sacrifices as gods, so they tore their clothes confessing that they were only mortal men and not gods and forbade them to do so.[17] We read also in the Apocalypse that an angel, after having prevented John from worshiping him, in a vision, said to him, 'See thou do it not: I am thy fellowservant, and of thy brethren that have the testimony of Jesus: worship God.'[18] For already Christ had been raised above the angels. But, earlier, we read that the angels were adored, as was said in Book Four, in the chapter *The Fourth Part of the Canon*. Mordecai also refused to worship Aman, because he wanted to pay a tribute of worship that is due only to God.

6. One must therefore honour the saints by imitation, and not adore them by religion. They must be honoured with an honour of charity, and not of servitude, as has been said in the abovementioned chapter. We therefore pray to the saints for three reasons, as was said in Book Six, in the chapter *The Rogations*. And notice that we must remain standing when we venerate the saints, as was said in the *Preface* of Book Five, where consideration is given to the responsory. Now, regarding days, there are ordinary days and holy days or solemn days. Ordinary days are not marked by any special solemnity, and they are called, *profesti*, 'open,' as if it were said, *procul a festo*, 'far from the festivals.'

7. Also, notice that the Hebrews give a particular name to the days of the week, the Gentiles and their priests another, and the Christians a third. The Hebrews named all other days from the Sabbath, which is their main day. Thus, the day following the Sabbath, they call, 'the first day after the Sabbath,' the next they

---

[16] Latria is a theological term used in Eastern Orthodox and Roman Catholic theology to mean *adoration*, a reverence directed only to the Holy Trinity.
Dulia is of a lower order and refers to the *veneration* of angels, Mary and other saints.
[17] See Acts 14:11-15
[18] Revelation 19:10

call, 'the second day after the Sabbath,' and so on. On the seventh day, they simply call it, the 'Sabbath,' and sometimes, the 'Sabbath of the Sabbaths.'

8. They call the sixth day of the week, Parasceve'[19], from the Greek *para* which in Latin is *prae* (before) and *skeue*, which is *structio*, as like *praestructio*, or 'preparation.' The reason for this was because the Jews were preparing their food for the Sabbath, according to what was ordained to them on the subject of manna. Namely, 'on the sixth day they shall prepare that which they bring in; and it shall be twice as much as they gather daily,'[20] because they were not allowed to prepare food or gather manna on the Sabbath. For us, however, this is a name that is common to all Jewish Sabbath watches, we keep it on the Friday before Easter, because the food or manna is then prepared for us which the Church Militant now enjoys and will enjoy, when it will be in the Church Triumphant and in eternal rest. And note that *paraskeue*, is a Greek word; but the Jews, because of their various captivities having been scattered among the Greeks, borrowed some terms from the Greeks, such as, *paraskeue* and *sunagoge*,[21] and some others.

9. The Gentiles, both the crowd and the philosophers, call the days after the planets. Therefore, according to them, the first day is called the day of the sun; the second, the day of the moon, etc. Sacred Scripture has not admitted these names, although they are now in common use. This is discussed in Book Eight, in the chapter *Of the Week*. Now the people called them this, because they believed that the sun, the moon, Mars, and the other planets whose names they gave to the days, were gods. On the other hand, the philosophers named them in this way, because they said that it is the name of the planets, which, by their revolutions and their nature, give vegetation and life to all.

10. Now, Christians only designate two days by proper names, for they call Saturday *Sabbatum,* or simply Saturday or Sabbath, because of the authority of the Hebrew language. The next day they call the Lord's Day or Sunday, because of its primacy, which

---

[19] Good Friday
[20] Exodus 16:5
[21] synagogue

we shall speak soon of. Or because that day is so named in the legend of St John, where it says, 'John, on Sunday after Mass went down to the place that had been dug for burial.' Sunday could also be called first day of the week. The day following Sunday, Monday, would be called the second day of the week, the day after the third weekday, and so on the other days until Saturday.

11. Now, *feria*,[22] by interpretation, means, so to speak, a, 'solemn day,' and comes from *feriando*, 'cessation;' from which it follows that the first day of the week is solemn. Therefore, we call the festivals, *feriando*, 'to break because of a holiday,' because at all times we must feast, that is to say we abstain from vices, and not that it is necessary to abstain from the works necessary for life. Or this word comes from, *fando*, 'to be spoken of,' or *loquendo*, 'that which is spoken of or told,' because, as it says in Genesis that the Lord spoke, and all was created.[23] Indeed, Blessed Sylvester, not wishing to imitate the Jews who speak of, the first day after the Sabbath, the second day after the Sabbath, etc., nor the Gentiles who say, Sunday, Monday, etc., invented that name of *feria*.

12. However, at the end of the week, he kept, *sabbatum*, 'Saturday,' for the reason or for the figure, because, *Sabbath*, 'Saturday,' by interpretation, means *requies*, 'rest.' For it was then that the Lord, 'rested on the seventh day from all his work which he had made.'[24] Therefore we too, throughout our life, which extends over the period of seven days, must work and make the greatest efforts so that we come to rest and happiness.

13. So, the day is named in three ways. First, in itself, as day of the moon, day of Mars, etc. Secondly, according to the custom of the Church, as first weekday, second weekday, etc. Thirdly, in relation to the months, and this is in three ways. First, the day of the calends,[25] the day before the calends, the third of the calends;

---

[22] In the Catholic Church, *feria*, refers to a weekday other than Sunday. If a Saint's feast day falls on a day other than Sunday the liturgy either for that day or for the feast of the saint. So *feria*, a word which is seldom used nowadays, means a day of the week when no specific feast is celebrated. In this translation, *feria*, has been replaced by, 'day of the week'

[23] See Genesis 1

[24] Genesis 2:2

[25] The first day of the Roman month. See Book Eight

secondly, the day of the ides, the eve of the ides, the third of ides; thirdly, the nones, the day before the nones, the third of the nones.[26]

14. Now, Sunday obtains primacy and is the greatest among the other days, because Christ was announced, resurrected, and sent the Holy Spirit to the Apostles on that day, and because on that day God also made the world, that is, heaven and earth. It is on this same day also, it is said, that the world will be destroyed. It is called, *dominica*, 'Sunday,' because of the Resurrection of the Lord that we are celebrating on this day. Now, although some Sundays outweigh all others, such as those of Easter and Pentecost, because of the Resurrection and the sending of the Holy Spirit, yet there are five others which are called principal and solemn, in which the Offices are changed. These are the first Sunday of Advent, the Sunday in the octave of Easter, the Sunday in the octave of Pentecost, the Sunday on which *Laetare, Jerusalem*, 'Rejoice, Jerusalem,'[27] is sung, and Palm Sunday. Others add a sixth Sunday, namely the one where *Invocavit me*, 'He shall call upon me, and I will answer him, etc.,'[28] is sung. Some other Sundays are called privileged, namely which have Offices of their own.

15. Also note that there are certain days that are privileged during the time of Lent, namely four Wednesdays which are, Ash Wednesday, the Wednesday of the following week, the Wednesday after *Loetare, Jerusalem*, and the Wednesday before our Lord's Supper or Holy Thursday. There are also four Saturdays, namely the Saturday of the first week, when the orders are celebrated, also the fourth Saturday, the fifth Saturday and the Saturday which is Easter Eve. There are also three Sundays, namely the Sundays *Invocavit me, Loetare, Jerusalem*, and Palm Sunday. There is a Thursday, Holy Thursday (the Lord's Supper). There is a Friday, namely Good Friday (Parasceve). There is also a whole week, the last one, which is the biggest, as it was said in Book Six, in the chapter *The Sixth Sunday of Lent or Palm Sunday*.

---

[26] See Book Eight, Chapter 4
[27] Isaiah 66:10-11 The fourth, or middle, Sunday of Lent, which gets its name from the first words of the Introit at Mass, *Laetare Jerusalem*, 'Rejoice, O Jerusalem'
[28] Psalm 91:15 Quadragesima Sunday

We spoke in this place of these privileges. And note that Easter and Pentecost are weekly festivities, as it was said in Book Six, in the chapter, *The Seven Days after Easter*, and in the chapter *The Holy Day of Pentecost*.

16. The natural day, according to the Egyptians, begins at sunset or at the beginning of the night, and lasts until the evening of the following day, according to these words, 'And the evening and the morning were the first day.'[29] According to the Persians, the Greeks, and the general public it begins at sunrise; according to the Romans, in the middle of the night; according to the Athenians, the Arabs, and the astronomers, from the sixth hour of the day. We imitate all these different uses. For the celebration of the Divine Offices, the day begins at Vespers, according to these words, 'from even unto even, shall ye celebrate your Sabbath.'[30] With regards the observation of the truce,[31] at sunrise. As for contracts, the day begins and ends in the middle of the night. For the night fast it begins after supper until daybreak. As for judgments, it begins in the morning and ends in the evening, at the end of the day, before the darkness of the night. Now, the supposition of the Egyptians seems to be true, since it contains the rising and setting of the stars; however, it can be said that, according to the Church, the natural day begins in the middle of the night, because it is then that the true sun, that is to say the Christ, has risen, according to these words, 'For while all things were in quiet silence, and the night was in the midst of her course, Thy Almighty word leaped down from heaven, etc.'[32] Or more truly at Vespers, as has been said above, because the night has preceded and the day has then approached. For again, although of course the days precede the nights, yet in the Paschal night it is the opposite which takes place, as was said in Book Six, in the chapter *The Mass of Holy Saturday*.

---

[29] Genesis 1:5
[30] Leviticus 23:32
[31] The Truce of God, first proclaimed in 1027 at the Council of Toulouges, attempted to limit the days of the week and times of year that the nobility engaged in violence. The movement survived in some form until the thirteenth century
[32] Wisdom 18:14-15

17. Now solemn or festive days are those on which, in honour of God and of the saints, we must abstain from all servile work and spend time singing the praises of God. And it must be noted that a solemnity is a festival commonly instituted for some sanction. This word comes from, *solo*, 'of the ground,' that is, which is common to all, or, *absoluto*, 'of what is completed,' that is to say firm and solid, because the religious solemnities must not be altered. Or else, 'solemnity,' is said of the solemnities which it is customary to celebrate during the year (*solet in anno*). It is called, 'celebration,' because it does not deal with earthly things, but only with the things of heaven. Now, some are the solemnities of the festivities, others that of the stations, others that of the litanies, others that of the fasts. Let us speak successively of all these solemnities.

18. The solemnity of feasts, which marks the death of the saints, is designated by various names because it is called a festival; a celebration; a nativity, a natal, *natalis*, or *natalilium*; a *transitus*, which is a transit, passage or exit; an *obitus*; a passion; an assumption; or a deposition and sleep. A festival is called a *festis diebus*, a 'feast day,' as a celebration, because during the days of festivity, one only deals with divine things. These are the opposite of *fasti*,[33] 'pomp,' days when justice is done, for then, *jus fatur*, 'rights are addressed.' A festival may sometimes be called the nativity or day of birth of a saint, although properly a nativity is called the feast of birth which takes place in the flesh and in the world; and this applies only for the birth of Christ, Blessed Mary and Blessed John the Baptist, which are the only nativities that are celebrated in the Church. So why do we say that saints are born when they die? This is what we will see in a while; and we shall speak of it again when treating of the octave. We have already spoken of celebration. The date of death of the saints of this age is called a natal, *natalis*, *natalitium*, or day of birth because when they die then they are born to God and pass from the world to glory by the nativity which tends to eternal life. These terms natal, *natalis*, or *natalitium*, are used indifferently. *Transitus*, or the passage, is said of the feast of the death of the saints, because their

---

[33] The calendar in Ancient Rome, which gave the days for festivals, courts, etc.

souls, at the end of their bodies, pass through various regions unknown to them, as for example through the celestial space, ethereal and crystalline or transparent air, to finally arrive at the empyrean.[34]

19. And notice that the feast of the passage of some saints is greater than of others. We will speak of this in the chapter *The Assumption of the Glorious Virgin Mary*. *Obitus*[35] is also said, a journey that one makes to meet someone, because then the angels come to meet the soul of the saint, as it is said regarding St Martin. It is also called, *passio*, 'passion,' because the body suffers especially then, and even the soul, when these two substances are violently separated from each other. The journey of each, or the death of each, may be called a passion, because no soul separates from its body without bitterness and without some violence. 'Assumption,' is properly used of the journey of Blessed Mary. 'Deposition,' is said to be especially of the deposition of Blessed John the Evangelist, who, as has been said above, entered the place of burial alive and thus deposed himself. We call *obdormitio*, 'sleep,' the death of the saints, which is like a rest. For just as after sleep one is more vigorous and stronger, so the saints are resurrected without difficulty in glorified bodies, as if waking from sleep. Which is why the Lord to said of Lazarus, who was dead, 'Our friend Lazarus sleepeth.'[36] So that the Apostle says, 'But I would not have you to be ignorant, brethren, concerning them which are asleep, etc.'[37]

20. We need to talk now about the stations. A station according to St Isidore, is the observation of marked or determined days or times, like the fasting of the fourth and sixth weekdays, which are ordered according to the old law. Regarding this, 'station,' is mentioned in the Gospel where it says, 'I fast twice in the week,'[38] that is to say, on the fourth and sixth day of the Sabbath.[39]

---

[34] The region of pure light; the highest heaven
[35] *Obitus* has various translations including, *perishing*, *destruction*, or *death*. It can also be the act of going down, hence, *setting*, or *sunset*. Or the act of approaching or going toward, hence, *approach*, *encounter* or *visit*
[36] John 11:11
[37] 1 Thessalonians 4:13-14
[38] Luke 18:12
[39] Wednesday and Friday

Regarding the seasons, it is those which were determined at times prefixed by the institutions of the law and the prophets, such as the fast of the fourth, fifth, seventh and tenth months. The procession, which is made to some church, to render thanks to God, is also called a station; and we call it a station, because we must then pray standing (*stantes*) and give thanks to God, without bending our knees. So we do not fast and we do not take time for supplication; all of which things are practiced in the litany, where one puts on clothes that mark humility.

21. It seems that the stations derive their origin from the old law, because then the Jewish people, and also a large number of Gentiles, gathered in great solemnities, namely at Easter and Pentecost, to pray in the temple, to render and offer thanksgiving to God. The Church still observes this, especially in Italy where, during the weeks of Easter and Pentecost, the people of the neighbouring towns and countryside gather at the cathedral church.[40] Other stations originated with the Romans, who often practice them. These people, after having escaped great perils by the intercession of the saints whose suffrages they demanded, came in procession to the church of the saint, by whose patronage they had been delivered, and glorified God with thanksgiving. St Isidore says in the sixth book of his *Etymologies* that 'station' is a military import, or takes its name from a military example, in that, as there was no accord in the camps, the military stations were conceived of, in order to dispel the sadness of the soldiers.

22. Now, there are two kinds of stations, for there are some general and some particular ones. The general stations are those that are done during the two weeks mentioned above at the cathedral church. The particular stations are those which are made in various churches, for the reason mentioned above. The stations are sometimes also observed, if there is no reason opposed to it, when, on the feast of some saint, the procession proceeds from the principal church to the church of this saint. They are also celebrated when, on various feast days, they go in procession to various altars, to venerate the saints. The institution of the stations is evident from what we have said, adding, however, that, just as the Romans established the stations at

---

[40] The seat of the bishop

Rome to escape danger; in the same way, other peoples instituted them in their cities for similar reasons. On the days of the stations songs or hymns of joy are heard, namely the responsories or the antiphons, or something similar. Sometimes we also celebrate Mass in the church where we go, and sometimes it is not so; but after the station, we return when the prayer is over.

23. And notice that the people begin to congregate in some church near the place where the station is to be made, as was said in Book Four, in the chapter *The Collect*. Blessed Gregory, who regulated the stations in the city of Rome, ordered that, at different times or at various renewals, twenty homilies of the Gospel should be said, and that various persons should pronounce them successively and in turn, in order to avoid stomach fatigue. The solemnity of litanies has been spoken of in Book Six, in the chapter *The Rogations*.

24. Note, however, that the stations are made for past perils, while the litanies, which are expounded through rogations or supplications, are made to avoid perils to come, as has been said above. We have spoken of the solemnity of the fasts and vigils of the saints in Book Six, in the chapter *Other Fasts*. Notice again that Christmas is the feast of the Father, because it is through Him that the Son has been made known in the world. 'In this was manifested the love of God toward us, because that God sent his only begotten Son into the world,'[41] as Blessed John says. The feast of the Father, however, is the feast of the Holy Son and Spirit, for by saying 'the Word,' we mean the Father of the Word. Yet another reason is that the Son has manifested the Father to the world. Easter is the feast of the Son, because then Christ rose from the dead and appeared true God.

25. Note that the solemnity of Easter is said to be, 'the Solemnity of solemnities,' as they say, 'the Holy of Holies,' and, 'the Song of Songs,' because the Holy of Holies has primacy over all things holy, just as the Song of Songs prevails over all other hymns. Hence it is that we repeat it every Sunday, that is, every Sunday is the octave of Easter. It is also called, 'the Festivity of festivities,' both because it is the first of all festivities, and because all the faithful must commune on this Sunday. However, in some places,

---

[41] 1 John 4:9

Easter is called, 'the great feast of Easter,' as one would say a passage, because we must pass from vices to virtues. Pentecost is the feast of the Holy Spirit; and each of these solemnities belongs to the whole Trinity, because the works of the Trinity are indivisible, although, as has already been said, each of these solemnities is more suitable especially to one Person than to the other.

26. It must not be forgotten that the people of Israel celebrated three main solemnities. The first was the day of Passover or the day of unleavened bread, which is Easter, because then God delivered them from the power of Pharaoh and from the bondage of Egypt. Also from the blows of the Exterminating Angel, for God ordered them to dye their doors with the blood of the immolated lamb, for there were no houses of Egyptians where there were no dead, there were only the houses of the Israelites where there was none. The second feast was Pentecost, because it was then that the Israelites received the law, as it was said in Book Six, in the chapter *The Holy Day of Pentecost*. The third was *Scenopegia*,[42] in the month of September; it is a Greek word which signifies the dedication or the construction of tabernacles or tents, for the people of Israel lived forty years in tents. In memory of which the Jews still celebrate this festival, as if they lived under a tent. The Greek *skenos* is *tabernaculum*, in Latin or, 'tabernacle.' These feasts which were prolonged for seven days were said to be chief, and the Sabbath which was enclosed there was called, *sabbatum sabbatorum*, 'the Sabbath of Sabbaths,' that is, *sabbatum sanctorum*, 'the Sabbath of saints,' or holy feasts par excellence.

27. But they also added other feasts, because of various events, such as *Encaenia* or the festival of Dedication,[43] which the Hebrews celebrated in the winter, namely in October, and they called *Encaenia* the new dedication of the temple; for *neoe* in Greek is called *novum*, 'new,' in Latin. It is from this point that we call *Encaenia* all the dedications of new objects that we make; for if someone puts on a new tunic, he is said to be, 'enchanted,' or to wear a new garment. For us, we keep two of these feasts, namely

---

[42] Feast of the Tabernacles. Durandus has *Scenopkegia*
[43] The eight days of celebration for the dedication of the church of the Holy Sepulchre in Jerusalem

Easter and Pentecost, but for a different reason than the Jews. For they celebrate the Passover, because it was then that they were delivered from the slavery of the Egyptians. However, we do so because we have been redeemed by Christ. The Jews celebrated Pentecost in memory of the law they received then, and we, because on this feast we receive the Holy Spirit. The Jews received the law engraved externally on stone tablets, to mark the hardness of their hearts, because they could not understand the spiritual sense of the letter, but the Holy Spirit was given to the seventy-two disciples, and the finger of God engraved in their hearts the understanding of the spiritual sense. We also celebrate, in a way, *Scenopegia* at the feast of the Ascension of the Lord. For by the tabernacle we mean the body of the Lord, in which the divinity resides hidden under humility, according to these words of the Psalmist, 'Which is as a bridegroom coming out of his chamber.' Thus Christ did not fix His tent in mortal flesh, since He, 'rejoiceth as a strong man to run a race,'[44] flying from place to place to fulfil the mystery with the execution of which He was charged. However, He then definitively fixed His tent, that is to say, His body, when He was taken up to heaven where He sits at the right hand of God the Father and where He rests in the heritage of His heavenly Father until He uses His enemies as a footstool.[45] It is therefore appropriate that we celebrate these three feasts in a spiritual way in the Gospel or the new law. For, according to the Psalmist, Christ, 'led captivity captive,'[46] when, having been raised up at Easter He, 'sent forth thy prisoners out of the pit wherein is no water.'[47] He rose in the womb, when in His ascent He; 'rideth upon the heavens of heavens, which were of old.'[48] He, 'gave gifts unto men,'[49] when on the day of Pentecost He rained His Holy Spirit on all flesh. Now, the fourth day of the week after the Sunday of the Passion belongs to the

---

[44] Psalm 19:4-5
[45] See Psalm 110:1
[46] Psalm 68:18
[47] Zechariah 9:11
[48] Psalm 68:33 The Vulgate has, 'Who mounteth above the heaven of heavens, to the east' (Ps 67:34)
[49] Ephesians 4:8

feast of *Neomenia*[50] or Dedication, as it was said in Book Six. There were also four other solemnities, though less solemn than the previous ones, namely the Sabbath, the Feast of Trumpets, the Feast of Atonement, and the *Neomenias*, that is, the New Moon. Among the Hebrews, in fact, they said *neomenism*, because they calculated the months following the course of the moon. *Mene*[51] in Greek means 'moon;' from this comes, *neomenia*, that is to say, 'new moon.' With us, the *neomenias* are the calends;[52] among the Hebrews, the very days of the calends were solemn, according to the legal institution.

28. The Emperor Constantine, visiting the overseas parts of the empire, saw Eusebius, bishop of Caesarea, a man of great holiness, and said to him, 'Ask me what is in your church which needs to be enriched?' 'My church is rich enough; but here is the request and the prayer that I address to you. It is that you send legates charged with writing the names of the saints to all parts of the world, including the time of their passion, under what emperor, how and where they have suffered,' and this was done. Eusebius records that every day of the year there are more than five thousand feasts of saints that coincide, except the day of the calends of January, a day the Gentiles devoted to feasts and solemnities, and not to martyring the saints. Furthermore, Blessed Jerome says the same thing in the epistle preceding his calendar; which made Gregory say, 'The whole world is full of saints.' And Haymon,[53] likewise speaking of angels, says that if anyone could see spiritual creatures, he would see them swirling in the air, similar to the smallest atoms that appear in the rays of the sun.

29. And note that no one's name should be inscribed on the catalogue or in the number of saints, unless it is by the Roman pontiff, nor before one has knowledge that excludes the smallest doubt about his life and his miracles. Now, 'catalogue' comes from the Greek *kata*, 'about', and *logos*, 'word' or 'speech.' The litany or calendar, which lists the saints approved by the Roman Church, is called the 'universal discourse.' Moreover, according

---

[50] An accepted variant spelling of *noumenia*, which means 'new moon' and refers to the first days of a lunar month
[51] A variant of *mene*, 'moon'
[52] See Book Eight
[53] A Benedictine bishop of the ninth century

to the decree of the Council of Africa, 'we must not honour or solemnize the memory of any martyr, except where the body and the authentic relics of the martyr are, or where it originally was, and in the place where one possessed them from.' For the altars that are uplifted in any place are utterly reprobated, as a result of the dreams and imaginary revelations of some individuals. Similarly, it was ruled in the Council of Orleans, 'that the bishop, unless he is hindered by some infirmity,' says book five, 'should not be absent on Sunday at the nearest church, such as the Episcopal Church.'

30. Which festivities must be celebrated? The Council of Lyons teaches us about this in the following decree, 'We must celebrate Sundays from the Vespers of one day to that of the next. Likewise, the festivals of the Nativity of the Lord, of St Stephen, of St John the Evangelist, of the Innocents, of St Sylvester, of the Circumcision, and of the Theophany or Epiphany. Also Easter, with all the previous week and the following ones. The three days of the Rogations, the Ascension of the Lord, Pentecost and the two following days. Also St John the Baptist, the feasts of the Twelve Apostles and St Lawrence. And the festivities of Blessed Mary. Every Sunday, the dedication of St Michael, the feast of All Saints, and the feast of St Martin. Likewise all the festivities, namely of canonized saints, which each bishop orders and decrees the clergy and to the people in the churches of his diocese to celebrate. As for the other festivities of the year, we must neither compel nor prevent people from observing or celebrating them. It has been said in Book Five, in the chapter *The Night Offices*, the number of psalms, responsories, or lessons which are said in festivals, and why they are said.

31. Now, there are certain feasts that are double (in totality), others simple doubles, and some semi-doubles. Some are said to be double in some churches, because the major responsories, as well as the short responsories and the verses, are sung in two voices. This is because everything that is to be sung is by two voices, and because we also redouble the antiphons at Matins and Vespers; for they are said entirely both before and after the psalm. Examples of this are at the feasts of Christmas, of St Stephen the first martyr, of St John the Evangelist, the Circumcision of the

Lord, the Epiphany, the Purification, the Annunciation, the Resurrection, the Ascension, and Pentecost. Also of St John the Baptist, the Apostles Peter and Paul, St Lawrence, the Assumption of the Blessed Virgin Mary, the Nativity of the same, and the Dedication of the Church.

32. The aforementioned feasts are double-majors. The double-minors are the second and third working day in the octave of the Resurrection, so is the second and third working day in the octave of Pentecost, the Commemoration of St Paul, the octave of the Apostles Peter and Paul, of St Lawrence, of the Assumption, and every feast that every church wants to be celebrated as double-major.

33. Semi-double festivals are those in which the above-mentioned rules are not fully observed, and where the third, sixth, and last responsories are sung by two singers. The intonation is not done in two voices; the antiphons are not doubled, although the verses and short responsories are said in two voices. These semi-double festivals are the festivals of the saints St Andrew, St Nicholas, St Lucy, St Thomas, an Apostle and the Holy Innocents. Also, the octave of Epiphany, of St Agnes, the Conversion of St Paul, St Agatha, St Mathias, the Chair of St Peter, St Gregory, St Augustine, St Jerome, St Ambrose, St Philip and St James, and St Mark the Evangelist. Also that of the Finding of the Holy Cross, of the Revelation of St Michael, of the Octave of the Ascension, of St John Latino, of St Barnabas, the Apostle; the octave of St John the Baptist, St Mary Magdalene, the Apostle St James, and the Chains of St Peter the Links. In addition, the octave of St Lawrence and of St Bartholomew, an Apostle. The Decollation of St John the Baptist, the octave of the Nativity of Blessed Mary, the Exaltation of the Holy Cross, and of St Matthew the Apostle, of St. Luke the Evangelist, of the Apostles St Simon and St Jude, St Martin, St Cecilia, St Catherine, and others, according to the custom of each church. Now, this variety is preserved in festivals; for, as the Apostle says, 'for one star differeth from another star in glory. So also is the resurrection of the dead.'[54] Now, as, according to Blessed Dionysius, the ecclesiastical hierarchy represents in some manner in its actions and ordinances the

---

[54] 1 Corinthians 15:41-42

celestial hierarchy, in which the saints are disposed according to the diversity of their merits, it is to represent this that we find in our holy Church the variety of the various Offices.

34. Now, what festivals must we call doubles in totality and which ones should we call semi-doubles? This is evident from the mystical understanding. For, according to the holy fathers, the vision of God will be the reward of the blessed. Now, this vision will be greater or smaller, depending on whether they have progressed to a greater or lesser extent in charity while on earth, which is the root and source of all merits. However there are some special merits according to which, in the future glory, some special rewards will be granted to those who will have special merits. Thus a special and more excellent[55] reward will be given to martyrs, doctors and virgins, and this reward is called a halo. So, with regards to this, some saints will have a double reward, namely the essential, which is called the vision of God, and the accidental, which is the halo. And, according to this, the feasts of saints can be called major or minor, that is to say, where one can find more or less reasons for reward. As, therefore, the Blessed Virgin enjoys a reward more excellent than all the other saints, with regards to the essential reward, and the reasons for accidental reward also suit her, so her feast is said to be entirely double. It is the same with the festivities established in honour of Christ. Now, after them the angels occupy the first degree, then afterwards come the Apostles and the martyrs, then the others; that is why, according to their greatest or smallest number of rewards, essential and accidental, their feast must be celebrated, either entirely double, or semi-double, or simple, by the Church Militant, which traces and conforms to the Church Triumphant.

35. Sometimes also the festivals are called double, due to another consideration, namely when two festivals coincide on the same day; and then the least gives way to the most considerable, For, on this day, we celebrate the service of the feast which carries it in excellence, and we content ourselves with remembering the least important, the service of which is postponed until the next day. An example of this occurs with the blessed Peter and Paul. If, therefore, several festivals of saints coincide on the same day,

---

[55] Super essential

and all these saints are martyrs, we will have to celebrate the Office of the one who, among all the others, has the greatest renown. If one is a confessor and the other martyr, or there are several martyrs; if the confessor has more celebrity than the martyr, or is privileged as blessed St Martin, and the Church has generally adopted his Office, the Office of the confessor must be said and martyr remembered; otherwise we must celebrate the Office of the martyr. Similarly, if the feast of St Andrew comes on the first Sunday of Advent, it will be celebrated on Monday.

36. We say the same thing regarding every feast of the Apostles and martyrs that could coincide with Sundays, which are more privileged. Similarly, if a feast having a vigil falls on a Monday, the vigil and fast take place on the preceding Saturday. Again, if the feast of an Apostle or of some distinguished martyr, or of another saint who has his own Office, arrives on some other Sunday among the privileged Sundays, that is to say, those which have a history or a proper Office, it is necessary to examine if the following week or a day of this week has a clean Office. If there is one, they will do Sunday service, and they will hand over to Monday the service of the saint; if they do not have one, we will serve the feast on Sunday, and the Sunday service will be postponed until Monday. Thus Sunday sometimes gives way to the feast, and vice versa.

37. Regarding the vigils of the saints, we said; in Book Six, in the chapter *The Office of Wednesday of the Advent Ember Days*, during the third week of Advent, why they are so called and what their origin is. Regarding the festivals that coincide with Septuagesima or the time of the Passion, or that arrive before this time, such as the feasts of St Agatha, the Chair of St Peter, St Mathias, the Annunciation of the Lord, and the feast of St Gregory the following applies. If one of these festivals happens, or even the patronal festival of some church or the annotative Easter, that is to say the anniversary of baptism, we say that it is generally adopted that the singing in these festivals are the songs of joy, namely, the *Te Deum laudamus*, etc., the *Gloria in excelsis Deo*, etc., *Vite, Missa est*,[56] and all that one would sing in these festivities, if

---

[56] Namely, 'We praise Thee, O Lord, etc.,' 'Glory to God in the highest, etc.,' and 'Go, the Mass is said'

they arrived at other times, except the Alleluia. The reason is because the festivals where it is sung belong to Easter time. Yet why do we not say the Alleluia then, since we sing the other hymns of joy? I answer that the Alleluia is more a hymn of joy than the other songs in question, which are rather expressions of respect or a way of rendering to God our homage and thanksgiving rather than hymns of joy and elation, although these canticles are not deprived of any joy, especially in the expression of the chant. Now it could be objected that the *Gloria in Excelsis Deo*, which is a chant proper to the birth of the Lord; the *Vita, Missa est*, which is the hymn or the praise of the Resurrection; and the *Te Deum laudamus*, which means the joy for the new found penny, should not be sung at the feast of the Annunciation of the Lord. This is because the said canticles did not yet exist during the advent of the Lord, or in the time that preceded the coming of the Lord and which corresponds to Advent. For the Lord had not yet justified these songs according to the ordinary course of human affairs, or had not yet reached the time when these hymns appeared following the ordinary revolutions of time. However, those who claim that we must then sing these canticles respond that this feast, namely the feast of the Annunciation of the Lord, is like the source, the origin or the principle of all the festivals of Christ. This is because, if the birth or the Passion of the Lord and the discovery of the penny was not a *fait accompli* in reality and in relation to time, it was an accomplished fact in hope, because the wonders that made us hope had started by preceding their production.

38. The Annotative Easter takes place when someone annually celebrates the anniversary of their baptism, a custom that may come from the Gentiles who were celebrating, under the name of *Natalitium diem*, 'Birth Day,' the day they were born into the misery of this world. In this feast we must sing the Easter service, except the Alleluia, if we are in Lent. And note that these three hymns, namely *Te Deum laudamus*; *Gloria in excelsis Deo*, and *Vite, Missa est*, follow each other and accompany each other; here is the reason. The *Gloria in Excelsis Deo* indicates this ineffable joy that the Angel announced to the shepherds by saying to them, 'I bring you good tidings of great joy, which shall be to all people. For

unto you is born this day in the city of David a Saviour.'[57] *Vita Missa est*, which, as has been said, means, 'Go to your business or go to your home, the Mass is over,' designates the shepherds approaching the place of the birth of Christ, and saying in their hearts, after the announcement made by the Angel, 'Let us now go even unto Bethlehem, and see this thing which is come to pass, which the Lord hath made known unto us.'[58] As the approach of the shepherds of the manger followed the news that the Angel had announced to them, that is why, when the priest says *Gloria in excelsis Deo*, in which he represents the Angel, he must also and with good reason say, *Vita, Missa est*. Likewise, when one says or omits these two hymns, one also says or one omits at night the *Te Deum laudamus* at the Night Offices, because in this hymn are designated the joy and the praises of heaven and earth, creator and creature, head and limbs. For in *Gloria in Excelsis Deo*, heaven and earth are called with praise and gladness, creator and creature, head and limbs; moreover, almost all that is explicitly enclosed in the first is implicitly contained in the second. It is therefore right that, when we say one, we must not omit the other. However, the aforementioned hymns do not always accompany each other. Indeed, in the feast of the Blessed Peter's Chair, even when it occurs in Lent, there are churches that say the *Te Deum Laudamus* and suppress the other hymns of praise, because we are accustomed to sing this hymn for the enthronement of bishops in their seats; and the blessed Peter, on that same day, was enthroned in the seat of Antioch. Likewise, on Holy Thursday, one says *Gloria in Excelsis Deo* and *Vite, Missa est*, when the bishop is present and celebrates the Office of chrism. Also on Holy Saturday, they say *Gloria in Excelsis Deo* and not *Vite, Missa est*. However, on those same days, one does not say *Te Deum laudamus*. Similarly, on the day of the Nativity, *Gloria in Excelsis Deo* is said at the first Mass; but they do not say *Vite, Missa est*, lest the people, believing themselves dismissed, should go away without having heard Matins. That is why there are also some who suspend the final Collect of the first Mass, until the end of Matins, and then finish the Mass with, 'Thanks be to God.' We give another reason

---

[57] Luke 22:10-11
[58] Luke 2:15

in Book Four, in the chapter *The Last Prayer and the 'Go, the Mass is Said*. They also finish the second Mass in the same way. However, in some churches, 'All things are accomplished,' is said and the people are not given permission to retire, so that they may know that they must hear a third Mass, at the end of which they say, 'Go, the Mass is said'. In other churches where the Ambrosian Office is being followed, no feast is celebrated during the Lenten season; any are merely remembered, and ancient decrees prescribed the same thing in other churches, and formerly this custom was commonly established. In still other churches we consecrate, before reading or singing the Gospel. We have spoken in Book Six, in the chapter *The Time of Advent*, of the Office of festivals coinciding with the time of Advent.

39. Regarding the feasts that take place during the period from the Resurrection to the octave of Pentecost, it is a rule generally observed in some churches to sing at all the festivals of the saints the antiphon, 'Blessed is the man, etc.,'[59] and this is done for the Apostles, martyrs, confessors, and virgins, when there is only one saint, and also when there are many of them. For, 'this blessed man', is Christ, who is at the same time both the head and the members. For it is He who is the martyr of whom it is said in the antiphon, 'Daughters of Jerusalem, etc.,'[60] that God crowned Him as head, that is to say, as the head of the robe of immortality, at this time of solemnity and gladness, and will then crown Him in His members at that time, by which is meant for eternity and glory. For it is He who speaks in the Office which is celebrated at this time, namely, *Deus*; 'Hide me from the secret counsel of the wicked, etc.'[61] It is He who is the true vine and the saints are its offspring, as it is said in the Gospel, 'I am the true vine, and my Father is the husbandman, etc.,'[62] which is also read in this time. Furthermore, from what we have already said, it is evident that in the festivals of two or more saints one must say in the above-

---

[59] Psalm 1

[60] Daughters of Jerusalem, come and see this martyr wearing the crown with which the Lord has adorned him this solemn day of rejoicing. Alleluia. For he has strengthened the bars of your gates, and has blessed your children within you. Glory be to the Father, etc.

[61] Psalm 64:2, 1

[62] John 15:1-7

mentioned antiphon, 'Daughters of Jerusalem, come and see the martyr,' that is to say Christ, and not 'the martyrs,' nor to put the rest in the plural as some do. In this time, for the festivities of the saints, we sing identical Offices, to designate or signify that the penny will be the same for all, and because then we will be glorified in unity with Christ, as those glorified at this time are.

40. But we ask why, during Easter time, we do not celebrate the feasts of the saints who are resurrected with Christ or who went up to heaven with Him. For we must rejoice in their glorification and solemnize it, as we do for the other saints, since we are certain that they have ascended to heaven. I answer that we do not solemnize the festivals of these saints, because they have descended into limbo; for we celebrate the birth of the saints, when they were born for heaven, as it was said above, but not when they went down to hell or when they were born into limbo. We talked about this in Book Six, in the chapter *Holy Friday, Good Friday or Parasceve*. We can also say that we should celebrate their glorification in soul at Easter, or at least at Ascension; but we cannot, because of the authority and the solemnity of the Offices of those days. This is because the solemnity of these saints would be crushed and disappear under the authority of a greater solemnity, because at the arrival of the prince the magistrate is effaced. That is why it was decreed that at other times of the year their feasts would be celebrated on the day of the dedication of the churches placed under their name. Or, according to Bede, they are celebrated at the dedication of the Church, during which nine lessons are said. For example, the feast of St John the Baptist is at the end of August, although this saint died at Easter; and that of St James of Compostela in July, although he was put to death in the Easter season. It was also at this time that the Blessed Apostle Peter was incarcerated. The change of the above-mentioned festivals was made, for such was the greatness of the festivity of the prince of all the saints, which one could not celebrate then the feasts of His satellites, according to this adage, 'Give way to the most worthy.'

41. It is said, however, that the feasts of the Old Testament saints, such as Abraham, Isaac, David, Daniel, and others, are celebrated in Greece and Venice. It is also said that in these countries there

are churches dedicated to the Maccabees, as will be seen in the chapter of these Saints.

42. As far as the octaves are concerned, it should be noted that Leviticus seems to insinuate the eighth day, or the celebration of the octave, by saying, 'on the eighth day shall be an holy convocation unto you.'[63] Undoubtedly, the octaves of the saints are celebrated in the same way that the first day refers to the nativity of the saints. That is to say, how they are born for heaven and are to be received into the society of angels and holy fathers when their souls are separated from their bodies. Thus, in the octaves recalling the resurrection of bodies, we rejoice with them in the resurrection of these bodies.

43. Note that we celebrate the octave of some saints and, so that this mystery[64] does not become too common, we do not celebrate it[65] for all the saints; for if we cannot celebrate the feasts of all the saints, how can we celebrate their octaves as well? And if other saints have solemn octaves, will the octave of the Holy of Holies, that is to say, the Nativity of the Lord, be much more solemn? But it seems that the Nativity of the Lord has no octave, since the intent was His death.[66] In fact, one gives an octave to the death of the saints, because in dying they are born from that birth which leads them to eternal life. For it is after this nativity which arrives at death, that we must hope for the glory of the resurrection which is given in the octave; but this does not happen after the birth which must lead to death. According to this, it also appears that the nativities of Blessed Mary and St John the Baptist have no octave, nor even the Resurrection of the Lord, in which the Lord has received the robe of His body, which will be given generally to all the faithful in the octave or the eighth age, because already the Resurrection of the Lord had taken place in reality.

44. Since, therefore, there are various churches celebrating the octave of various festivities, we say, in order not to appear to blame them, that there is a double octave, namely one of reverence, veneration or devotion, and one of institution. The

---

[63] Leviticus 23:36
[64] of the resurrection of the body
[65] the octave
[66] The purpose of His birth was that He should die

octaves of reverence or veneration are those of Easter, Pentecost, and the nativities of the Blessed Virgin Mary and Blessed John the Baptist, for these octaves are celebrated by devotion only, and not for any other mysterious reason. The octave of devotion also takes place for the holy patrons of the churches, as for example, St Nicholas, Blessed Mary Magdalene, and other similar ones who have no octaves. However some churches celebrate these octaves by devotion. As for the octave of institution, it is subdivided into four octaves, which are the octave of significance, the octave of suppletion, the octave of signification of another thing, or which designates something else, and the octave of future glorification. 45. The octave of significance is, for example, that of saints who have a vigil and that of the feast of the dedication, which is done to mark that the Church will be dedicated or consecrated. That is to say, it will be consecrated by a last and much more complete dedication, that is, it will be united to Christ; for to be consecrated or dedicated is to be united. Also those of the martyrs, because of, and by, the sufferings that they endured, and by the little event which they made of this life, they testified that there is an immortal life. We can also call the octave of the Innocents an octave of meaning, because it designates our resurrection, as will be said in the chapter of their Feast. The same can be said of the octaves of the blessed Peter and Paul and of some saints, who represent the second robe, that is to say the glorification which we will enjoy in the eighth age. But why, for the same reason, do we not make or celebrate the octave of the Passion of the Lord? For just as Christ, who was born a sun of righteousness, was not born for Himself, but to illuminate our souls plunged into the darkness with His light. Just as He was baptized, not for Himself, but to cleanse us from our sins, so He died, not for Himself, but so that we might die to sin and thus tear ourselves away from death. I answer that it is because the festivity of joy that occurs covers and removes any memory of sadness. Moreover, although the reason for the above-mentioned octaves are explained, it is not the case that octaves are celebrated everywhere for such festivities or in such cases. For Christ was circumcised in His flesh, that we might observe spiritual circumcision. He fasted, that we might fast. He washed our feet so that we could do the same. For we celebrate not only the octave of these festivals of saints or the like, but the octave of the saints is also celebrated for different reasons, as has been said above. Moreover, there are still other reasons why the mystery or the ministry of the octave does not take place. One is given here however. It is because of the eight beatitudes which one receives in this solemnity, as it has been said in its place. The octave of Pentecost is also celebrated only to mark the consummation of the works of the Holy Spirit.

46. There is one more general reason for all octaves. The octave is the same as the first day of the feast; which takes place for the eight beatitudes, of which the eighth enters into the first. In the book, 'of Christian Doctrine,' St Augustine assures us that the eighth day or octave of the Lord is the same as the first day. Therefore the Resurrection of the Lord is said to have taken place in the octave, that is, the day of the Lord, on Sunday. Now, we also observe the celebration of the octaves, so that we return to the first state of innocence, in memory of which innocence we practice circumcision on the eighth day, so that the soul becomes circumcised of any carnal contagion.

47. The octave of suppletion is the octave of the Nativity of the Lord, because in this octave we make up for what has been missed at the feast of the Nativity. In fact, as in the Nativity, there was much talk of childbirth and little of the birth, so in the octave we treat the child more fully, as we can see in the responsories, in the antiphons of Lauds and in the day Offices of the same octave. It is for the same reason that we celebrate the octave of Epiphany. The octave of meaning of another thing is also the octave of the Nativity, as we have just said, and the octave of St Agnes; for in this last octave it is represented, and it appears, that Blessed Agnes appeared glorious to some faithful on the eighth day, as will be said at her feast. The octave of future glorification is, for example, the octave of the death of some saint.

48. Note also that only the blessed Stephen and Lawrence have octaves of institution among the martyrs, and only the blessed Martin among the confessors. In Book Six, in the chapter *Easter Day*, we have spoken of the octaves of Easter, Ascension, and Christmas. Now, normally in the octave of the feasts, the Office of the Mass is the same as the Office of the feasts themselves, since the octave is supposed to be made on the same day with the

feast. However, this induces an error in the octave of the Apostles Peter and Paul, in which the Office of the Martyrs is said, for although both of them have suffered together and on the same day, the Church does not solemnize the feast of these two Apostles on the same day, as we shall say in the chapter of their feasts. Now the Office of both cannot be done in the octave, since both have only one day for an octave. It was therefore necessary that on their octave there should be some common Office, and as their martyrdom has been of excellent merit, which is why the Office of the Martyrs is said to be in their honour, although in the Office itself mention is made of the principal acts of each. This is also misleading in the octave of St Lawrence, who made himself especially commendable by three things. Namely, his charity to give alms, his invincible firmness in the confession of the faith and his special martyrdom. There is talk of the first thing in his vigil, of the second in his feast, and that is why it was necessary to speak of the third in the octave.

49. Now, in the *Preface* to Book Six we have spoken of the Offices of the Church, beginning with the Advent of the Lord, the time of renewal. However, in this book, adopting a simpler method, we will treat, following the calendar and starting from January, some festivities of the year, intermingling successively some special festivities, namely those of saints Fabien and Sebastian, of St Agnes, of the Conversion of St Paul, of St Julien, of St Agatha, of the Purification of Blessed Mary, of the Chair of St Peter, of the Annunciation of Blessed Mary, of St Philip and St James, the Exaltation of the Holy Cross, the Revelation of St Michael, the saints Gervais and Protais, of St John the Baptist, of St Peter and St Paul, of the feast of the seven Brothers, and of St James, an Apostle. Also of the Seven Sleepers, of St Peter the Links, of the Maccabees, of the Finding of the Body of St Stephen, of the Transfiguration of the Lord, of St Lawrence, of the Assumption of the Blessed Mary, of St Bartholomew, of the Decollation of St John, and of saints Felix and Audacte. In addition, that of the Nativity of Blessed Mary, of the Exaltation of the Holy Cross, of St Matthew an Apostle, of St Maurice and his companions, of Blessed Luke, of Blessed Simon and Jude, the Feast of All Saints, the Office of the Dead, of the Four Crowned Saints. Also of St Martin, St Andrew, St Nicholas, the venerable Bede who was a

BOOK SEVEN

priest, of the Apostle St Thomas, and celebrations of saints Stephen and John the Evangelist, the Innocents, the Apostles, Evangelists, martyrs, confessors, virgins, and finally the Office of the Feast of the Dedication of the Church.

2 SAINTS FABIEN AND SEBASTIAN

1. On the feast of the blessed Fabien and Sebastian, two Collects are said in certain churches and usually they are both terminated under one, 'Through our Lord.' The reason for this is that in both these cases it was through the mediation of the only-begotten Son of God, Jesus Christ, that they obtained the palm of martyrdom. Although they suffered at different times, the Church, however, because of the great merits of both, celebrates them both equally and mainly, and finishes the two Collects with a common end.

3 SAINT AGNES

1. The feast of Blessed Agnes lacks an octave, that is, an octave of institution; however, it has an octave of meaning of something else, as already mentioned in the *Preface*. So, what is said in the Calendar, 'Second Agnes,' is not said in the sense that we celebrate the feast of the octave of this saint. The octave of Agnes is not a recognized point in the Church, nor inscribed on the Calendar. It is another solemnity which is repeated in honour of the same saint, because of a certain miracle which arrived eight days after her death, at her tomb, at the sight of her parents weeping. This is what we mean by 'second,' that is to say, the second feast of Agnes; which makes it better to say, 'Second Agnes.' And as the son of the prefect loved her with passion, that is why, and appropriately, the Introit, 'The wicked have waited for me to destroy me, etc.,'[67] is sung at her feast.

---

[67] Psalm 119:95-86, 1

4 THE CONVERSION OF SAINT PAUL

1. The conversion of St Paul, an Apostle, took place the same year that Christ suffered and that Stephen was stoned, not in the natural year, but in the emergent year. For Christ suffered on the eighth of the calends of April, while St Stephen was stoned in the same year, on the third day of August, and St Paul was converted on the calends of February. However, one celebrates his conversion rather than that of the other saints, for three reasons.
2. First, to serve as an example, so that no one, no matter how great a sinner, need despair of their forgiveness, seeing such a great sinner became so great and so blessed with grace. Secondly, by a motive of joy, for just as the Church suffered great affliction by the persecution of Saul, so she experienced the greatest joy from Paul's conversion. Third, because of the miracle that the Lord has manifested in making the cruellest persecutor the most faithful of preachers.
3. On this feast they say the Epistle is, 'And Saul, yet breathing out threatenings and slaughter against the disciples of the Lord, etc.,'[68] and the Gospel is, 'Then answered Peter and said unto him, Behold, we have forsaken all, and followed thee, etc.'[69] The capitulum,[70] 'And there was a certain disciple at Damascus, etc.,'[71] is also sometimes said.

---

[68] Acts 9:1-22
[69] Matthew 19:27-29
[70] A short reading
[71] Acts 9:10

5 SAINT JULIEN

1. This Julian, whose feast is celebrated on the day of the calends of February, was bishop of Le Mans. It is said that he was the same Simon whom the Lord cured of leprosy and who invited God to a feast. It is also said that it is this Julian whom travellers invoke to find a good lodging, because the Lord received hospitality in his house. Others say that it was this Julian who killed his father and his mother, and of whom we relate the following, 'There was another Julian, a native of Germany, who, burning to suffer martyrdom, presented himself to the persecutors, which caused the proconsul Crispinus to order him to be put to death. On hearing this sentence, Julien immediately rushed out, presented himself intrepidly to the executioner, and immediately received the mortal blow.' There was also another Julian, brother of the blessed Julian, who, with the permission of the Emperor Theodosius, together with his brother overturned the temples of idols, and at the word of whom a man who carried the dead on a cart died in reality. There was another Julian, who, without knowing it, killed his father and mother; then, after a long penance, he received in the form of a leper's beggar an angel in his house, and deserved to hear from his mouth that the Lord had sanctioned his penance. There was also a fifth Julian who, far from being a saint, was the most villainous of the apostates. First monk, he was later Roman emperor, as it will be said on the feast of the Finding of the Holy Cross.

6 THE BLESSED AGATHA

1. Blessed Agatha, after many tortures, died in prison. At the head of this saint, on her tomb, an angel visibly placed a tablet with this inscription, 'Holy soul, full of good will, the honour of God and the salvation of her country.' That is why it is customary to make the procession with a tablet, on which is the description of her virtues.

7 THE PURIFICATION OF SAINT MARY

1. Among all the saints, the glorious mother of God, Mary always virgin, ranks first as the most worthy and the most excellent of all creatures.
2. The Church, in her honour, celebrates four solemn festivities at four times of the year, namely the Annunciation, the Assumption, the Nativity and the Purification. For all the time we must have in our memory the one who, at all times, intercedes with her Son for us, sinners. Two of these festivities are common to the Virgin and our Lord and these are the Purification and the Annunciation. Now, these four festivities are made according to the four blessings which are enclosed in the greeting of the angel to the Virgin herself. The first blessing is, 'Hail, Mary, full of grace,' which is appropriate for the first festivity, which is the Annunciation, namely, when the angel greeted the Virgin, and when she conceived by the operation of the Holy Spirit, and so became full of grace. The second is, 'The Lord be with you,' which relates to the Assumption, that is, when she was raised to heaven, because then she was joined with her Lord, that is to say, her Son, and to God, for before she had not seen Him, as Lord God, so manifestly in His essence.
3. The third blessing is, 'You are blessed among women,' which suits the Nativity, because then she was born after being sanctified in her mother's womb. For there is no other woman who was sanctified in her mother's womb, and that is why she was called, 'fortress,' because of her special privilege; because the demons never broke nor invaded this fort. The fourth blessing is, 'Blessed is the fruit of your womb,' which adapts to the fourth

festivity, namely to the Purification, because then she offered this blessed fruit in the temple.

4. There are also some who celebrate a fifth feast, that of the Conception of Blessed Mary, saying that, just as we celebrate the feast of the death of the saints, not because of this death, but because then they have been admitted to the eternal marriage, so the feast of the conception of the Virgin can be celebrated. The reason given is not because of her conception itself, since she was conceived in sin, but because of her conception as mother of God. This clarity was revealed to a certain abbot who had been shipwrecked; which, however, is not authentic and that is why we must not approve it, since the Virgin was conceived in sin, that is to say by carnal commerce. However, although conceived in sin, this original sin was erased in her, since she was sanctified in her mother's womb, like Jeremiah and St John the Baptist. That is why, and appropriately, we celebrate his birth and that of Blessed John the Baptist. Understand that I speak here about the nativity or birth from the mother's womb, that is, when the children come to light or into the world. But their nativity in the bosom of the mother, that is to say, when their souls have been infused into their bodies, is not celebrated, as has been said above. There is also a sixth festival, which is the celebration of the birth of the child, that is to say the Christmas festival. However as it is at the same time as the feast of the Son and requires a full service and unity, that is why it is not solemnized in honour of the Virgin, except in the octave where this is so, as has already been said in the *Preface* to this book. There is also a seventh feast of Blessed Mary to the martyrs, to be discussed at the feast of All Saints. Now, as the feast of the Purification, according to the division of this seventh book, precedes in the order of time the other feasts of the Virgin, that is why we speak here of this feast.

5. Now there is a double feast today. First, it is to deliver the feast which is called the *Hupante*,[72] that is 'the meeting,' because in this solemnity Anne the prophetess and Simeon met Blessed Mary who came to present and offer Christ, her Son, at the temple. For

---

[72] A festival in memory of the meeting of the infant Christ and His mother with Simeon and Anna in the temple: same as the Western Purification or Candlemas. Alternatively called *Hupapante*

the Greek word *hupante*, which is Latin in *obviatio*, 'meeting,' comes from the verb that corresponds to 'go,' and from 'to the encounter.' The arrival of the Lord in the temple means His arrival or entry into the Church and into the soul of every believer, who is a spiritual temple. The Lord has foretold this arrival, coming, or entry, by the prophet who said, 'Behold, I will send my messenger, and he shall prepare the way before me: and the Lord, whom ye seek, shall suddenly come to his temple, etc.'[73] Or else it is called, *hupante* that is, 'presentation,' because this feast marks Christ being presented at the temple.

6. The second feast, which concerns the bringing forth in birth, is called the Feast of the Purification. Now the blessed Virgin, did not need purification, nor was she obliged to the law of purification, since she had nothing impure in her. She had not conceived according to the ordinary rules of nature, however, she wished to fulfil the precept of the law. Indeed, it is said in Leviticus, 'If a woman have conceived seed, and born a man child: then she shall be unclean seven days.'[74] She was sequestrated from the commerce of men and had to remain far from the entrance of the temple, or could not enter the temple. After the seven days passed, she was pure with regards to the commerce of men, that is to say, she could frequent the society of men. Yet she was still unclean with regards to her entering the temple until the thirty-third day, until she was purged through her monthly cycle, according to the law. And after the completion of the forty days, on the fortieth day she entered the temple and offered her child with gifts. If she had given birth to a girl, the time was doubled for her sequestration from men and her removal from the temple, just as the time for the formation of a female child is twice that of the formation of a male child.

7. For the body of a male child is completely organized in forty days, and most often, after forty days, his soul descends into his body by infusion. But it takes eighty days for the organization of

---

[73] Malachi 3:1
[74] Leviticus 12:2

a girl's body, and her soul comes to enliven her body at the end of this time, as it happens most often. Thus, if a woman had given birth to a male, the entrance to the temple was forbidden for forty days, from the day of the child's birth, and for eighty days, if it was a girl. However, today, she is allowed to enter the church immediately, only unless a punishment is imputed to her for some fault. However, a woman who feels the pain of childbirth should not enter the church, or at least must take precautions not to pollute it. Now, the priest must often warn the woman to admit when she is nearing her end, so that when she is pressed by the pains of childbirth, she will be ready to receive the Eucharist; for it would not be decent that the priest should remain with her for a long time during the time of confinement.

8. Now there were three reasons why the Lord commanded that the child was to be presented at the temple on the fortieth day. First, to note that, just as the fortieth day the child is led into the material temple, so, on the fortieth day after conception, the soul is introduced into his body as being his temple, as it is said in the scholastic history, although the doctors say that the body is organized only after forty-six days. Secondly, that the soul which, the on fortieth day, is introduced into the body, is defiled by the same body, so it needs to be purified by offerings. Third, to indicate that those who have observed the ten precepts of the Decalogue with the law of the four Gospels deserve to enter the heavenly temple. So when the days of cleansing were complete, the mother would enter the temple, offering her son or daughter, and presenting a gift on the child's behalf. For a son a young pigeon or a turtledove and for a daughter she offered a burnt offering. One who could not afford a burnt offering offered two turtledoves or two young doves. One as a burnt offering instead of her travail, the other for herself, that is, for her sin. That is why it is said in the Gospel that Mary went to the temple, 'to offer a sacrifice according to that which is said in the law of the Lord, A pair of turtledoves, or two young pigeons.'[75] Therefore, to imitate

---

[75] Luke 2:24

the Blessed Virgin, in certain places women, after leaving their beds, enter the church after forty days, designating that if they imitate the Virgin, according to the present life they will enter with her into eternal life. This feast is therefore celebrated forty days after the Nativity of the Lord, because the blessed Virgin, forty days after the Nativity of Christ, came to the temple and presented her son according to the law.

9. Again, this festival comes after the festivities of Christmas, the Circumcision and Epiphany, because of a mystery or for a mysterious reason the Lord wanted to be presented to the temple for two reasons. Here is the first mystery. It consists in that first God is born in man by faith; and circumcision follows. For when faith is in man, man is purified, hence it is read in the Acts of the Apostles, 'purifying their hearts by faith.'[76] Now those who have a good and sincere faith abandon all evil deeds, and then God manifests Himself. However it is then also necessary for one to do penance, so that He may remain in us as in His temple. Then there is an offering of a pair of turtledoves, that is to say that one offers purity of heart and body, which can only take place by a continual mourning, as the turtledove moaned for a place to sing. We also offer two little doves, that is to say, double simplicity.

10. The second mystery is that He came to the temple on that day to mark His coming into the soul of every believer or into the Church, into which He is always ready to enter. That is why in the Introit it says, 'We have thought of thy loving-kindness, O God, in the midst of thy temple, etc.,'[77] because Christ is the tree of life in the midst of paradise, ready to meet the needs of all equally and to bestow His blessings. 'According to thy name, O God, so is thy praise unto the ends of the earth, etc.,' as if it were said, 'Just as You have created all men, and has renewed them, so are you to be praised throughout the whole world,' and so You must be praised by everyone. This was further explained in Book Six, in the chapter *The Eighth Sunday after Pentecost*. Now, so that the Lord

---

[76] Acts 15:9
[77] Psalm 48:9-10, 1

may descend into our soul, the Church exhorts her children to meet Him. Thus she says at the beginning of the morning service, namely in the Invitatory, 'Behold, the Lord the Ruler cometh unto His holy temple; Rejoice and be glad, O Zion! Go forth to meet thy God!' namely by faith and good works. That is why this feast is called the *Hypapante*, that is to say 'the meeting,' because if we want to receive Him in our soul, we must receive His image. This is why it is said in the first responsory, 'Adorn thy bridal chamber, O Zion,' that is, purify yourself with virtue; 'and receive Christ the King,' 'and receive,' implies virtues, for that is how He will come in you. The Epistle is, 'Behold, I will send my messenger, and he shall prepare the way before me, etc.'[78] The Gospel, 'And when the days of her purification according to the law of Moses were accomplished, etc.'[79] The Post Communion is, 'And it was revealed unto him by the Holy Ghost, etc.'[80]

11. And notice that in the time of the Emperor Justinian there was a great death at Constantinople, and that is why the solemnity of the Purification of Mary, through veneration for the Virgin, was established for the reasons mentioned above. But as an infinity of heresies are also abundant, it is customary to ask how what is said in the ninth responsory can be true, namely, that the Blessed Virgin has exterminated all heresies. To this we answer that she did it as much as it was in her, because it was she who made visible the One who was invisible. Because at first we could not find Him. Some looked for Him among the delights of the flesh, others in the midst of riches and others in the books of philosophy, and He was not there. As it says in the Song of Songs, 'I sought him, but I could not find him.'[81] Now no one can get lost in the way unless he wants it,; regarding which it is plainly said in Isaiah, 'This is the way, walk ye in it,'[82] so that the fool himself may not go astray in his way. And what will this path be?

---

[78] Malachi 3:1-4
[79] Luke 2:22-32
[80] Luke 2:26
[81] Song of Songs 5:6
[82] Isaiah 30:21

'I will place salvation in Zion for Israel my glory.'[83] Today we say the capitulum, 'Behold, I will send my messenger, and he shall prepare the way before me,'[84] and this one, 'And I took root in an honourable people,'[85] and also, 'I was exalted like a cedar in Libanus.'[86]

12. On this day we must make a general procession that signifies the procession that Blessed Mary and Joseph made to the temple. Those who are in the procession sing, 'And it was revealed unto him by the Holy Ghost, etc.,'[87] in front of the railings, and they represent the prophets announcing the Nativity of the Lord and His mercy. The melody of those who respond to them is the joy of those who receive this mercy from God. They hold candles in their hands and sing, 'We have thought of thy loving-kindness, O God, in the midst of thy temple, etc.'[88] 'Then took he him up in his arms, etc.,'[89] which is sung in the procession and read in the Gospel, shows that we must not only carry Him in our heart, but also in our arms. Therefore, in the Song of Songs it is said, 'Set me as a seal upon thine heart, as a seal upon thine arm,'[90] for, as St. Paul says to the Corinthians, 'For ye are bought with a price: therefore glorify God in your body.'[91] We must therefore not only bear divinity or humanity, but both, as Simeon did, which is signified by the candle that we carry in the procession. For the wax that bees produce with honey by a work that is all virginal (for this production is not due to any impure union) designates humanity or the flesh that Christ has taken in the womb of the Virgin. The light of the candle marks divinity, 'For the Lord thy

---

[83] Isaiah 46:13
[84] Malachi 3:1
[85] Ecclesiasticus 24:16
[86] Ecclesiasticus 24:17
[87] Luke 2:28
[88] Psalm 48:9-10 'We have thought of thy loving-kindness,' is also sometimes translated as, 'We wait for thy loving-kindness,' or 'We have received thy mercy'
[89] Luke 2:28
[90] Song of Songs 8:6
[91] 1 Corinthians 6:20

God is a consuming fire.'[92] The wick that is in the wax designates His soul, the purest and whitest of all, or the divinity hidden in the flesh, or, according to others, mortality.

13. The lit candle that is carried by hand also designates faith with good works. For as it is said, a candle without light is dead, and that the light cannot shine by itself and apart from the candle, but seems to be dead. So also works without faith and faith without works are said to be dead. The wick hidden in the wax is the right intention. Of which comes Gregory says, 'Act in such a way before men, that your intention remains in secret.' Now, the candles are blessed so that all may be worthy, for there are many who carry darkness in the depths of their hearts, although they seem to shine outwardly. Those are worthy of the candles are those who, as they shine outwardly by the light they carry in their hands, so also they shine within by a true and sincere faith. It is in this that the festivity and the great joy consist.

14. There are lit candles in the procession for six reasons. First, so that each one becomes enlightened and in shining gives to others the example of his works, manifested by the light. Secondly, so that the ordinances of the Christian religion may change and improve, following a custom observed among the Gentiles. For the Romans, on each fifth year, on the calends of February, in honour of Februa, the mother of Mars, whom they considered the god of war, illuminated the city all night long with candles and burning torches. This was so that Mars, her son, might grant them victory over their enemies, for the sake of the solemn honours they rendered to his mother. This festival was named *Burbale*. In the month of February they also sacrificed to Februus,[93] that is, to Pluto, and to the other infernal divinities, for the souls of their dead. They offered solemn victims to these gods, that they might be propitious to these deaths, and the Roman ladies themselves spent all night singing their praises, and celebrated the Festival of Lights. Now it is said that Pluto, having

---

[92] Deuteronomy 4:24
[93] The god of purification in ancient Roman religion

fallen in love with the beautiful and incomparable Proserpine, took her away at the beginning of this month and made her a goddess, and that Ceres, her mother, and her parents, having lit torches, searched through the night for a long time on Etna, a mountain of Sicily. However the Gentiles mark these things as the fictions of the poets. Nevertheless this is the reason why they themselves, at the beginning of February, in memory of this event, roamed the city at night, and there they circulated, carrying burning torches; idolatrous caries, as it is said in the book of Wisdom,[94] who did things hidden or mysterious.

15. Pope Sergius,[95] exchanging and improving these (Gentile) uses and illuminations established the feast of Purification in honour of the Mother of God in the same month and decreed that one would make processions then. So all the people, carrying lit candles in their hands, would march in procession in the churches, in memory of the celestial kingdom, while all the chosen ones, with the bright lamps of their good works, would go to the front with the Bridegroom and will soon be coming with Him to the wedding hall of the celestial city.

16. Thirdly, so that we may imitate the wise virgins of whom the Blessed Virgin is the head, so that, bringing forth in us the lamp of chastity and good works, we deserve to enter with them into the temple of glory, with the true Bridegroom. Fourth, because it is on this day, as Simeon says, that the light has been presented to serve as a torch to the Gentiles. So this procession is Simeon's. Fifth, to mark the divinity and humanity of Christ, as it has been said above. Sixth, to show the purity of the virgin, lest, when they hear of her purification, one might believe that she needed to be purified. We carry lit candles, as if the Church were thus saying, 'The Blessed Virgin does not need purification, for she is all brilliant, all resplendent.' And, for the reasons mentioned above, this festival is called Candlemas.

---

[94] See Wisdom 17
[95] The Feast of the Purification dates from the fourth century in Jerusalem, which predates Pope Sergius I. It gradually evolved and spread in usage over the following centuries

17. This feast has no octave, because although Christ, according to the law, was presented in the temple, yet no doctor gives us, as an obligation, to present children in the temple forty days after birth. Thus, just as the presentation of the children to the temple, according to the ancient writ, has fallen into disuse, since it takes place in baptism, so also there is no octave of the *Hypapante*. For, just as by the first day we recall what was done in the octave, so by the octave we recall the thing for which what happened was done. We will speak in their place of the celebrations of the Annunciation, the Assumption and the Nativity of the Virgin.

8 THE CHAIR OF SAINT PETER

1. The Church solemnizes the feast of the Chair of St Peter, an honour which he obtained at Antioch, when the siege of which city is reported to have been lifted. Some claim that he was promoted to this dignity by Theophilus, prince of Antioch, whose son Peter was revived, having died at the age of fourteen. Peter also converted the people of the city, who, because of this, built a church in the midst of which a high pulpit was placed, and they enthroned the Apostle, who, thus elevated, could be heard and seen by all the world. He sat there for seven years. The Church, then, made the solemnity of this honour rendered to St Peter, because it was then that the prelates of the Church began to have places of distinction and to receive the honours due to their dignity. Then this word of the Psalmist was fulfilled, 'Let them exalt him also in the congregation of the people, etc.'[96] And notice that Peter was raised or exalted in three ways and that is why we are giving him a triple festival.

2. First, he was exalted in the Church Militant, of which he was head, and governed in a manner worthy of praise both in faith and morals. It is to this elevation that the festival of this day is related, as has been said. Second, he was exalted in the church or assembly of the wicked and the ungodly by dispersing them and converting them to faith. This is why the second celebration is called, 'St Peter in Chains,' for then he dispelled the church from the wicked, and converted a great number of men to the faith. Thirdly, he was exalted into the Church Triumphant, namely,

---

[96] Psalm 107:32

happily entering into it, to which the third feast, that is to say, that of his martyrdom or his passion, relates.

3. It is also a triple festival for five other reasons. First by privilege, for he was privileged above all others, and that is why he is more honoured and in greater consideration, for he was the Prince of the Apostles and received the keys of the kingdom of heaven. His love for Christ was also more ardent and his power more effective, for his shadow healed the sick. Second, because of his office or dignity. For he had the dignity or the office of prelature over the universal Church, a prelature which spread over the three parts of the world, namely Asia, Africa and Europe. That is why the Church celebrates three solemnities in honour of St Peter during the year. Third, because of his blessings, because this Apostle, who had the power to bind and untie, delivers us from three kinds of sins, namely sins of thoughts, words, and deeds, or because we sin towards God, to our neighbours and to ourselves. Or this benefit may be a triple good that the sinner acquires in the Church by virtue or the power of the keys. The first is the absolution by declaration of debt.[97] The second is the commutation of the sentence from purgatory to temporal punishment. The third is the relaxation in part of the temporal pain. Fourthly, because of debt, namely because Peter feeds and nourishes us in the triple pasture, namely, that of speech, that of example and that of temporal help. Fifthly, because of his example, so that no one would despair, even though he would have denied Christ three times, like Peter, provided that he also wants, like Peter, to confess God with heart, mouth, and works.

4. It must not be forgotten that this feast of the enthronement of St Peter was formerly called the Feast of St Peter's Dishes.[98] For it was once a custom among the Gentiles, according to Master Jean Beleth, every year in February, to offer to God on this day wine and food on the sepulchre of their parents, perhaps moved by this precept of Tobit, 'Lay out thy bread, and thy wine upon the burial of a just man,'[99] and these dishes were eaten during the night by the demons. Yet the Gentiles thought that these dishes

---

[97] *Mea culpa*, beating one's breast while declaring, 'through my fault'
[98] *Sancti Petri epularum*
[99] Tobit 4:18

were absorbed by wandering souls around the sepulchres which they called shadows. The Holy Fathers, wishing to abolish this custom, decreed that we should celebrate the feast of the enthronement of St Peter, which took place both in Rome and in Antioch, on the same day that the Gentiles observed these ceremonies. It is from these dishes that the custom has come to call this feast the 'Feast of the dishes of Blessed Peter.' On this day, however, there is only one Collect relating to the enthronement at Antioch.

5. Now one says the Epistle, 'Peter, an apostle of Jesus Christ, etc.,'[100] and the Gospel is, 'When Jesus came into the coasts of Caesarea Philippi, etc.'[101] The trait is, 'thou art Peter, etc.,'[102] or sometimes, 'Peter, an apostle of Jesus Christ, etc.' At the feast of Blessed Mathias,[103] an Apostle, the Epistle, 'And in those days Peter stood up in the midst of the disciples, etc.,'[104] is said, and the Gospel is, 'At that time Jesus answered and said, I thank thee, O Father, etc.'[105]

---

[100] 1 Peter 1:1-7
[101] Matthew 16:13-19
[102] Matthew 16:18-19
[103] February 24 or 25
[104] Acts 1:15-26
[105] Matthew 11:25-30

9 THE ANNUNCIATION OF THE VIRGIN MARY

1. The feast of the Annunciation of the Blessed Virgin Mary is the day when the Angel announced to Mary the good news after which she conceived the Saviour. Then the prophecies were fulfilled. That is why the Church reads and sings extracts from the prophets. That is also why we sing the Introit., 'Drop down, ye heavens, from above, and let the skies pour down righteousness, etc.'[106] Now this is to say that the preachers, 'rain,' that is, announce the Just, that is, Christ, because Christ is called the Just; 'let the earth be opened,' that is to say, the Blessed Virgin, that she opens herself, I say, by her consent; 'and bud forth a saviour,' that is, Christ. We talked about this in Book Six, in the chapter *The First Sunday of Advent.* The Epistle is, 'And there shall come forth a rod out of the stem of Jesse, etc.,'[107] while other churches say, 'Moreover the Lord spake again unto Ahaz, saying, etc.'[108] The Gospel is, 'And in the sixth month the angel Gabriel was sent from God, etc.'[109] Now the words from this Gospel, 'In the sixth month, etc.,' are explained in this way, 'the sixth month,' namely, the month of March, in which the Blessed Virgin conceived, 'is the sixth from that,' that is to say, from the conception of that, namely of Elizabeth, 'who is called barren,' because Elizabeth conceived Blessed John the Baptist on the calends of October.

---

[106] Isaiah 45:8 The Vulgate has, 'Drop down dew, ye heavens, from above, and let the clouds rain the just: let the earth be opened, and bud forth a saviour: and let justice spring up together: I the Lord have created him.' which is the text examined here
[107] Isaiah 11:1-5
[108] Isaiah 7:10-15
[109] Luke 1:26-38

During the Hours, the capitulum, 'In those days, and at that time, will I cause the Branch of righteousness to grow up unto David, etc.'[110]

2. This festival is well suited to the time of spring, because it is in spring that God became man and everything was renewed. Now this feast belongs to the Lord and to Blessed Mary; that is why Christmas and the Annunciation of the Lord have the same Preface. It is customary to call this feast, 'Annunciation of the Lord.' 'Gloria in Excelsis,' 'Go the Mass is said,' and *Te Deum laudamus* should not be sung in this festival. We have explained the reason for this in the *Preface* of this book. If this festival happens to fall on the Sunday of the Passion or Palm Sunday, it is moved to Monday. This is usually done on special Sundays. If it arrives during the three days before Easter, it will be celebrated by anticipation on the Saturday before Palm Sunday, according to some; but there are some who put it back to the octave. Likewise, if it falls on Easter Day, the service of this feast, which is compiled or extracted from Advent, cannot be properly celebrated in this week; that is why it is better to send it back to Monday after the Easter octave.

3. On this day, at various times, it is said that God has performed a great many works, which a poet has concisely rendered in the following beautiful verses:

> *Salute, feast day, which closes our wounds,*
> *Where the angel was sent, where the Christ suffered and was crucified,*
> *Creation day and all at once of the fall of Adam.*
> *On that day, because of the merits of his offering, Abel perished by the sword of Cain;*
> *Melchizedek offers his sacrifice, and Isaac is placed on the stake.*
> *On that day Blessed John, who baptized Christ, took off;*
> *Peter is put on the cross; James put to death under Herod;*
> *Many bodies of saints are resurrected with Christ.*

---

[110] Jeremiah 33:15

THE ANNUNCIATION OF THE VIRGIN MARY

On this day the thief receives from the mouth of Christ such consoling assurance. Amen.[111]

---

[111] Today the familiar hymn. 'Hail thee, Festival Day.' These are the words which Durandus gives them without saying where he drew them from:
Salve festa dies, quae vulnera nostra coercet.
Angelus est missus, est passus et in cruce Christus. Est Adam factus, et eodem tempore lapsus.
Ob meritum decimae cadit Abel fratris ab ense.
Offert Melchisedech, Isaac supponitur aris.
Est decollatus Christi Baptista beatus.
Est Petrus erectus, Jacobus sub Herode peremptus.
Corpora Sanctorum cum Christo mulla resurgunt.
Latro per Christum tam dulce suscipit amen

10 SAINTS APOSTLES PHILIP AND JAMES

1. Easter time, as has been often said, refers to the eighth age, where the good that will belong to each, in an unequal charity, will belong to everyone, because everyone will rejoice in the good of others as his own.
2. Therefore, in order that Easter time should be in harmony with the solemnities that come in this time, and especially because the Apostles had no particular solemnities in the early Church, it was decreed that in May we would celebrate solemnities in honour of all the Apostles. This meant that various days of solemnization would not separate those who have been elevated by the same dignity and the apostolate that has been raised to celestial glory. It is said that the Greeks celebrate this festival at the feast of the Apostles Peter and Paul. It is also on this day that the feast of the Apostles Philip and James is found, perhaps because they suffered on that day. This James is called the Minor, to distinguish him from St James of Compostela, son of Zebedee, who is called the Greater, not by his age, but by his vocation. For this happens for the bishops who replace the Apostles, because the one who was first consecrated in a way outweighs the others who have the same dignity Thus James the Major was called first by the Lord, became he was the first and became more intimate with Him. And He called to His inner circle James the Major, namely, when He was transfigured and when He revived a dead man in the name of the Lord.
3. This James is also called son of Alphaeus, because he was, in fact, the son of Alphaeus. He is also called the brother of the Lord according to the flesh, because it is said that he resembled His face, or because he was the son of Alphaeus, brother of Joseph

husband of Blessed Mary, and Mary, his sister. For those who were cousins on both sides were called brothers among the Jews and Jesus was the supposed son of Joseph. Or he is called the Lord's brother, that is, his cousin, because he is the son of the sister of Blessed Mary. The Tuscans still retain this use. But Joseph is also called the Lord's parent, either because he is his supposed father, or because he was a relative of the Lord on the side of his mother, Blessed Mary.

4. Now, to establish the more incontestable evidence of the things mentioned above, it must be noted that Joachim, father of Blessed Mary, married Anne, who had a sister named Imeria. And this Imeria begot Elizabeth and Eliud; and Elizabeth begot John the Baptist. From Eliud was born to Emineud the holy St Servatius, whose body rests at Maestricht on the Meuse, a bishopric of the country of Liege. Now it is said that Anne had three spouses, namely, Joachim, Cleophas who was brother of Joseph, and Solomon. From the first she had a daughter, namely, Mary, mother of the Lord, who was married to Joseph. From her Christ was begotten. We talked about the generation of Joseph and Mary in Book Six, in the chapter *The Christmas Office*. After the death of her first husband, Anne had a second daughter named Mary, and gave her in marriage to Alphaeus, of whom she had four sons, namely James the Minor, Joseph the Just who was also called Barsabas, also Simon and Judas. By her third husband, Solomon, whom she had after the death of the second, she had two sons, James the Major and John the Evangelist.

5. Now, this James is called the Just, by merit of his birth or his condition. For it is said that he was holy from the womb, or sanctified in the bosom of his mother. He was ordained the first bishop of Jerusalem by the Apostles Peter, James, and John. It is he who, with Basil, bishop of Caesarea, has left us in his writings a liturgy of the sacrifice of the Mass. According to tradition, St James celebrated the first Mass at Jerusalem, after the Passover of the Lord, and St Peter, the first at Antioch. St James did not drink wine or other fermented drink. He did not eat meat. He never shaved or healed himself, he never took a bath, he prayed for so long with his knees on the ground that his knees were harder than a camel's skin

6. The Jews threw him from the pinnacle of the temple, while he was preaching the name of Christ, and he was slain with fullers' poles. Now, the fuller is the workman who whitens the pieces of linen. Some have said that it was because of the crime of this murder that the Jews had been destroyed, as a body of a nation, by Titus and Vespasian. So they do not attribute their destruction to the death of Christ.

7. In this festival there are churches that say the Introit, 'in the time of their trouble, when they cried unto thee, etc.'[112] The Epistle is, 'Then shall the just stand with great constancy, etc.,'[113] the Gospel is, 'Let not your heart be troubled, etc.,'[114] and the Post Communion is, 'Jesus saith unto him, Have I been so long time with you, etc.'[115] At times, one says the capitulum, 'Then shall the just stand, etc.,'[116] and this one, 'We fools esteemed their life madness, etc.,'[117] then this other, 'They shall hunger no more, neither thirst any more, etc.'[118]

---

[112] Nehemiah 9:27, Psalm 33:1
[113] Wisdom 5:1-5
[114] John 14:1-13
[115] John 14:9-10
[116] Wisdom 5:1
[117] Wisdom 5:4
[118] Revelation 7:16

11 THE FINDING OF THE HOLY CROSS

1. Our second hope is in the Holy Cross of the Lord. For just as the Blessed Virgin carried the Lord, so did the Holy Cross in its own way. And as the Lord gives to the waters of baptism and to the other sacraments the virtue which sanctifies, in the same way, by its contact with the flesh of the Lord, the wood of the Cross was sanctified, so that in its own way it could sanctify us. Furthermore, as the Cross saves us by such effects and by the virtue which it possesses, that is why we sing the following in its honour.

2. 'O Cross! brighter than all the stars, you alone were worthy,'[119] that is, after having received the privilege, 'to bear the price of the redemption of the world, etc.' And since the end of the Cross is glory, then at the end of many of the antiphons of the Cross, 'Alleluia,' is said. It is said during the Hours with the captulum, 'But God forbid that I should glory, save in the cross of our Lord Jesus Christ, etc.'[120]

3. Two festivals of the Cross are celebrated, namely that of the Exaltation, which we will speak of in its place, and that of its Finding, because the Holy Cross was found in the time of Pope Eusebius,[121] by blessed Helen, mother of Constantine, by means of a man named Judas, who was then Jewish. That is why, in the canon of the same Eusebius it reads, 'We command that the cross

---

[119] O cross, brighter than all the stars, you alone were worthy to bear the price of the redemption of the world, sweet wood, sweet nails, holding up the sweet body; save your flock assembled here to sing your praises
[120] Galatians 6:14
[121] Reigned for only four months, in 309 or 310

of our Lord Jesus Christ, which has just been discovered lately, on the fifth day of May, under our pontificate and our government of the Holy Roman Church, is celebrated by a festival, on the aforesaid day of the calends of its finding.' Now, this feast is greater than the feast of the Exaltation, as will be said here.

4. Now it is read, regarding the aforesaid Judas, that, having converted to the faith, he afterwards became bishop of Jerusalem, and having changed his name, he took that of Cyriacus. It is said that the devil prophesied to him saying, 'Judas delivered Christ to death, but this Judas exalted the dead Christ, and discovered or unveiled the art of the magicians. But Julien, my intimate and friend, will soon become king and avenge me for him.' This is what happened.

5. For the monk Julian, having apostatized and abandoned his monastery and his order, and acquired the consulate in Rome by crime, thus became emperor and persecutor of the Christians and afflicted them with various penalties and put them to death. We also read that a certain soldier named Cyriacus then killed this Julien. One also reads of this Julien that an unbearable stench escapes from his tomb in Constantinople.

6. If we ask why we make a feast of the Cross on which Christ was hated and scourged, and not that of the donkey on which he was honoured, and also of the things which the Lord touched, we can answer that the praises and honours which were rendered to Him on the donkey are transient and of this world. Moreover, that is not where our salvation came from, and we must not worry about it. In addition, it is not said that these other things that the Lord touched have worked miracles and healings. It is not by them either that we were redeemed, while the outrages that Christ suffered on the Cross produced our redemption. Today, we say the Introit, 'But God forbid that I should glory, etc.,'[122] and we read the Epistle, 'But I trust in the Lord that I also myself shall come shortly, etc.,'[123] because it says, 'But God forbid that I

---

[122] Galatians 6:14 Psalm 67:1

[123] Philippians 2:24-30 There appears to be an error as the next quotation is not found here

should glory, save in the cross of our Lord Jesus Christ.'[124] Other churches say, 'Let this mind be in you, which was also in Christ Jesus, etc.'[125] The Gospel is, 'Again, the kingdom of heaven is like unto treasure hid in a field, etc.,'[126] because the Lord's Cross was found literally in a field, or morally in the field of the Church. The Cross of the Lord is called the treasure, because it is through it that the kingdom of heaven was purchased for us. He who sees this treasure in the Church goes and sells all that he has, that is to say all the transient pleasures, and he buys this field of the Church. Others say, 'There was a man of the Pharisees, named Nicodemus, a ruler of the Jews, etc.'[127] And it must be noted that the feast of the Cross is always done with the feast of Martyrs, because the cross means martyrdom. And that is why in the festivities of the Holy Cross we read, in certain churches, six lessons of the martyrs, and there is a mixture of the two Offices. We have spoken of the sign of the cross in the *Preface* to Book Five.

---

[124] Galatians 6:14
[125] Philippians 2:5-11
[126] Matthew 13:44-46
[127] John 3:1-15

12 THE APPARITION OF SAINT MICHAEL

1. The Church celebrates the Feast of Angels for two reasons. The first is because, 'Are they not all ministering spirits, sent forth to minister for them who shall be heirs of salvation?'[128] The second reason is because they fight in our favour against the evil angels, and they do not allow us to be tempted above our strengths. Regarding this fight is said in the Apocalypse, 'And there was war in heaven.'[129] This war will take place especially in the time of the Antichrist, and took place at the death of the martyrs, and it still exists. 'And the great dragon,' that is to say, the devil, 'was cast out,'[130] of heaven, that is to say, far from heavenly men, and sent back to the heart of the wicked. Now the chief of this war is the most blessed Michael and that is why a feast is celebrated in his honour, although he is of the last hierarchy, that is to say of the lower order of the angels, for there are nine orders of angels, as was said in the *Preface* of Book Four. There are, I say, nine orders of angels who, although they are all sent, since they are the ministers of the Spirit and Isaiah says that one of the seraphim was sent to him,[131] they are, however, seldom sent.

2. Of which Daniel says, 'thousand thousands ministered unto him, etc.'[132] Michael is the prince of those who are sent. Michael was the prince of the Church of the Jews, as we see in Daniel,

---

[128] Hebrews 1:14
[129] Revelation 12:7
[130] Revelation 12:9
[131] See Isaiah 6:6
[132] Daniel 7:10

now he is the prince of the Church of Christians, for the Church, which is now among Christians, was formerly with the Jews.

3. This feast, which is the commemoration of St Michael's victory, has its origin in the following fact. While the barbarians ravaged Apulia, the Christians, by a fasting of three days, which had been prescribed, implored the assistance of St Michael. By the visible help of this angel, the barbarians were put to flight three times and the Christians won the victory. It is also called the Feast of the Apparition, because it was on Mount Gargano, as we shall see, that St Michael revealed himself. Assuredly Michael, Gabriel, and Raphael, are personal names that belong to angels, but there are other names which belong to the orders of the angels, as was said in the *Preface* of Book Four.

4. But since this festival is common to all angels, why is it spiritually called the feast of St Michael and not Gabriel or Raphael? I answer that Michael is the angel who was sent to Egypt, who made these famous plagues of Egypt, who separated the Red Sea, leading the people through the desert and into the Promised Land. He is the chief and guardian of paradise, it is he who is in charge of receiving the souls and who is the prince of the Church. That is why we must venerate him more than others. The second reason is that he founded the Church and consecrated the altar, from where it is said, 'And another angel came and stood at the altar, etc.'[133] This took place on Mount Gargano. Then the angel revealed it to men by means of the bishop of this region. The third reason is that men, venerating the angels, manage to share their fate, and it is for this reason that, on Sundays and solemn feasts, nine psalms, nine lessons and nine responsories are sung, so that by this singing we may reach the society of the nine orders of angels, whose charge is to celebrate God in their songs.

5. Now the Church, sharing the joy of the angels, says to them in the Introit, 'Bless the Lord, ye his angels, etc.,'[134] and as the angels praise God, we must also praise Him. That is why follows the verse, 'Bless the Lord, O my soul, etc.' The Epistle is 'The

---

[133] Revelation 8:3
[134] Psalm 103:20, 1

Revelation of Jesus Christ, which God gave unto him, etc.,'[135] in which it says, 'John to the seven churches, etc.' By the seven churches or by the seven spirits, for that is the understanding or meaning that belongs to this day, we understand the universality of the angels, and by the seven days we hear the course of the present life. Then follows the, 'Bless the Lord, ye his angels, etc.,' responsory and verse,[136] for the reason given above. The Alleluia is, 'Before the gods will I sing praise unto thee, etc.'[137]

6. Now, the Church speaks in this way because the angels are ready to carry our prayers before the throne of God. For they ceaselessly stand at our side, watching and listening to us, which comes from reading in the Song of Songs, 'Thou that dwellest in the gardens, the companions,' that is, the angels, 'hearken to thy voice.'[138] Their compassion is for the good, and the suffering and the kind of jealousy and sorrow they experience on the occasion of the wicked, causes them to keep their eyes on us. Then follows the Gospel, 'At the same time came the disciples unto Jesus, saying, Who is the greatest in the kingdom of heaven, etc.,'[139] in which we are commanded to be careful not to tempt little children to sin, because there is mention of angels, namely, 'That in heaven their angels do always behold the face of my Father which is in heaven.'

7. It is shown in the Offertory that they are always ready to carry our prayers before God: 'And another angel came and stood at the altar,' and, 'there was given unto him much incense,'[140] that is to say, the prayers lit by the fire of charity; 'And the smoke of the incense, which came with the prayers of the saints, ascended up before God,'[141] that is to say, the prayers presented by the Angel ascended to the throne of God. In the Post Communion, it pleases the Church to bless as before, that is why there are

---

[135] Revelation 1:1-15
[136] Psalm 103:20, 1
[137] Psalm 138:1 The Vulgate has, 'I will sing praise to thee in the sight of the angels. (Ps 137:1)
[138] Song of Songs 8:13
[139] Matthew 18:1-10
[140] Revelation 8:3
[141] Revelation 8:4

churches that say, 'Bless the Lord, ye his angels, etc.'[142] Now, what is said, namely that St Michael fought against the dragon, is understood in an allegorical sense. In this sense, Michael means Christ. In the historical sense, one reads or describes in the Church that the devil, in favour of the faithful or because of the faithful, was driven out by the ministry of Michael and the other angels. On this feast we say the capitulum, 'The Revelation of Jesus Christ, which God gave unto him, etc.,'[143] and this one, 'Blessed is he that readeth, and they that hear the words of this prophecy, etc.,'[144] and, 'John to the seven churches which are in Asia, etc.'[145]

---

[142] Psalm 103:20
[143] Revelation 1:1
[144] Revelation 1:3
[145] Revelation 1:4

13 SAINTS GERVASE AND PROTASE

1. At the feast of Saints Gervase and Protase, according to the institution of Gregory, the Introit, 'I will hear what God the Lord will speak: for he will speak peace unto his people, etc.'[146] is sung. For it was on this day that peace was cemented between the emperor of the Romans and Agisulphus, king of the Lombards, whom the most Christian queen, Theodosia, his wife (to whom Gregory wrote a book of dialogues), converted to the faith. Now the Offices of the saints belong, in part to the saints themselves, in part to the events that took place at the time of their feast.

---

[146] Psalm 85:8, 1

14 SAINT JOHN THE BAPTIST

1. As, 'Among them that are born of women there hath not risen a greater than John the Baptist,'[147] the Church with good reason celebrates his feast. She celebrates two festivities in his honour, namely that of his Nativity and that of her Decollation.[148] Of his Nativity, for four reasons. First, because of history, because the Lord says of him through the mouth of an angel, as seen in the Gospel, 'many shall rejoice at his birth;'[149] Second, because of allegory and his ministry, because by John is figured the origin of the grace that Christ brought us, for John preceded Christ by his annunciation, his nativity, his preaching, his passion and his descent into hell. Third, because as the Blessed Virgin was sanctified in her mother's womb, so was John the Baptist. Fourthly, because he first announced the eternal joys, and that is why he is called Lucifer and Dove; hence it is said in the Canticles, 'the voice of the turtle is heard in our land,'[150] and Job says, 'Canst thou bring forth Mazzaroth in his season?'[151] And his birth was announced by Gabriel.

2. Now, John was named Lucifer, *Luciferum*, because he inaugurated the new time. Hence, in some churches, Mass is said in the morning, because the nativity of John was like dawn, and the Nativity of Christ was like the rising of the sun. Or we say

---

[147] Matthew 11:11
[148] Beheading
[149] Luke 1:14
[150] Song of Songs 2:12 'turtle' here can also translate as 'dove' or 'turtledove'
[151] Job 38:32 The Vulgate has, 'Canst thou bring forth the day star in its time,' where the Latin word for 'day star' is *luciferum*, which is a grammatical form of the word 'lucifer,' which can also be translated as, 'light bearer'

Mass at daybreak, because we read in the Gospel of St Luke that John was sanctified and filled with the Holy Spirit in the womb of his mother. This is why it is right to praise, at the beginning of the day, his Creator who has deigned to honour him in his mother's womb.

3. He also has another proper Mass like the other saints, which is said around the time of Terce. Or the first Mass is the vigil of the Evangelist. Or else a second Mass is celebrated, because John the Baptist was at the same time both martyr and precursor, hence this Mass is the one for the martyr, and the Introit is, 'The righteous shall flourish like the palm tree, etc.'[152] For Isaiah and Jeremiah have prophesied about him, Jeremiah, by his own life, which was like that of John, and Isaiah, as we see in this day's Epistle, 'Listen, O isles, unto me; and hearken, ye people, from far, etc.'[153] from which is taken the Introit, 'The Lord hath called me from the womb, etc.'[154] Then follow these words, 'he hath made my mouth like a sharp sword.' The sharp sword is the language of the preacher who cuts off superfluities. Then these words, he 'made me a polished shaft.'[155] The chosen arrow is the preacher who practices his own teachings. John was a sharp arrow when he said, 'O generation of vipers, who hath warned you to flee from the wrath to come?'[156] The responsory is, 'Before I formed thee in the belly I knew thee, etc.,'[157] and relates to the nativity of John. The Alleluia is, 'And thou, child, shalt be called the prophet of the Highest, etc.,'[158] and this one, 'Among them that are born of women there hath not risen a greater than John the Baptist, etc.'[159] The Gospel is, 'Now Elisabeth's full time came, etc.'[160] On this day the capitula are, 'Listen, O isles, unto

---

[152] Psalm 92:12-13
[153] Isaiah 49:1-3, 5-7
[154] Isaiah 49:1-2, Psalm 92:1
[155] The Vulgate has, 'hath made me as a chosen arrow'
[156] Matthew 3:7
[157] Jeremiah 1:5,9
[158] Luke 1:76
[159] Matthew 11:11
[160] Luke 1:57-68

me, etc.,'[161] and this one, 'Before I formed thee in the belly I knew thee, etc.,'[162] and this other, 'Kings shall see and arise, etc.'[163]

4. Now, we fast on the vigil of Blessed John the Baptist, as if to sympathize with his fasting in the wilderness and his austere life. And his vigil has a full Office, because after the decollation of John, Christ ate the Lamb, and was crucified. For John was like the cornerstone, that is, the stone cementing in a common union the Old and New Testaments. That is why we are solemn then, more because of the mystery than because of the very person of the saint. Also because he held the middle ground between the Testaments, for he was the end of the Old and the beginning of the New. For the law and the prophets extend to John inclusively, hence the Office of that day belongs partly to the Old and part to the New Testament.

5. It was on this day that John the Evangelist died but his festivity has been moved, as will be said in the chapter of his Feast. The Church does not solemnize the feast of the Decollation to the same degree as this one, as it will be said. St John was then, as it was said above, sanctified in the bosom of his mother, like Jeremiah. Therefore Jeremiah is read, which is proved by what is said in the Gospel, 'Elisabeth was filled with the Holy Ghost,'[164] and, 'the babe leaped in my womb for joy.'[165] But we do not read with what kind of sanctification John was sanctified.

6. Yet there are those who say that he was cleansed from all sin, but in the explanatory note made on this passage, 'You want to be baptized by me;' then, 'it is I who must be baptized by you,'[166] that is, to be purified from original sin, it is said that John spoke in the person of all men in general. However, he was conceived in original sin.

7. Paul, historian, deacon of the Roman Church, monk of Monte Cassino, on wishing one day to bless the paschal candle, found that his voice had become hoarse. In order that his voice should be restored to him, he composed in honour of Blessed John the

---

[161] Isaiah 49:1
[162] Jeremiah 1:5
[163] Isaiah 49:7
[164] Luke 1:41
[165] Luke 1:44
[166] See Matthew 3:13-14

Baptist the hymn, 'Since thy servants desire to sound forth, etc.'[167] at the beginning of which he asks that his voice be restored to him, which was granted (as formerly to Zechariah) by the merits of St John.

8. On this feast we do not sing Alleluia, as frequently as we do at the festivities of Peter and Paul and others, in the last Night Office during which we make it ring out. The reason for this is that John the Baptist represents the law, and his birth predates the Resurrection of Christ and our joy is the joy of the Gospel. There are, however, those who celebrate the Office without an Alleluia, at the beginning of the night, because of the figure of the law; and then they redouble the Office with the Alleluia, in the middle of the night, and finish it at the beginning of the day, in memory of the ancient observance. We talked about this and we said in Book Five, in the chapter *The Night Offices*, why on this feast we sing the Night Offices at the beginning of the night.

9. Note that formerly it was customary to celebrate a Quadragesima before this feast, and another before the Nativity of the Lord but afterwards, because of human frailty, it was reduced to three weeks before Christmas and three before this feast. As a result it has been forbidden in the canons to celebrate a wedding during these three weeks. But this has been abolished, as it has been said in the chapter *The Sacraments of the Church*, in Book One.

10. Three special ceremonies take place in this festival. In some countries, on the eve of this feast, to conform to an ancient observance, the bones of men and children and other unclean objects were gathered and attached to a wheel. They would then set fire to the wheel causing a thick smoke to rise. Then, carrying brands or torches, they would roll the wheel as they walked through the fields. They obtained this custom from the Gentiles, for formerly the dragons, excited to pleasure because of the heat of the season, often dropped their sperm while flying through the air, which would fall into wells and fountains which corrupted the waters. Then, the year was catastrophic in its rate of mortality,

---

[167] The first stanza is, 'Since thy servants desire to sound forth with vocal chords well strung, thy wondrous deeds, from all uncleanness free the lips of the guilty ones, O holy John!'

because those who drank from these waters perished or contracted serious diseases. That is why the philosophers had ordained that fires and wells should be frequently lit here and there and that unclean objects should be burned to obtain an impure smoke.

11. They knew that this smoke could put the dragons to flight and as it is in this time especially that this was done, so that is why some still observe this practice. Dragons are animals and it is because of this that one reads, in the psalm, 'Praise ye the Lord from the heavens,'[168] but it says *dracones*, 'dragons,'[169] and not, *thracones*, that is to say the fissures of the earth, as some have interpreted it. Now these animals fly in the air, swim in the water and roam the earth. They tolerate nothing impure and are put to flight by resinous smoke, like elephants by their own grunts.

12. There is another reason for burning animal bones which is that it is in memory of the fact that the bones of John the Baptist were burned by the Gentiles in the city of Sebastia. Alternatively, this may relate to the New Testament as the children throw and burn old objects, to indicate that at the arrival of the new law the Old Testament must cease. For it has been said, 'And ye shall eat old store, and bring forth the old because of the new.'[170] We carry firebrands or torches, and we make fires, to signify that St John was the light, the lamp lit, the predecessor and the precursor of the true light, 'which lighteth every man that cometh into the world.'[171] This is why it is said, 'He was a burning and a shining light,'[172] who prepared the way for the Lord in the wilderness.

13. A wheel is rolled in certain places to indicate that, just as the sun, when it has reached the highest point of its course, can no longer rise but then descends into its circle. So also the fame of John, who was looked upon as the Christ, diminished when He appeared, as he himself says, 'He must increase, but I must

---

[168] Psalm 148

[169] The Hebrew word, *tanniyn*, translated here means a monster of some kind, either of land or sea. For example, it is translated as 'a great serpent,' (Ezekiel 29:3) and, 'whale,' (Genesis 1:21, Job 7:12)

[170] Leviticus 26:10

[171] John 1:9

[172] John 5:35

decrease.'[173] Some say that it is because at this time the days begin to decrease, while they start to lengthen again at the time of Nativity of Christ. But as they start to decrease before the feast of St John and they begin to increase before the Nativity, we must hear these words as referring to the nativity in the bosom of his mother, namely when both, Christ and John, were conceived. For John was conceived at the time of the decay of days in September, and Christ at the moment of their growth in April. Again, this can be understood as the day of the death of one or the other, for the body of Christ was lifted up on the Cross, and John the Baptist was beheaded.

---

[173] John 3:30

15 SAINTS PETER AND PAUL

1. The question that arises concerning these two saints is if they suffered on the same day. Henry the Solitary suggests that St Paul suffered on the same day, but a year later. The Popes Pelagius and Nicholas, St Ambrose and the other holy Fathers, suggest that they had suffered on the same day and at the same time, under the Emperor Nero, namely in the fourteenth year of his reign. Otherwise, the histories written of these two Apostles would be false. However, they suffered neither in the same place of Rome nor the same torture. St Peter was crucified in the city itself but St Paul, who was a Roman citizen, as we read in the Acts of the Apostles, although he was of Tarsus, was beheaded outside the walls of the city, a punishment which seemed more honourable. And one reads that milk escaped from his body instead of blood. Later, after the Emperor Constantine had raised churches in honour of the two Apostles, the Roman pontiff wanted to separate their bodies. However as there was doubt about the identity of their relics, a heavenly voice was heard which said, 'The largest bones belong to the preacher and the smaller ones to the fisherman.' Thus we distinguished their relics, which were placed in the churches which were respectively dedicated to them. Then Pope Sylvester, wishing to consecrate these churches, weighed the bones big and small with great respect, placing half in one and the other half in the other church. That is why there are some who celebrate this division at None[174] and on the eighth day before the ides of July, because it was on this day that this division took place. Others celebrate it on the fifteenth or sixteenth day of

---

[174] One of Canonical Hours, see Book Five

the same month. Others say that the feast of the division of St Peter and St. Paul is made on this day, because of their separation which took place in Jerusalem after twelve years,[175] when they separated to go and preach to the Gentiles. On this feast they sing the great sequence, 'The heavens declare the glory of God, etc.,'[176] and the Gospel of the Ascension, 'Afterward he appeared unto the eleven as they sat at meat, etc.,'[177] beginning at the end, 'So then after the Lord had spoken unto them, etc.'

2. Although the feasts of the two Apostles fall on the same day, however, the blessed Gregory has decreed that one would say only the Office of blessed Peter on this day, both because it is on this day that the church of Blessed Peter was dedicated, and because he was the first to convert. Also because he was more dignified, having obtained the pontificate in the Roman Church. The Introit, 'Now I know of a surety, that the Lord hath sent his angel, etc.,'[178] is said at Mass. The Collect is common to the two Apostles, 'O God, Who hast consecrated this day, etc.,'[179] this is why we do not remember St Paul. The Epistle is, 'Now about that time Herod the king, etc.,'[180] and the Alleluia is, 'That thou art Peter, and upon this rock I will build my church, etc.'[181] The Gospel is, 'When Jesus came into the coasts of Caesarea Philippi, etc.,'[182] where we read these words, 'Whom do men say that I the Son of man am?' According to Jeremiah, in the Hebrew text we read, 'The son of Adam.' During the Hours one says the capitula, 'Now about that time Herod the king stretched forth his hands, etc.,'[183] and this one, 'And, behold, the angel of the Lord came upon him, etc.,'[184] and this one, 'And when Peter was come to

---

[175] Or twelve years after the Ascension
[176] Psalm 19:1-5
[177] Mark 16:14-20
[178] Acts 12:11 Psalm 139:1-2
[179] O God, Who hast consecrated this day to the martyrdom of Thine apostles Peter and Paul, grant to Thy Church in all things to follow their teaching from whom it received the right ordering of religion in the beginning. Through our Lord
[180] Acts 12:1-11
[181] Matthew 16:18
[182] Matthew 16:13-19
[183] Acts 12:1
[184] Acts 12:7

SAINTS PETER AND PAUL

himself, etc.'[185] The following day, the feast of St Paul is celebrated, and the Introit, 'I know whom I have believed, etc.'[186] is said at Mass. The Collect is, 'O God, Who didst teach the multitude of the nations, etc.'[187] The Gradual is, 'For he that wrought effectually in Peter to the apostleship, etc.,'[188] and the verse is, 'his grace which was bestowed upon me was not in vain, etc.'[189] The Epistle is, 'But I certify you, brethren, that the gospel which was preached of me is not after man., etc.,'[190] the Alleluia is, 'Go thy way: for he is a chosen vessel unto me, etc.,'[191] and the Gospel is, 'And Simon Peter answered and said, etc.'[192] In other churches it is said, 'This is my commandment, etc.'[193] The Communion is, 'Verily I say unto you, That ye which have followed me, etc.'[194] Likewise, at the service of Blessed Paul's Night Office, some small verses are preceded by the antiphons of Lauds,[195] as was said in Book Six, in the chapter *Holy Trinity Sunday*, and we say the capitulum, 'I have fought a good fight, etc.'[196]

3. At the octave of these Apostles, it is said, 'I will give glory to thee, O Lord, O King, etc.,'[197] but in the vigil one says the Introit, 'When thou wast young, thou girdedst thyself, and walkedst whither thou wouldest, etc.,'[198] and the Epistle, 'Now Peter and John went up together into the temple, etc.'[199] The Gospel is,

---

[185] Acts 12:11
[186] 2 Timothy 1:12 Psalm 139:1-2
[187] O God, Who didst teach the multitude of the nations by the preaching of the blessed Apostle, Paul, grant us, we beseech Thee, that, venerating his natal day, we may experience the benefits of his intercession with Thee. Through our Lord
[188] Galatians 2:8-9
[189] 1 Corinthians 15:10
[190] Galatians 1:11-20
[191] Acts 9:15
[192] Matthew 16:16-19
[193] John 15:12-16
[194] Matthew 19:28
[195] The Night Office and Lauds are two of the Canonical Hours, see Book Five
[196] 2 Timothy 4:7
[197] Ecclesiasticus 51:1-3
[198] John 21:18-19 Psalm 10:1
[199] Acts 3:1-10

'Jesus saith to Simon Peter, Simon, son of Jonas, lovest thou me more than these, etc.'[200] This festival contains three things, namely, fasting, solemnity and an octave. Fasting, because if we want to reign with these Apostles, we must suffer with them. On the day of the festival, we rejoice in their glorification. On the octave, certain of the beatitude of their souls, we rejoice in the future blessedness of their bodies, and we await the merit of eternal glorification. We have spoken of this octave in the *Preface* of this book. And note that Pope Leo II,[201] praying for the citizens of Naples, who fought at sea against the Saracens, composed the Collect, 'O God, whose right hand upheld blessed Peter, etc.'[202] After completing the strengthening of the Leonine city, placing locks at the doors, he prayed and Collect, 'O God, Who, upon blessed Peter, etc.'[203] At the feast of St Madeleine, we say the Epistle, 'Who can find a virtuous woman, etc.'[204] The Gospel is, 'And one of the Pharisees desired him that he would eat with him, etc.'[205]

---

[200] John 21:15-19
[201] In office from 682 to 683
[202] O God, whose right hand upheld blessed Peter walking upon the waves, lest he should sink, and delivered his fellow apostle Paul when shipwrecked for the third time from the depth of the sea; hear us in Thy mercy, and grant that through their merits we may obtain the glory of everlasting life
[203] O God, Who, upon blessed Peter, Thine apostle, didst bestow the pontifical power of binding and loosing, and didst give to him the keys of the kingdom of heaven: grant that his intercession may ensure our deliverance from the bondage of sin. Who livest and reignest, etc.
[204] Proverbs 31:10-31
[205] Luke 7:36-50

16 THE SEVEN BROTHERS

1. Concerning the Feast of the Seven Brothers, it should be noted that there were three mothers who each had seven children and suffered after the torment of their children. These mothers are, the mother of the Maccabees, whose name is unknown, Felicitas, mother of the seven brothers and Symphorosa, virtuous woman, who is among the saints.

17 SAINT JAMES

1. James the Major, son of Zebedee, brother of John the Evangelist, was sent to evangelize the Spaniards, but having been able to convert only one prince, he returned to Jerusalem. Finally, he was beheaded by Herod, and again transported to Spain. Those whom he could not convert during his life, by a divine miracle, he converts after his death. His feast is celebrated one day before the calends of August, not that he died then but because it was on that day that he was transported to Compostela. He was put to death by Herod in the days of unleavened bread, namely the eighth before the calends of April, at the Annunciation of the Lord, that is, about the time of Easter, as we read in the Epistle of this day, 'Now about that time Herod the king stretched forth his hands to vex certain of the church, etc.'[206] So he had no feast then, because of those very days, instead he was buried on the calends of January, because the construction of his tomb was prolonged from August until the time when one celebrates his feast. Now we make this feast on the eighth day before the calends of August, because it was on this day that we dedicated a church in Compostela to St James. It was said at the feast of the Apostles St Philip and St James, why this saint is called St James the Major. This holiday does not have vigils or fasting, as it was said in Book Six, in the chapter *The Office of Wednesday of the Advent Ember Days*. On this day, some churches say the Epistle, 'Now therefore ye are no more strangers, etc.,'[207] others say, 'Blessed be

---

[206] Acts 12:1-11
[207] Ephesians 2:19-22

the God and Father of our Lord Jesus Christ, etc.,'[208] and the Gospel is, 'Then came to him the mother of Zebedee's children, etc.'[209]

---

[208] Ephesians 1:3-14
[209] Matthew 20:20-23

18 THE SEVEN SLEEPERS

1. We must now speak of the Seven Sleepers. Six of them were powerful in Ephesus from the time that Caesar Decius persecuted the Church of God. As soon as they heard of the persecution, they fled to a mountain and hid in a cave, carrying with them a large sum of money, but little food. Their names were Maximillian, Mark, Martin, Dionysius, John, Serapion and Constantine. Being in the cave the first day, they consumed all that they had to eat and said to their servant, 'Tomorrow you will buy us food, because we have eaten little today,' and then they fell asleep. Now Decius looked for them, for he heard that they were Christians and it was reported that they had fled to other countries or hid in the mountains. Informed of this, Decius had them butchered in the cave with stones. Long afterwards, about three hundred years later, a man wanted to build a table near this cave, so he made a great fire which calcinated the stones which obstructed the entrance of the cave and immediately the light of the fire shone from underground. The seven Sleepers awoke, and the six who were rich said to the seventh who was their slave, 'The day has come, go buy us food,' because they thought they had only slept for one night. The slave therefore went to the city and came to the market, astonished at the number of crosses in the towns, squares, and crossroads. After buying his meat, he offered the coin he had. The butchers, not knowing it, said to him, 'Where did you get that money?' 'I acquired it by my work,' he replied. So they asked him, 'Where are you from?' 'From this country,' he answered. Then they asked him, 'Who are your parents?' He answered, 'These are so and so.' And the butchers knew none of those whom he named, for their names had long

been buried with them. They then asked him, 'Under what emperor were you born?' 'Under Decius,' he replied. Then they were surprised both because of the coin, and because of the words the slave told them, so they took him for a fool. They tied him and took him to the bishop of the city. The latter having questioned him carefully and asked him who he was, where he had found this coin and many other things, the slave told him everything he had told the others. Then the bishop, with all the people of the city, having gone to the cave, found the six other sleepers who had fallen asleep again. They were awakened, and after having conducted them to the city, the bishop asked them what had happened to them. He was convinced that they had remained in the cave for nearly three hundred years. There were also in the cavern the leaden strips which had been placed by those whom Decius had sent to block the entrance. The emperors who reigned at that time were Honorius and Arcadius, who previously doubted the resurrection of the dead, and they believed firmly at the sight of this prodigy. The seven young men mentioned above remained with the bishop for a few days and then died without pain. They were called martyrs, because of this long stay in the cave.[210]

---

[210] This is obviously a legend historically found in several versions and cultures. There is uncertainty as to whether it should be celebrated

19 THE FEAST OF SAINT PETER'S CHAINS

1. The feast of Blessed Peter's Chains was instituted in the following manner, according to Bede. Theodosia, wife of the Emperor Theodosius II, going to Jerusalem, saw in Alexandria in August a feast in honour of Augustus Caesar marking his triumph over Cleopatra, Queen of Egypt, and Mark-Anthony, her husband. Theodosia complained loudly that a great honour was bestowed on one who was damned and a Gentile. Having arrived at Jerusalem, she acquired the chains which had bound St Peter under Herod and, on her return to Rome, she presented them to the pope, who had acquired the other bonds which had chained the Apostle under Nero. These chains, by contact, adhered and met together in a miraculous manner, as if they had always been the same. So Theodosius built a church in honour of St Peter and placed these chains there. Its dedication was set for the calends of August, so that the solemnity of the fisherman effaced that of the emperor, and the chain of stone eclipsed the collar of Augustus.
2. The second reason for the institution of this feast is the memory of the deliverance of Blessed Peter, whom an angel drew from his prison, breaking the bonds of which he had been charged by order of Herod Agrippa, as it is read in the Epistle of this day. From this, it appears that this feast should be called, 'Feast at the Chains,' and not, 'in Chains.'
3. The third reason is that the tribune Quirinus, having a daughter afflicted with goitre, at the command of Pope St Alexander, sixth successor of the blessed Peter, asked for access to the shackles or chains which had bound the blessed Peter at Rome, under Nero. His daughter kissed them and was healed. Quirinus was baptized

with all his family. Then Pope Alexander decreed that this feast should be celebrated on the calends of August and built a church in this city in the honour of Blessed Peter where he laid the chains. He named this church, *ad Vincula*, 'at the Chains,' and dedicated it on the calends of August. In this festivity the people, in Rome, kiss these bonds on this day.

4. A fourth reason, perhaps, is that the Lord miraculously delivered Peter from his bonds and gave him the power to bind and loose.[211] For ourselves, we are chained and held in the bonds of sin, and we need absolution. That is why in this solemnity, which is called, *ad Vincula*, 'at the chains,' we honour St Peter, so that, just as he deserved to be delivered from his chains, and he received from the Lord the power to absolve, so he also procures for us to be delivered from the bonds of our sins.

5. On this day we read the Epistle, 'Now about that time Herod the king stretched forth his hands to vex certain of the church, etc.'[212] The Gospel is, 'When Jesus came into the coasts of Caesarea Philippi, he asked his disciples, saying, etc.'[213]

---

[211] Before the invention of keys the ancients used only ropes to close their doors. Therefore when our Lord speaks of the keys He gives to His Apostles, He refers to the ancient keys that could be used to bind or untie the ropes that shut doors; for he attributes to the keys the facility of binding and loosening; which would make no sense, applied to our modern locks and keys
[212] Acts 12:1-11
[213] Matthew 16:13-19

20 THE MACCABEES

1. These Maccabees are those of the family which Judah Maccabee, who is mentioned in the second book of Maccabees, was from. Although the Church of the West no longer celebrates the feast of any Old Testament saint, as it was said at the beginning of this book, however, it does remember the feast of the Maccabees and the Innocents. She remembers the Maccabees for four reasons.

2. First, because they suffered for enforcing the law because they refused to eat pork meat which was prohibited by the law. Secondly, because of the prerogative of martyrdom, as we read in scholastic history, because they endured unheard-of tortures and suffered more than other Old Testament saints. That is why they are privileged and why we celebrate their passion. Thirdly, because they were seven brothers and the number seven is the number of the universe. That is why in them are designated all the martyrs of the Old Testament worthy of memory, and they are all venerated in the person Maccabees. Fourthly, because the Maccabees are presented and offered as an example of the martyrs of the New Testament, so that just as they suffered for the observance of the old law, so we especially, if it is necessary, we are prepared to suffer for the Gospel. So, according to this, this feast is celebrated for the thing signified rather than for the signifying thing. There are some who have said that these Maccabees are those seven brothers who were the children of Felicity.

21 THE FINDING OF SAINT STEPHEN'S RELICS

1. The Finding of the Body of St Stephen, the first martyr, was made on that day when his passion is celebrated; and he suffered on the day when one celebrates his discovery, namely in August. But his feast was transferred by the Church for four reasons. First, because, as Blessed Stephen was the first martyr, and the martyrdom of the saints is their birth for heaven, so it is appropriate that immediately after the Nativity of the Lord is celebrated, that of the first martyr, Stephen, is observed. Second, because of dignity, for the feast marking death is more worthy than another, and that is why it was rightly placed, as more worthy, after the Nativity. Third, because the Office of his passion accords with the Christmas Office, hence these words, 'Yesterday, Christ was born on earth; today, Stephen is born for heaven.'[214] Fourthly, because at his Finding there was an immense multitude, who, seeing the many miracles that God did on this occasion, celebrated this annual feast with more solemnity than the very day of the death of this saint. So, the holy Fathers decreed that the feast of his passion would be postponed to the day of his Finding, and that the feast of the Finding would be postponed the feast of his passion, because the feast of his passion is worthy of a greater veneration, so that the people would celebrate the day after Christmas with more fervour than they would have done, on the feast day of the same saint, in the month of August. Another reason will be given in the chapter *Saint Stephen*.

---

[214] This is the beginning of a homily by St Fulgence on St Stephen

22 THE TRANSFIGURATION OF THE LORD

1. Then follows the feast of the Transfiguration of the Lord, which is also the day of Pope Sixtus II, [215] not that the Transfiguration took place on this day, but because it was manifested, published and preached by the Apostles who were with the Lord on the mountain. For the Lord had forbidden them to speak to anyone before He was raised from the dead. They kept the secret until this day for it is agreed that the Transfiguration took place towards the beginning of spring, namely the day when the Gospel of the Transfiguration is said, that is to say, in the second week of Lent.

2. Notice that in certain places, on this day, we consecrate the Blood of Christ with new wine, if we can find some, or at least we express into the chalice a little juice from a ripe bunch. We also bless the bunches of grapes with which the people communicate, and here is the reason. On the day of the Last Supper, Jesus Christ said to His disciples, 'But I say unto you, I will not drink henceforth of this fruit of the vine, until that day when I drink it new with you in my Father's kingdom.'[216] For the new word which He pronounced, and also the Transfiguration, belong to that glorious innovation which Christ possessed after His Resurrection, and which the faithful will enjoy. Therefore, on this feast, the Blood of Christ is consecrated with new wine, and because of that also we bless the new clusters on this day.

---

[215] Pope Sixtus II, in office from 257-258. He was martyred (on August 6) along with seven deacons, including Lawrence of Rome
[216] Matthew 26:29

THE TRANSFIGURATION OF THE LORD

3. Pope Eutychian[217] decreed that the first fruits[218] of corn and beans should be blessed on the altar on this day.

---

[217] In office from 275 to 283
[218] New crops

23 SAINT LAWRENCE

1. Blessed Lawrence has a vigil, because after Blessed Stephen he has the primacy among the other martyrs. This is not because he has borne a greater torment than the others, for a great number, like St Vincent and Blessed Gregory, suffered as much as he did, but because of the Office of preaching and the place of his martyrdom, which was at Rome, and because of his good administration, the treasures of the Church.

2. That is why the Introit of his vigil is, 'He hath dispersed, he hath given to the poor, etc.'[219] During the day, it has its own Office, namely, 'Honour and majesty are before him, etc.'[220] This is said, because he was roasted and exalted for confessing the faith, and his holiness was manifested when he did not fear to suffer this torment for Christ. As he was full of joy in the midst of torment and sang the praises of God, so follows the verse, 'O sing unto the Lord a new song, etc.' In the Collect, 'Grant us, we beseech Thee, O almighty God, etc.,'[221] the Church prays and asks to be delivered by the Lord from the fire of vices, and that her vices are annihilated in her, as Blessed Lawrence was released from the fire of torment; which made him say to the tyrant, 'Learn, unhappy, how great is the virtue of God; for these coals, far from causing me pain, give me refreshment.' In the Epistle, 'He which soweth sparingly shall reap also sparingly, etc.,'[222] it

---

[219] Psalm 112:9, 1
[220] Psalm 96:6, 1
[221] Grant us, we beseech Thee, O almighty God, to extinguish the flames of our evil dispositions, as Thou didst grant blessed Lawrence to overcome the fires of his torments. Through our Lord
[222] 2 Corinthians 9:6-10

SAINT LAWRENCE

says that alms must be given to the poor, a precept that Blessed Lawrence exacted, for he gave the poor the treasures of the Church. So that we may imitate it in this we say these words, 'His righteousness endures forever.' The responsory relates to his passion and to his being tested by fire, as gold is tested in the furnace, and this is what one says, 'Thou hast proved mine heart; thou hast visited me in the night, etc.,'[223] because by the letter he was roasted by night and visibly visited by the Lord. That is why he said, 'My night knows no darkness, but everything is resplendent with light.' The verse is, 'thou hast tried me, and shalt find nothing, etc.,'[224] that is, deviance, because, and always and perfectly, he was constant in the faith. The Alleluia relates to his noble ministry. Also since he was the chief minister, that is why he operated mainly by virtue of the Lord. 'The Levite Lawrence (he says) did a good work, he who, by the sign of the cross, illuminated the blind.'

3. 'Levite,'[225] has the same meaning as, 'assumption,' and, 'offering,' because, literally, Blessed Lawrence was raised to the divine ministry. This is why it is reported that he said to the blessed Sixtus, 'Where are you going without your son, my father? Did you think I am unworthy; test me with certainty, and be assured if you have chosen a minister worthy of the promise you made to him to consecrate the Blood of the Lord.' He was also a Levite, that is, for offering himself. That is why, while being tormented, he said, 'I have offered myself to God, like a victim in the odour of sweetness.' That is why the Church, during the Night Office, sings of him, 'Blessed Lawrence deserved to be a victim, he who, while he was roasted, did not renounce the Lord.' That is why he was found a sacrifice of praise and since God must be commended for such great patience being given to the martyr, which is why we sing the words above with the alleluia.

4. In the Gospel, 'Except a corn of wheat fall into the ground and die, etc.,'[226] the Lord speaks of his ministers and their reward. First He says, regarding their works, 'If any man serve me, let him

---

[223] Psalm 17:3
[224] The Vulgate has, 'thou hast tried me by fire: and iniquity hath not been found in me.' (Ps 16:3)
[225] The Latin comes from, *levitar*, 'to levitate'
[226] John 12:24-26

follow me,' and then, regarding the reward of his ministers, 'where I am, there shall also my servant be: if any man serve me, him will my Father honour.' So, as Blessed Lawrence was the first among the ministers, this is why we sing this Gospel at his festivity. Then, as the preaching and confession of the name of the Lord before kings and princes is a privileged ministry, therefore the Offertory which follows is, 'Honour and majesty are before him: strength and beauty are in his sanctuary.'[227] The Post Communion is also about the ministers and their merits, 'If any man serve me, let him follow me, etc.'[228] At times, we say the capitulum, 'He which soweth sparingly shall reap also sparingly, etc.'[229]

5. Now note that this saint, because of the three prerogatives of which we spoke of above, is privileged. First, because he alone, among the martyrs, has a fast of institution. Second, because he has an octave, and he is the only one among the martyrs, with Saint Stephen, who enjoys this privilege, like Blessed Martin among the confessors. We have spoken of this octave at the end of the *Preface* of this book. Third, because of the repetition or resumption of the antiphons, for in this feast the antiphons are preceded by certain small verses, as it was said in Book Six, in the chapter *Holy Trinity Sunday*. Blessed Lawrence was archdeacon of Rome, and no one after him, it is said, has been archdeacon of that city.

---

[227] Psalm 96:6
[228] John 12:26
[229] 2 Corinthians 9:6

24 THE ASSUMPTION OF THE GLORIOUS VIRGIN MARY

1. St Jerome reports how Blessed Mary was received[230] in heaven. Whether she was in body, or if she was out of her body, I do not know, God knows it.[231] St Augustine says that she was in body. The truth is, however, that at first she was received in soul but whether her body remained on the earth is uncertain. It is better to be pious than to say something rash about it. Nevertheless, we must piously believe that she was received in body and soul. A certain woman of great merit, named Elisabeth, of Saxony, assured us that it had been revealed to her that the body of the Blessed Virgin was received in the heavens forty days after the assumption of her soul, and she composed on this subject a certain treaty which, however, is not authentic. Ephirius reports that the Blessed Virgin, when she conceived Christ, was fourteen years old, that she gave birth to Him in her fifteenth year, and that she remained with Him for thirty-three years, then after the death of Christ she survived Him for twenty-four years. According to this she was seventy-two years old when she died.

2. It seems more probable, according to others, that she survived her son for twelve years, and so her assumption took place when she was sixty years old. The Apostles preached that many years in Judea and the surrounding countries.

3. In this feast we say certain things that we sing at the dedication of churches, because they relate to the Virgin. There are also

---

[230] The Latin is *assumpta*, hence 'assumption'
[231] Adapting the words here from 2 Corinthians 12:2

excerpts from the Song of Songs, that is, 'Let him kiss me with the kisses of his mouth, etc.,'[232] responsories, antiphons and lessons are from the same book. This book deals with love because the Virgin, in her flesh, had a greater love than any living creature in the flesh except Christ. Therefore, because of the excellent charity she had on earth she deserved to rise above the angels, apart from the flesh, as if one were out of the flesh, which is not an earthly life but a heavenly life.

4. This festival is well suited to the summer season because charity goes up by the heat of fire. We also read and sing extracts from the Song of Songs because the Blessed Virgin is the Church. For just as she is a mother, a virgin, and a wife, so is the Church the mother of the saints, she has the name of virgin and wife. She is virgin, I mean, by the spirit and the faith, which prevail over the virginity of the flesh, and spouse, since she is the bride of Christ. This is why the Apostle says, 'I have espoused you to one husband, that I may present you as a chaste virgin to Christ.'[233] Now there are some who say that one must read half of the Song of Songs at the octave, and reserve the other half until the Nativity of the same Virgin. So, with this addition, that at this feast Solomon's books are also read, and furthermore, the antiphons are preceded by certain versets, as was said in Book Six, in the chapter *Holy Trinity Sunday*. In the Council of Chalcedon, held by Blessed Leo, it was decided that the Virgin Mary would be called Mother of God. However others say that it was in the Council of Ephesus, held by order of Pope Celestine.

5. Note also that the discourse of the blessed Jerome, which begins with, 'You constrain me, O Paul and Eustochie, etc.,' which some read in the church, is said on this feast. However it should not be read other than in the refectory or chapter, because it was composed for that. In the Hours the capitulum, 'in all these I sought rest, etc.,'[234] is to be said. At the vigil of the Assumption, we say the Epistle, 'From the beginning, and before the world, was I created, etc.,'[235] while other churches say, 'As the vine I have

---

[232] Song of Songs 1:2
[233] 2 Corinthians 11:2
[234] Ecclesiasticus 24:11-13
[235] Ecclesiasticus 24:14-16

THE ASSUMPTION OF THE GLORIOUS VIRGIN MARY

brought forth a pleasant odour, etc.'[236] The Gospel is, 'And Mary rising up in those days, etc.,'[237] and other churches say, 'And it came to pass, as he spake these things, a certain woman of the company lifted up her voice, etc.'[238] Otherwise, at the Mass of the day, one reads the Epistle, 'In all these I sought rest, etc.,'[239] because in everything and everywhere she sought eternal life, and that is why she got it. Then follow these words, 'and he that made me, rested in my tabernacle,' that is, in my womb. And as the Lord rested in the womb of the Blessed Virgin Mary, that is why He also gave her His tabernacle, that is, heaven. And as the Virgin was raised by God to a sublime and illustrious throne, that is why she herself says, 'My soul doth magnify the Lord.'[240] And it is said in the book of Kings, King Solomon, 'made a great throne of ivory.'[241] Likewise, the Lord made her a magnificent throne in heaven, raising her above the angels.

6. We read the Gospel of Martha and Mary, namely, 'Now it came to pass, as they went, that he entered into a certain village: and a certain woman named Martha received him into her house, etc.'[242] Now at first sight this does not appear to be suitable for the subject and yet it agrees with it in the allegorical sense. For Jesus entered a certain, *castellum*, that is, a castle or a village, that is to say in the Blessed Virgin, who is called, *castellum*, a strong castle, because she is formidable to the demons, and was fortified carefully against demons and vices. Now she is called *castellum*, which is a diminutive, because of her humility, they say 'a certain,' because she is unique, and no one like her ever lived before and no one will like her will ever live again. Martha, that is the active life, receives the Lord. For the Virgin, with the most diligent care, nourishes her son and carries Him to Egypt. And first she proved herself in the active life, by visiting Elizabeth and serving her. And just as she was Martha in active life, so she was also Mary Magdalene in the contemplative life. This is why, in another

---

[236] Ecclesiasticus 24:23-31
[237] Luke 1:39-41
[238] Luke 11:27-28
[239] Ecclesiasticus 24:11-13
[240] Luke 1:46
[241] 1 Kings 10:18
[242] Luke 10:38-42

Gospel, it says, 'Mary kept all these things, and pondered them in her heart.'[243]

7. The two sisters, Martha and Mary, designate the active life and the contemplative life, which were united in the highest degree in the Blessed Virgin Mary. It is by this means that she received Christ in herself, in a sublime and honourable manner, and with great delight. It should be noted that there are four Gospels dealing with the Blessed Virgin Mary.

8. The first is, 'And in the sixth month the angel Gabriel was sent from God, etc.,'[244] which is to be said only at the Advent of the Lord and at the Annunciation. The other three can be sung indiscriminately whenever a particular, or special, Mass in honour of the Virgin is sung. They are, 'And it came to pass, as he spake these things, a certain woman of the company lifted up her voice, etc.,'[245] 'And Mary arose in those days, and went into the hill country, etc.,'[246] and, 'Now there stood by the cross of Jesus his mother, etc.'[247]

9. It should be noted that this festival has a fast and also an octave, which does not take place for other feasts of the Virgin, for this feast is the most solemn of all those celebrated in her honour. In the same way, for every other saint, the feast of death is greater than any other that can be celebrated in his honour (because he has gone from misery to life), except for St John the Baptist.

10. The legend of the Virgin will indicate why we collect and bless herbs on this feast. Blessed Mary is compared to the rose and the lily, hence this verse, 'Just as the thorn brings forth the rose so Judea bought forth Mary.' The Office of the Blessed Virgin Mary must be said every day, and solemnly on Saturday, as was said in Book Six, in the chapter *The Time of Advent*. However, in some churches it is not said, from the Holy Thursday of the Lord's Supper to the octave of Pentecost, alleging that then, in the Church, everything must be short. Yet we read that a certain priest who, knowing no other, celebrated the Mass of the Blessed Virgin every day, having been banned by the bishop, the Blessed

---

[243] Luke 2:19
[244] Luke 1:26-38
[245] Luke 11:27-28
[246] Luke 1:39-47
[247] John 19:25-27

Virgin made the most serious reprimands to the latter, he therefore released the priest from his prohibition.

25 SAINT BARTHOLOMEW, APOSTLE

1. Blessed Bartholomew, according to the blessed Abbot Theodore, preached first in Lygdonia, then in India, then in Albania, a city of Armenia, where he was first flayed and then beheaded. Afterwards he was, it is said, transported to Benevento, although it is said today that he was at Rome. There are some who celebrate the feast of his denunciation and others that of his beheading, as it was said in Book Six, on the chapter *The Office of Wednesday of the Advent Ember Days*.
2. It should be noted by those who seek Blessed Bartholomew that the devil thus gave his description as follows. 'His hair is black and curly, his skin is white, his eyes are large, his nose well-proportioned and upright and his long beard has a few white hairs. His height is well taken. He wears a long white and purple tunic and wears a white coat which, at each corner, is adorned with purple-coloured beads.'

26 THE BEHEADING OF SAINT JOHN THE BAPTIST

1. The Church celebrates the feast of Blessed John the Baptist, because he died for the truth, but it does not celebrate it as solemnly as that of his Nativity, because he descended into limbo, as Gregory says in commenting on this passage, 'Art thou he that should come, or do we look for another?'[248] He was beheaded in the paschal season by King Herod, in the year thirty-two of the birth of the Lord, namely the year that preceded the Passion of the Lord, and he himself began to preach at thirty, and so this feast is that of his Beheading.

2. And notice that there were three Herods whose atrocious cruelty made them famous. The first is called Herod Ascalonite and it was under this Herod that the Lord was born, and it was he who had the Innocents massacred. The second is Herod Antipas, who cut off the head of Blessed John the Baptist. The third was Herod Agrippa, who put St James to death and imprisoned St Peter. From where we made these verses:

> *Ascalonite massacres children; Antipas puts John to death;*
> *Agrippa destroys James and locks Peter in a dungeon.*

3. What is certain is that after the taking off John's head his disciples buried his body in Sebastia, a city in Palestine, and his head was buried in Jerusalem near the tomb of Herod. God worked an infinite number of miracles where his body had been

---

[248] Matthew 11:3

buried, which attracted an immense number of Christians. Seeing this, Julian the Apostate ordered the Gentiles to dishonour St John, to break his tomb and to scatter his bones through the fields, which they did. But as the Christians were still going there and the miracles did not cease, the Gentiles gathered up the bones, which they burned. However it was not possible to burn the finger with which the saint had shown the Lord when he was going towards the Jordan, saying, 'Behold the Lamb of God, etc.' Yet many of the Christian monks of Jerusalem, being in the midst of the Gentiles who were collecting these bones, kept as much as they could hide, and bore them to Philip, bishop of Jerusalem, who sent them by the deacon Julien to Anastasius, bishop of Alexandria. Thereafter, Theophilus, bishop of the same city, deposited them in a temple of Serapis, and consecrated a basilica in their honour. Hence the Church, according to Master Guilbert, celebrates this feast of the Beheading and also the burning of the bones of St John, as if he had suffered a second martyrdom after the first, because he suffered somehow in his bones. Others say that Blessed Thecla brought the finger of Blessed John, which it had not been possible to burn, from abroad to Maurienne. There she founded, in honour of Blessed John, a church, which was dedicated to him on that day. That is why it was decreed by the Lord Pope that throughout the world this day would always be celebrated in honour of Blessed John and, from that, it seems that one must call this feast the Feast of the Beheading.

4. Moreover, Blessed John revealed the place where his head was buried to two monks from the East, who had come to Jerusalem to worship. They found him near the palace of Herod on the seventh of the calends of March. But in the aftermath other monks carried him to the city of Edessa where he was hidden without honour in a cavern, until this place was again revealed to the priest Marcel, and he was returned with the honours which he deserved by the bishop of that same city, on the fourth of the calends of September. From that time on, they began to celebrate in the same city the Beheading of Blessed John, on the day, in my opinion, when his head was revealed or discovered. So this feast could be called the feast of Revelation. This feast can therefore be called the Feast of the Beheading or Reunion of the Bones of

THE BEHEADING OF SAINT JOHN THE BAPTIST

St John, or the Dedication of the Church built in his honour, or the Feast of his Revelation.

5. On this day there are some who say the Epistle, 'The hope of the righteous shall be gladness, etc.,'[249] the Gospel is, 'For Herod himself had sent forth and laid hold upon John, etc.,'[250] and the Alleluia is, 'He was a burning and a shining light, etc.'[251]

---

[249] Proverbs 10:28-32
[250] Mark 6:17-29
[251] John 5:35

27 SAINTS FELIX AND AUDACTUS

1. It must be known that when Blessed Felix was dragged to death for the name of Christ, a certain man suddenly appeared in the midst of the crowd and exclaimed, 'I am a Christian.' The executioners exclaimed, 'Well! You will accompany us too;' and as his name was unknown, he was called Audacust. He is associated with Blessed Felix because of his audacity, just as Blessed John, bishop of Alexandria, was nicknamed the Chaplain because of his excellent charity towards the poor of Christ. His feast is celebrated on the day of the calends of February.

28 THE NATIVITY OF BLESSED MARY

1. The feast of the Nativity of the Blessed Virgin Mary, that is to say, the day she came into the world, is celebrated because the Virgin was sanctified in the bosom of her mother, according to these words of the Psalmist, 'the holy place of the tabernacles of the most High.'[252] In this festival we read the genealogy of the Saviour, which is also that of Blessed Mary, since she had the same genealogy, which one reads of in the Gospel of St Matthew, 'The book of the generation of Jesus Christ, etc.'[253] This was spoken of in Book Six, at Christmas, and under the feast of the Apostles Philip and James. The epistle is, 'As the vine I have brought forth a pleasant odour, etc.,'[254] while other churches say, 'The Lord possessed me in the beginning of his way, etc.'[255] We also sing the story of the praises of the Virgin Mary. However, in some churches one reads the Song of Songs, which is more fitting for the feast of the Assumption of the Virgin Mary, as it has been said in its place. The captulum, 'As the vine I have brought forth a pleasant odour, etc.,'[256] is also said, at times.

2. Assuredly, this feast once was not celebrated but a certain religious man, for several years, heard the angels who solemnized this festival on that night in heaven and as he asked the cause. It was revealed to him that the angels rejoiced because of the birth of Blessed Mary which had taken place on that night. The pope,

---

[252] Psalm 46:4 The Vulgate has, 'the most High hath sanctified his own tabernacle.' (Ps 45:5)
[253] Matthew 1
[254] Ecclesiasticus 24:23-31
[255] Proverbs 8:22-35
[256] Ecclesiasticus 24:23

having ascertained the authenticity of this revelation, decreed that this feast should be solemnized, in order to conform to the custom of the celestial court, or to unite with intent in the celestial court, by celebrating this solemnity.

3. This festival has no fast of institution however it can have one of devotion. Furthermore it had no octave, but Pope Innocent IV[257] instituted one. This came about when the chair of Rome became empty due to the death of Pope Gregory. The cardinals could not assemble to elect a new pope as the Romans kept them shut up for several days. These cardinals promised the Queen of Heaven by a vow that if, by her merits, they could freely assemble they would then decree the celebration of the octave of her Nativity, which had long since been neglected. They were delivered and their choice fell on Pope Celestine. But the same Celestine lived only eighteen days and could not fulfil this wish and it was Pope Innocent, who was elected later to succeed him, who fulfilled it.

4. Also note that the Church solemnizes three nativities, namely that of St John the Baptist, that of Blessed Mary and that of Christ. Indeed, John was, so to speak, Lucifer, the morning star, for just as this star precedes the day, so he himself preceded Christ, and he first preached publicly. Mary was the dawn of the day and the Nativity of Christ was the sunrise, because in it appeared the splendour of the Father. Now, the three aforementioned nativities designate the three spiritual nativities, for with John man is reborn in water, with Mary he is reborn through penance, and with Christ we are reborn in glory. So, as it is necessary that contrition precedes the nativity of baptism in adults, and also the nativity in glory, that is why, with good reason, these two nativities of John and of Christ have vigils. But as penance replaces the whole vigil, it is not necessary for the nativity of the Virgin to be preceded by a vigil and that is why this festival has no vigil or fast. And it must be known that Blessed Fulbert,[258] cardinal-bishop, composed three responsories. First, 'The rod of Jesse produced a branch, and the branch a flower: And upon the flower rests the Spirit of love.' Second, 'In order to bring forth

---

[257] In office from 1243 to 1254
[258] Bishop of Chartres, c. 952-1028

the sun of justice, the sovereign King: Mary, the star of the sea, to-day arose in the heavens.' Third, 'Ye choirs of new Jerusalem.'

29 THE EXALTATION OF THE HOLY CROSS

1. This is the origin of the Feast of the Exaltation of the Holy Cross. Chosroes, king of Persia, came to Jerusalem, bringing with him the standard of the Cross, and, having built a palace which represented heaven, he built a throne. To the right of the throne he placed the Cross, which took the place of the Son, on his left was a cock, which represented the Holy Ghost, and he, standing in the middle, called himself God. At this news, Heraclius, Roman emperor, went with an army on the Danube river of Persia (it is not the river that has its source in the Suevia, but another of the same name), defeated the son of Chosroes in a single fight and took hold of the Cross of the Lord. As he approached Jerusalem with great pomp, an angel shut the gates of the city to forbid his entry. At this Heraclius was greatly astonished, then a voice from heaven was heard, saying that the king of kings had not entered so equipped into Jerusalem, when he had come to suffer for all men, but with humility and sitting on a donkey. Immediately recognizing his pride, the Emperor dismounted and humbled himself deeply, and the doors opened of their own accord before him. He entered the city barefoot, and at his entrance a great number of people afflicted with various kinds of diseases were healed by the Cross. The Emperor himself uttered these praises full of piety in honour of the Cross, and exclaimed, 'O Cross, brighter than all the stars, more famous than all the great men of the world, etc.!' He therefore exalted the Cross and ordered, in agreement with the bishops, that the day of the Exaltation of the Cross should henceforth be solemnized in his empire. Pope Sergius, a long time later, found in the sanctuary of Blessed Peter a chest or box of money, and in this chest a cross made in great

part of the salutary wood of the Cross, or which bore the salvation of the world, and adorned with precious stones. This Cross, placed in the Basilica of the Saviour, is worshiped by the people on the day of Exaltation.

2. The feast of the Finding is greater than that of Exaltation, because of the authority of him who instituted it. For the first was instituted by a pope, namely Pope Eusebius, and the other by an emperor.

3. In this feast we say the Epistle that is sung on Palm Sunday, because in this Epistle it deals with the exaltation of the Holy Cross. Others read this, 'And being found in fashion as a man, he humbled himself, and became obedient unto death, etc.'[259] In some churches the Gospel which is read also deals with the advent of Christ, 'For as the lightning cometh out of the east, etc.,'[260] which is commonly said in the time of Advent. In other churches one reads the Gospel which relates to Nicodemus, which some say at the feast of the Finding of the Holy Cross, and in which it is said, 'And as Moses lifted up the serpent in the wilderness, even so must the Son of man be lifted up.'[261] Commonly, however, we say (which is preferable) the Gospel, 'Now is the judgment of this world, etc.,'[262] in which it is said, 'if I be lifted up from the earth, will draw all men unto me.' One reads the Preface which is said before Easter, for a fortnight, or, in certain churches, for only five days, or, as others wish, that which is read in the Easter season. At times the capitulum, 'And being found in fashion as a man, he humbled himself, etc.,'[263] is also said.

---

[259] Philippians 2:8-9
[260] Matthew 24:25-35
[261] John 3:14
[262] John 12:31-36
[263] Philippians 2:8

30 THE FEAST OF SAINT MATTHEW, APOSTLE AND EVANGELIST

1. Blessed Matthew was of the race of Levi. He was therefore a Hebrew, and he wrote in Hebrew for the Hebrews in Judea. But later his book was translated into Greek, and then into Latin. And notice that the Gospel which he wrote with his own hands, in the year forty of the Lord, was found with the bones of Blessed Barnabus. Blessed Barnabus carried this Gospel with him, and, placing it upon the sick, they were immediately healed, both by the faith of Barnabus and by the merits of Blessed Matthew. St Matthew proclaimed or preached the Gospel at Aquileia, in the year of the Lord forty-four. The Epistle said on this day is, 'But unto every one of us is given grace, etc.,'[264] others say, 'As for the likeness of their faces, they four had the face of a man, etc.'[265] The Gospel is, 'And as Jesus passed forth from thence, he saw a man, named Matthew, etc.'[266] At the vigil, we say the Gospel, 'And after these things he went forth, and saw a publican, etc.'[267]

2. St Matthew preached under the emperor Caius Caligula, so named because he was born during a military expedition, and he was wearing the military boots called *caligis*. John wrote under Nerva, Mark under Nero. We are not certain of the time when Luke wrote but there are some who say that it was under Nero.

---

[264] Ephesians 4:7-13
[265] Ezekiel 1:10-14 These four faces represent the four Evangelists
[266] Matthew 9:9-13
[267] Luke 5:27-32

31 SAINT MAURICE AND HIS COMPANIONS

1. While the Gauls were making war against the Romans, the prefect of Egypt raised an army of which Maurice was a part and he commanded a legion of six thousand, six hundred and sixty-six men. As they were in the army, the tyrant wished to compel them to adore idols but they refused. This is why the tyrant decimated them, that is to say, he destroyed the tenth part. Seeing this, Blessed Maurice addressed his companions and asked them to persevere with courage. Thus animated by Maurice, they suffered martyrdom. However they had been baptized before coming to Rome.

2. And note, concerning Maurice and the Theban Legion, that there are several Thebes. There is one in Egypt, inhabited by the Moors, another in Greece, where the Thebans are and another in India, who are the Thesbytes. The companions of Maurice were from Egypt.

32 THE FEAST OF SAINT LUKE, EVANGELIST

1. St Luke was Syrian of origin and he was patriarch of Antioch and priest in Bithynia, where he ended his life by a natural death and not by martyrdom. He was also a painter and a physician and, according to St Jerome, he was a disciple of the Apostles and not of the Lord, for he only embraced the faith after the Resurrection of the Lord, as it is read in his explanation of Exodus, although some said he was one of the sixty-two disciples of the Lord. He wrote his Gospel in Achaea. Now he lived for eighty-four years and he composed the Gospel and the Acts of the Apostles.

2. He was a disciple of Blessed Paul, from whom he learned what he taught, as Blessed Mark was instructed by Blessed Peter. However, in the prologue of his Gospel it is found that he learned many things from certain people who, in the beginning, lived with the Lord. But Blessed Paul was not from the beginning with the Lord, so he did not learn from him what he taught. The explanation is that he learned some things from Paul, other things from others, but it was especially through Blessed Paul that he was instructed. However, it is believed that he had recourse to the Blessed Virgin, as from the Ark of the Testament, and that he received from her a great deal of information, especially for those things which concerned her alone, for example concerning the Annunciation of the angel, the Nativity of Christ and other events of this kind, which of the Evangelists, St Luke alone deals with.

33 THE FEAST OF THE APOSTLES SIMON AND JUDE

1. James the Minor, brother of the Lord, and Simon and Jude, and Joseph, (who was nicknamed Barsabas and the Just, so that we could not imagine that he was rejected from the apostolate by injustice), were brothers, and the children of Marie Cleophas, who was married to Zebedee. Now this Simon was called the Zelote and Simon the Canaanite, or from Cana, a town of Galilee, which means the same thing; for Cana, by interpretation means, 'zeal,' or 'emulation,' for he had great ardour for the salvation of souls. 2. Jude received many nicknames. He was called, 'of James,' which means 'brother,' as was said previously. He was also called Thaddeus, from, *tracha*, purple, which is a royal garment, and, *Deus*, God, or Thaddeus, which, by interpretation, means, 'who seized the prince.' For he himself was a royal garment by the ornaments of virtue, by which he knew how to take hold of the Prince, Christ. He is also called, *Lebaeus*, a word which means *cor*, 'heart,' or *corculus*, that is to say, *cordis cultor*, 'who cultivates the heart.' A lot was drawn of which one would be choose for an Apostle, of the aforementioned Joseph and Matthias, and it is said of Simon that he died crucified. Others, however, say that it was not this one, but that Simon, son of Cleophas, who was crucified. 3. This Simon preached in Egypt, then he came to Jerusalem and was bishop, after Blessed James the Minor, (who was called the Lord's brother), and was crucified there. Now he lived for a hundred and twenty years, and before his death raised thirty who were dead; which is why in his legend we find that he restored to human life thirty dead who had perished in the waves. He also

restored to life the son of his host who had drowned. He died in the Bothoro and not in the Postophorus, which is, as some want, the portico of the temple where the guards of the temple slept. For St Jude preached to the Persians and the Medes and died among the Armenians.

34 THE FEAST OF ALL SAINTS

1. As each of the idols of the Romans could not have a temple in Rome, the Romans built one in honour of Cybele, mother of the gods, and in honour of all the gods themselves. This temple was called *Pantheon*,[268] from *pan*, 'all,' and *theos*, 'god.' In the course of time, Pope Boniface asked Phocas, emperor of Constantinople, who ruled the Romans, to give him this temple.

2. Having obtained it, he had the idols removed and then consecrated it on the fourth day of May, in honour of the blessed Virgin Mary and all the martyrs; and this solemnity was called the feast of Blessed Mary and the Martyrs. For the feasts of confessors was not yet celebrated but only that of the martyrs. Hence it was that the feast of Blessed John before the Latin Gate was instituted, because of the martyrdom he bore, as much as was in him. So the same pope ruled that every year, on this day, the feast of martyrs would be celebrated, as, a the calends of the same month, the feast of the Apostles was celebrated; and in honour of Blessed Mary and all the martyrs they sang, 'How dreadful is this place, etc.,'[269] which is usually said only at the Dedication of a Church

3. However Gregory IV[270] transferred this feast of the Martyrs to the calends of November, while the fruits of the earth were collected, for then one would find more abundantly the things necessary for life, which would be well for this feast. He also established that then we would celebrate, not only the Apostles

---

[268] This Greek word is *pantheion*, 'temple to all gods'
[269] Genesis 28:17 Psalm 84:1-2
[270] In office from 827-844

and martyrs, but also the Trinity, the angels, the confessors and generally all the saints, and also the elect, as can be seen in the hymn; and he regulated the service of this feast.

4. This festival was instituted for four reasons. First, because of the aforementioned dedication of the Pantheon. Secondly, to make up for the festival which had been omitted; for because of the multitude of saints, we cannot celebrate them all in a special way. Third, because of our neglect in the feasts we celebrate and for the expiation of our sins. And this reason is touched on in the sermon that is recited on this day in the Church, where it is said, It was decreed that on that day all the saints should be remembered, in order to make provision in this holy solemnity for all that might have been lacking in the festivals of the saints, as a result of human frailty, by ignorance, negligence, and by consequence of the involvement in temporal things.' Fourthly, so that our prayers are more easily answered. For we will more easily obtain what we ask if all the saints at the same time intercede for us; for it is impossible for the multitude not to be answered. That is why in the prayer of this day we say, 'multiply Thy graces upon us, and grant that joy may follow in the holy praise of those whose glorious festival we anticipate.' We have said in the *Preface* to this book why we celebrate the feasts of the saints.

5. This feast has a fast of institution, and no one on this day should eat until evening, nor change the fast, as some do, because of St Quentin.

6. Now, as this festival is common to all the saints, the Office varies according to the variety of all the saints. Indeed, we sing the first antiphon, the first lesson and the first responsory in honour of the Trinity, because it is the feast of the Trinity. In the second place, they sing in honour of Blessed Mary. Third, in honour of the holy angels, fourth, of the prophets, fifth of the Apostles, sixth of the martyrs, seventh of the confessors, eighth of the virgins and ninth, of all at once.

7. The authority of this Office is observed in the lessons. For in this feast, in some churches, the oldest in the church, namely the bishop if he is present, reads the lesson of the Trinity, namely, the first; or it is the dean, or at least a priest, and we continue the lessons in order, descending from mature people to children. So it is a child who reads the eighth lesson of the virgins; for it always

belongs to the highest in dignity or age to sing the ninth. The eighth responsory, in honour of the virgins, is also known as, 'And I heard as it were the voice of a great multitude, etc.,'[271] which is sung by five children before the altar of the Blessed Virgin. They hold candles in their hands, if there are any, to represent the five prudent virgins, having their lamps supplied and lit.

8. The capitulum, 'After this I beheld, and, lo, a great multitude, etc.,'[272] is also said. At Mass, we read the Epistle, 'I saw another angel ascending from the east, etc.'[273] The Alleluia is, 'O how glorious is the kingdom, etc.,'[274] in which all the saints rejoice with Christ, clad in robes of white they follow the Lamb wherever He goes. The Gospel is, 'And seeing the multitudes, he went up into a mountain, etc.'[275] At the vigil, we say the Epistle is, 'And I beheld, and, lo, in the midst of the throne etc.,'[276] and the Gospel is, 'And he came down with them, and stood in the plain, etc.'[277]

---

[271] Revelation 19:6, Revelation 12:10
[272] Revelation 7:9, 11
[273] Revelation 7:2-12
[274] Based on Revelation 7:9 'O how glorious is the kingdom in which all the saints rejoice with Christ, clad in robes of white they follow the Lamb wherever He goes'
[275] Matthew 5:1-12
[276] Revelation 5:6-12
[277] Luke 6:17-23

35 THE OFFICE OF THE DEAD

1. Here we have to talk about the Office of the Dead. Sometimes it is called *agenda*, from the verb, *ago*, 'to act' or 'I do,' because, among other meanings of this word, *agere*, 'to do,' is the same thing as, *celebrare*, 'to celebrate.' Hence the Office established for the dead and in their memory is called, 'agenda.' Again, it is sometimes called *exequiae*, 'funeral,' from the verb, *exequor*, *exequeris*, 'to execute,' 'to fulfil,' or 'to render the last duties,' because, among other meanings, *exequi* means the same thing as, *extra alla sequi*, 'to follow out,' or 'out of other things,' or, 'beyond other regions,' 'beyond life,' or, 'follow to the end.' So the Office or service for the burial of the dead is called, *exequiae*, because it is celebrated while one carries the dead out from the living, to bury them. Or because special and particular ceremonies are observed outside Canonical Hours. This Office is connected with the feast of All Saints because these two Offices, which last for three days, express or designate three different mysteries, or have three different mystical reasons. The vigil of All Saints is the day of affliction, the solemnity is the day of joy, and the day in question is that of prayer. In the first, we mortify ourselves by fasting, in the second, we rejoice and share in the bliss of the saints, giving thanks to God, in the third, we pray for the souls who are kept in purgatory, asking to obtain for them, by our prayers, either some relief from their sorrows, or an entire pardon.

2. Now, the Church has established that on this day we will commemorate all the faithful dead, so that they may be assisted by the general blessing of the prayers of all the other faithful. For in purgatory they are no longer capable of doing meritorious

deeds, and thus of obtaining spiritual merits, as has already been said in the chapter *The Feast of All Saints*. For, as Peter Damien[278] says, St Odilo,[279] having learned that near Mount Etna, in Sicily, the voice and the howling of the demons who complained that the souls of the dead were torn from their hands by alms and prayers, ordered that in his monasteries, after the feast of All Saints, the commemoration of the dead would be celebrated. This was subsequently approved and confirmed by the whole Church. First, let us examine by whom the Office of the Dead was instituted, secondly, where it began, third, how to celebrate it, fourth, how to bury the dead.

3. In the first place, it was instituted by the Apostles but, as St Isidore attests in his *Ecclesiastical Offices*, it was augmented and largely regulated and arranged by Origen. Hence St Augustine recommends it in his *Enchiridion*, saying that in the organization of ecclesiastical Offices it comes immediately after the Apostles.

4. This Office began in the old law for, as St Ambrose says, after the death of Jacob, Joseph and his other brothers, with a large number of Egyptians, brought him back to Ebron. But before that they cried in Egypt for forty days, and then wept for seven days in the field of Atad.[280] Similarly, it is read in that after the death of Moses the people of Israel wept for thirty days,[281] and the same for Aaron and Mary. In the same way, 'The mourning for the dead is seven days: but for a fool and an ungodly man all the days of their life.'[282]

5. Note that some remember the dead for three days, to represent the three days of the burial of the Lord, or for the sake of the Resurrection of Christ who rose on the third day, wishing the dead to resurrect with Christ. Or else because of the Trinity, or so that, as during their life they sinned in three ways, namely, by thoughts, words and actions, their sins are forgiven to them by the Trinity. Others celebrate Mass for seven days, that is, on all the seven days. Both of these are shown in the Book of Numbers, where it is said, 'He that toucheth the dead body of any man shall

---

[278] A reforming Benedictine monk and cardinal, c. 1007-1072
[279] Benedictine Abbot of Cluny, c. 952-1049
[280] See Genesis 50:1-12
[281] See Deuteronomy 34:8
[282] Ecclesiasticus 22:13

be unclean seven days. He shall purify himself with it on the third day, and on the seventh day he shall be clean.'[283] Surely the pollution or impurity contracted by touching the corpse of a dead man signifies a soul stained by dead works.

6. Now this Office is celebrated for seven days, first, so that the dead may come to the Sabbath of eternal rest. Second, that he may be forgiven all the sins that he has committed in his life, which is shut up in the space of seven days. Third, because of the seven elements that make up the soul and the body. Indeed, the soul has three forces, namely the reasonable faculty (or reasoning), the lustful and the irritable; the body is composed of four elements. So that the sins that man committed during this life, which is within the space of seven days, are destroyed, a seven-day service is celebrated for the dead. Fourthly, just as the sons of Jacob mourned their father's death for seven days, as has been said above, so also does the Church celebrates a seven-day service for the dead.

7. There are some who make the novena, that is to say, a nine-day service, so that by this Office the souls of the dead, delivered from their troubles, may be associated with the nine orders of the angels. Now there are some who do not approve of this, so that we do not appear to imitate the Gentiles, from whom this custom seems to be drawn. For they mourned their dead for nine days, and on the ninth they buried their ashes in pyramids or busts.

8. Others celebrate a thirty-day service or celebrate the thirty-first day for the dead. First, because the children of Israel mourned Moses and Aaron for as many days as previously said. Secondly, because three times ten are thirty; namely the number three,[284] in which we hear the Trinity, and by the number ten, the ten precepts of the Decalogue. We therefore observe for the dead an Office of three tens of days, so that the faults they committed in the observation or against the observation of the Decalogue or the precepts of Christ, and against the Trinity, may be forgiven them by the divine mercy. Third, because the number or course of the moon ends in the space of thirty days, therefore the Office

---

[283] Numbers 19:11-12

[284] The digits of a number are frequently added together until a single digit is arrived at in order to appreciate the symbolic significance

for the Dead lasts for thirty days, so that it may be understood that their works are full before the Lord.

9. There are also those who prolong the Office of the Dead for four times ten days, or forty days, so that the sins they committed against the doctrine of the four Evangelists and against the ten precepts of the law are forgiven them.

`10. Those who observe forty days of service represent the Lord's burial, wishing that the dead share the glory of Christ, who remained in the sepulchre for forty hours, including the hour when He returned the spirit and the last hour of the night of Sunday when he rose again, according to St Augustine. They also represent that after Jacob's death, his children cried for forty days, as previously said.

11. Others celebrate fifty days the reason for which Bede and Gregory give in commenting on the place where it is said that Abraham asked the Lord who wanted to destroy Sodom, 'Peradventure there be fifty righteous within the city: wilt thou also destroy and not spare the place?' To which the Lord replied, 'If I find in Sodom fifty righteous within the city, then I will spare all the place.'[285] They explain that the number fifty is a perfect number and refers to the jubilee year, that is, the eighth age where will be the remission of sins and full freedom. So for the souls of the deceased to acquire full freedom and the remission of their sins, an Office of fifty days is celebrated for them.

12. Others do a service of sixty days, because the Sexagesima designates the grief of the Church because of the absence of the Bridegroom, and that, to console her, two wings are given to her, as has been said in Book Six, in the chapter *The First Sunday of Lent*. Thus, those who act in this way mark the pain they feel at the absence of their dead, in order to console themselves and to purify the soul of the deceased, they offer the Lord a sacrifice and give alms to the poor.

13. Some also celebrate the hundredth day, so that the dead may pass from left to right, from combat to triumph, from earth to heaven, from misery to glory, from death to life. For they wish them eternal bliss, designated by the number one hundred, beyond which there are no more numbers designated.

---

[285] See Genesis 18:24, 26

14. Some mark the anniversary for three reasons. First, that the dead may go from years of misfortune to the years of eternity or to eternal life, which is endless and, like the year, turns on itself. Or else, because where there is identity there is no variety.

15. Secondly, because, just as we celebrate the saints' anniversary for their honour and our own usefulness, as it was said in the *Preface* of this book, so we celebrate the anniversary of the dead for their usefulness and to nourish our devotion.

16. Thirdly, we celebrate the anniversary of the dead, because, according to St Augustine, we do not know what their state is in the other life, and it is better for them that our benefits are superabundant and superfluous than to be lacking. Now, if the anniversary falls on a Sunday or coincides with some solemnity, it must not be put back to the next day, as is done at the solemnities of the saints, but we must celebrate it on the day before, so that as soon as possible it relieves the pain that the dead suffer in purgatory. For the dead need our help and our blessings, while the saints do not need it.

17. The anniversary of the dead should not be made on a feast day, nor should Mass be said for them, unless the body is present. The reason for this is because we can say Mass for the dead at any time when the corpse is present except on Good Friday, because then one can neither bury the body nor say the Mass for the deceased, since then one must not consecrate the Body of Christ. We must wait until the next day, and then, that is to say on Saturday, we can sing Mass for him and bury his body. Likewise, if someone dies on Easter day, one must keep his body above ground until the next day and then bury him, after having said Mass for him. For one must not bury a body without having said Mass for him, although the opposite occurs in many places.

18. Now, according to the Council of Chalons it seemed appropriate and fitting that one should pray and offer the sacrifice for the dead. However, in the days mentioned above, it is the friends of the deceased who do this especially. However, there are some who, at all times, except only on feast days, usually pray for the dead at both the evening and morning service. Others celebrate Mass every day for them. Others, at the beginning of the month, sing nine psalms, nine lessons, and nine responsories.

Now, it is a holy and salutary thought to pray for the dead so that they may be delivered from their sins.

19. In some places the Office of the Dead is not said in the church from Holy Thursday to the octave of Pentecost, because all the Offices of this time must be short, nor on Sundays. Now it is said that a certain abbot prevented his monks from celebrating for the dead on Sundays, but the dead, for that reason, ill-treated him and overwhelmed him with the most severe blows and that is why he revoked his defence.

20. Note that the suffrages which are made in the Church for the dead who have no more mistakes to expiate, are thanksgivings. For these souls, who are perfectly pure when they come out of their bodies, fly to heaven, and they do not need our help. For those who are only half good, that is to say, who are in purgatory, our prayers serve them as atonement for their sins. For those who are poorly bad, namely, who are in limbo, our prayers are favourable to them or cause a softening of their sorrows; for, according to St Augustine, our prayers are useful to them, or serve them to obtain a complete remission, or certainly render their condemnation more tolerable. The prayers which are made for those which are very bad, all turn to consolation or to the advantage of the living, for the help of our prayers is of no use to them, since these souls immediately descend to hell.

21. Note also that, according to St Jerome, when we say a psalm or a Mass for all souls at once, they receive no less than if they were said for each of them in particular. Yet, on this subject, it may be said that, if we make suffrages for certain souls in particular, these suffrages are more for those for whom they are specially made than for others. If they are done in general or in common, they serve more for those who, during their life, have deserved more than they were useful. For even though, according to St Augustine, these suffrages do not serve all those for whom they are made, nevertheless, as we do not know who they are useful for or not, we must do them for all, lest we come to deprive someone to whom they would be useful. For it is better that they be superfluous for those to whom they neither harm nor serve, than to fail those to whom they are useful, and that is why the day of the anniversary is marked, as it was said above.

22. But do the suffrages for him who, because of mortal sin, who is not in charity, serve him who died in charity? I answer that sacramental works, such as the Mass, the service for the dead, the Collects and other such things, made by the one who is in this state, are valid and useful to the dead. This is both because it is from God and not from the one who makes them that they draw their electiveness, because the one who does these works does not do them in his own name, but as the trustee or delegate of all. That is to say, he acts in this way in the name of the whole Church, according to what has been said in the *Preface* of Book Four. Now if as a private person he makes other suffrages, he may act in the name of another or in his own name. If it is in the name of another, for example by the order of a deceased or another who lives in charity, or if he gives alms to another, as minister, with his own property, then certainly it is useful to him. Because then he is supposed to act by order of the one in whose name he acts, and it is for the one who commands to execute, who is supposed to execute himself. This is why when a vow of pilgrimage has been issued by someone, another, by his order, can fulfil this wish. It is the same when two persons, one of whom is in charity and the other is not there, can read the psalter for a deceased, and when someone gives alms to a righteous person, so that he may pray for a deceased. Indeed, in these circumstances, it is useful to the deceased, because of the charity of the just on whose behalf he acts. However if it is in his own name and for his own good that someone gives alms, prays, fasts and does other austerities for a deceased, theologians almost all agree that these acts serve no purpose to the deceased; for we read in St John, 'Now we know that God heareth not sinners,'[286] but these words are those of the blind and not of the Evangelist. And Isaiah says, 'When ye make many prayers, I will not hear: your hands are full of blood,'[287] that is, sins. Moreover, according to Blessed Augustine, 'While the one who dislikes God intercedes, he provokes the soul of the judge who is irritated to still more severity, because God despises the gifts of the unjust and only the prayers of the just.' In the same way, the Lord says, through the mouth of the prophet Amos,

---

[286] John 9:31
[287] Isaiah 1:15

'neither will I regard the peace offerings of your fat beasts,'[288] that is to say, sinners. But as there are few who live without crime and such a feeling, which deprives the deceased of mercy and so many suffrages, and chills for the charity of the living, is too harsh and severe, that is why it does not seem necessary to follow it. For if we condemn the suffrages of men who have a conscience charged with sin, the dead will have only a very small number of faithful to relieve them.

23. It seems, therefore, that it must be said that although the suffrages of the one who is in a state of sin do not take place in charity, yet they take place in faith. So they are not useful to the person who died in charity, due to the lack of merits from a holy life. However, these suffrages may take place according to the doctrine of the Church and are produced by one who abides in the faith and one who has deserved to receive such a grace. In such a case it is the merit of faith and the charity of the Church which inspires, in the person who produces these suffrages, the thought of producing them, so that the deceased who draws the fruit from them is able to receive them. Moreover, because God is bountiful, and is full of compassion for us, He does not, according to Blessed Ambrose, revoke benefits, nor does He hoard the treasures of His liberality. Furthermore, He, by an effect of this liberality, considers the work done by others as if it had been made by the person for whom it is made. All this, I say, makes up for the lack of charity of the agent because, according to the law, when one person pays the debt of another, the debtor himself is released from the debt. For example, if liberty has been granted to a slave, and Titius has undertaken to pay ten crowns for his deliverance, however if Titius acquits himself of his engagement, the slave is nevertheless free. But, moreover, a person may acquire for others a legacy and an inheritance which he is incapable of acquiring for himself. Also, someone who, because of a crime which he has committed, is incapable of asking for himself, is permitted to ask for others and for those whose guardianship he has. According to St Augustine, although a stone canal produces nothing, yet the water that passes through this channel fertilizes the earth. Again, St Jerome says, 'If sometimes

---

[288] Amos 5:22

you see among many evil works some sinner doing something that is just, God is not unjust to the point of forgetting the little good they do, because of the great number of their iniquities.'

24. Assuredly, the deceased know in four ways, according to St Augustine, the suffrages that are done for them. First, by divine revelation, namely, when God reveals it to them. Secondly, by the manifestation or revelation of good angels. For the angels here below are continually with us, and, considering all our acts, they may in a moment, so to speak, descend to them, and announce it to them immediately. Thirdly, by the intimation of souls departing from hence. Fourthly, by experience, namely, when they feel a relief from their sorrows.

25. Now, it is necessary to know that the dead of the wickedest kind do not know what is done by the living unless they are permitted to do so. It is the same for those who are almost good, who are in the flames of purgatory, who do not yet enjoy the vision of God, except only so far as they are permitted to know, as said above. But those who are fully purified, who already enjoy this blessedness, know well what is happening in the heavenly country, according to these words of St Gregory, 'What can be ignored by those who see Him who sees everything?' There are, however, others who say that they know everything they need to and nothing else; of which Isaiah says, in the person of the afflicted people, 'Abraham be ignorant of us.'[289]

26. But do the dead care for the living? St Augustine expands on this subject in his book *On the Care One Should Have of the Dead*. He says that many believe that there are some who, either in dreams or in some other way, appear to the living, and that they often warned them of the place where their bodies were buried, or of building sepulchres and other innumerable things. And we find that this is true in the *Dialogues* of Gregory and in other writings, most of them authentic. However, as the same St Augustine says in the above-mentioned book, although the dead seem to say and ask for such things in a dream, we must not think, because of this, that these things are the reality. For even the living also may appear in dreams to those who are plunged into sleep, while they themselves, for the most part, do not know that they appear,

---

[289] Isaiah 63:16

when they hear from those who have had these dreams that they have seen them do or say something in a dream. Therefore, as he says, it must be believed that these are the operations of the angels, who, by a disposition of Divine Providence, serve to bring some consolation to the living. The Council of Ancyra says that most are often deceived by the illusions and ghosts produced by the demons.

27. The Office of the Dead is the complete imitation of the three days of the burial of Christ; for, as in these three days, so in this Office we suppress all the songs of praise and solemnity. For at Mass we do not ask for the blessings of the bishop and we do not say the ritual, 'Thou O Lord wilt open my lips, etc.,' nor, 'Incline unto my aid O God,' nor, 'Let us bless the Lord,' nor the Invitatory, unless the body is present. Neither is 'Glory be to the Father, etc.,' said at the responsories or at the end of the psalms. We do not ask or give blessings at the beginning of lessons. We do not say the, 'To You also, O Lord, etc.,' nor, 'Thanks be to God.' At the Mass the Alleluia is not said, nor the *Gloria in excelsis*, nor, 'Go, the Mass is said.' For in the old law it was forbidden to offer the oil of joy and the incense of sweetness for sin. Death, indeed, is God's punishment for sin, so that where there is sin, there is darkness. Nor must one make joy or sing hymns of joy where mourning and sorrow of heart reign; for we celebrate with mourning and sadness the funeral of the dead.

28. We also suppress Lauds, because, ignorant of where the dead pass to, we do not know whether we ought to praise God, His justice, or His mercy. We repress joy, because we enter the world sadly and sadly we come out of it. We must not say the sequence, which is a song of joy.

29. Moreover, although at a Mass for the living all must be praised, to mark that their prayers rise in the heavenly country; however, in the Mass for the Dead, incense should not be carried into the choir nor offered. That is to say, one must not incense the altar but only the body, because it has been prohibited by law, as has already been said previously. No one, therefore, is incensed in this Office, to show that the dead cannot merit anything by their prayers, of which the Psalmist says, 'The dead praise not the

Lord.'[290] However the bodies of the deceased are incensed and sprinkled with holy water, not for their sins to be erased, because they cannot be by this means, but to drive away all filthiness from them. It is also done, to mark the society and the communion of the sacraments they have shared with us as long as they lived. Consequentially Dionysius says that the living once embraced the dead as a sign of the unity they had with them. Now, these and similar things is also beneficial, as, by such ceremonies, it is God Himself that we honour. In the Introit for the Dead there is a double verse, namely, 'Praise waiteth for thee, O God, in Sion, etc.,' and, 'O thou that hearest prayer, unto thee shall all flesh come,'[291] as was said in Book Six, in the chapter *The Saturday Following the Third Sunday of Lent*. Similarly, at the Mass for the Dead, prayers for the living should not be intermingled, as was said in Book Four, in the chapter *The Collect*.

30. We do not give the peace for three reasons. First, because this Office, as it has already been said, is the representation of the three days of the burial of the Lord, where it is not given, in horror for the kiss of Judas. Secondly, because we do not communicate with the dead and they do not answer us, because we are in the sixth age, and they are in the seventh.

31. Hence the body of the dead must never be in the church, as long as the celebration of the Mass of the day lasts. Moreover, if it was there before, it must be carried out of the church into the vestibule, whatever his authority and dignity during his life, and then brought back for the Mass of the Dead.

32. Third, because just as a single loaf of bread is made up of a large number of grains, and wine is drawn from a large number of bunches of grapes, so the Church is made up of an agglomeration of a large number of faithful, some of whom are good and others bad. Now, since we do not know whether the dead are now in union or in conformity with the Church, whether he has peace with his Creator and whether he is reconciled with Him, which is why we do not give the peace at Mass. Nor do not praise God for the dead or because of the dead, for we have no

---

[290] Psalm 115:17
[291] Psalm 65:1-2

reason to do so, since their rest is still uncertain for us. The fourth reason was given in Book Four, in the chapter *The Kiss of Peace*.

33. It must also be noted that the Office of the Dead begins with Vespers. Afterwards follow the vigils, of which there are three kinds, for in some churches we read nine lessons from Job, the first of which is, 'Let me alone; for my days are vanity, etc.'[292] In others we read lessons from Wisdom, and they begin with this, 'It is better to go to the house of mourning, etc.'[293] In still others they are extracted from a sermon of St Augustine. But, whatever may be the source from which they are drawn, they are said absolutely without, 'May the Lord bless,' and without, 'But Thou, O Lord, have mercy upon us,' otherwise they begin and end as in the funeral we celebrate in the three days mentioned above of the burial of Christ. However, in some churches the, 'But Thou, O Lord, have mercy upon us,' is replaced by, 'Blessed are the dead which die in the Lord.'[294]

34. In this Office they say the psalm, 'Praise waiteth for thee, O God, in Sion, etc.,'[295] because it concerns the return of the children of Israel from captivity to the Promised Land. In the same way, the dead also come out of the misery of captivity, to enter into eternal life. The Psalm, 'O Lord, rebuke me not, etc.,'[296] is also said, which, although being the sixth in the order of the psalter, is however entitled, 'For the octave,' as if by this psalm we implored God for six ages, so that we could be the ornaments of the seventh and reach the octave of glory, or achieve the glory of the eighth. The Office of the Dead has no second Vespers, as was said in Book Six, in the chapter *Vespers*.[297]

35. In the Council of Toledo it was decided that the priest who would celebrate the Mass of the Dead, so that his enemy would find death, would be deposed, and that both himself and the one who would excite such an act would be punished with banishment for life. Now we must see how the body is to be buried. When a person seems to be in agony, one must place him

---

[292] Job 7:16-21
[293] Ecclesiastes 7:2
[294] Revelation 14:13
[295] Psalm 65
[296] Psalm 38
[297] The chapter *Of Vespers* is in Book Five

on the ground on ashes, or at least on straw, by which one insinuates that he is ashes and that he will return to ashes. This is done from the example of Blessed Martin, who, to give others a model to follow in his person, ended his life, lying on ashes. And if the dying man is a scholar or wise, one must read the Passion of the Lord or at least a part of the Passion, before him so that he may be excited to a greater compunction. The cross must be erected at his feet, so that, dying in sight of it, he may be more contrite and be converted. He must also be lying on his back, so that his face always looks at the sky, like the blessed Martin, and before he expires, his soul will be commended to the Lord.

36. When he has breathed his last, the bells must be sounded, as it was said in Book One, in the chapter *The Bells*. Then, if his body did not quite recently, before his death, received the last anointings, it must be washed, to mark that if the soul, by confession and contrition, was cleansed from sin, both, namely, the soul and the body, it will acquire glorification and splendour on the Day of Judgment. It is to designate that these, as Job says, really die in the Lord and are blessed who carry no stain of sin, but leave by penitence all uncleanness in this world. But since there is no mention of this phrase either in the Old Testament, namely in (Leviticus, chapter 10), or in the New (Acts, chapter 5), it should not be, according to some who worry about it a lot. St Augustine says in his book, *On the Care One Should Take of Mothers*, 'The duties which are rendered to the human body after its death are not an assurance of salvation, but a duty of humanity.' However, when Mary Magdalene anointed the Lord before His Passion,[298] she did for Jesus, who was going to die, what she could not do for the dead Lord. 'For in that she hath poured this ointment on my body,' said the Lord, 'she did it for my burial.'[299] By this it can be proved that the bodies of the dead must be washed; for, as St Jerome says, when commenting on, 'anoint your head.' For this parts of the body, perfumes were used instead of baths.

37. The thirteenth canon of the Council of Toledo has ruled that those who, called by God, come out of this world, will be carried

---

[298] See Matthew 26:7-12
[299] Matthew 26:12

to the place of their burial, accompanied only by the singing of the psalms and the voices of those who chant. However, the deceased should be carried by people of his profession; if he is a deacon, by deacons, if he is a priest, by priests, if there are any present. Otherwise, there is no absolute obligation that it be so, because necessity is law. If he belongs to some confraternity, he will be carried by those who belong to the same brotherhood. Women are not allowed to carry bodies, for fear of putting them in the situation of discovering their bodies, which could excite them to impurity, and this could easily happen. Now, while the body of the house is transported to the church or to the place of its burial, according to the custom of some countries, three breaks are made on the way. Firstly, to show that the deceased, while living on earth, exercised himself mainly in three things in order to be able to present himself with dignity before the Lord and to enjoy eternal rest with the other saints. These are the love of God, charity for his neighbour and the care of oneself; or that he lived and ended his life in the faith of the Holy Trinity. Secondly, to represent that the Lord rested for three days in the bosom of the earth. Third, there are three breaks on the way, so that, by the triple cessation of the psalmody that takes place in these three halts, he receives the triple absolution which are then pronounced, for the sins he has committed in three ways, namely, by thoughts, by words and by actions.[300]

38. Then we place it in the tomb together, in some places, with holy water and burning coals with incense. They put holy water in it, so that the demons, who fear it greatly, do not approach the body because they have a habit of exerting their fury upon the bodies of the dead. For that what they have not been able to do to them during their lifetime, they do at least hope to do to them after their death. Incense is placed there, to remove or dispel the bad smell of the body, or so that the deceased is supposed to have offered his creator the pleasant scent of good works, or to show that the prayers of the faithful serve the deceased. They put on

---

[300] This may shed light on Exodus 3:17-18 'And I have said, I will bring you up out of the affliction of Egypt… unto a land flowing with milk and honey… The Lord God of the Hebrews hath met with us: and now let us go, we beseech thee, three days' journey into the wilderness, that we may sacrifice to the Lord our God'

charcoal to indicate that this land can no longer be used for profane purposes, for charcoal subsists longer under the earth than any other matter. They also include ivy or laurel, and other things of this kind, which always preserve their verdure in the tomb, to designate that those who die in Christ do not cease to live. For, although they die in the world bodily the soul, nevertheless, lives and is revived in God. However, for another consideration, the ancients used the cypress in funerals, because, just as the cypress, once cut, no longer pushes up new offshoots but totally dies away, likewise, according to the Gentiles, a dead man does not live again. These ceremonies are also observed, not that the corpses have the feeling, but in the figure, that is to say, because we hope for the resurrection or the mercy of God, so either to provoke His benevolence to such acts of mercy, or because such honours rendered to the dead please God.

39. One must bury the dead so that his head is turned to the west and his feet to the east. In this position, so to speak, he prays, and this insinuates that he is ready to move in all haste from west to east, from the world or from the earth to the next age. And somewhere outside the cemetery where the Christian is buried, we must always place a cross at the head of his burial, to mark that he was a Christian, because the devil dreads this sign greatly and is afraid to approach the place that shines with the sign of the cross.

40. We must also bury the Christian faithful, after having wrapped them in a shroud, as the Provincials[301] observe, which they have borrowed from the Gospel where we speak of the shroud and the cloth in which we bury Christ. There are others who sew the dead in a hair shirt, to represent the insignia of penance, for ashes and haircloth are the weapons of penitents. They should not be clothed in common clothes, as they are in Italy and, as some say, hose must be put on their legs and shoes on their feet, to indicate that they are ready to appear in judgment.

41. Clerics, if they are ordained, are clothed or adorned with the insignia of their orders. If they are not in the sacred orders, they are buried as laymen. However, this will often be omitted for some in orders, if the deceased is poor. Nevertheless, for a priest

---

[301] Monastic superiors

and for a bishop, it must never be omitted, for the vestments designate the virtues, ornamented with which they signify that they are in a higher degree than the others. Pope Eutycian decreed that no one should bury martyrs without a dalmatic or purple collobium.

42. On this subject, we must consider whether Christ clothed himself in clothes after His Resurrection and whether He went up to heaven, clothed. Also whether He appeared clothed to the two disciples going to Emmaus and to the other women and to the disciples. Indeed, we read that the angels appeared clothed, according to these words of John, 'behold, two men stood by them in white apparel; Which also said, Ye men of Galilee, why stand ye gazing up into heaven? this same Jesus, which is taken up from you into heaven,'[302] Of course Christ was clothed when He ascended to heaven, according to where it says, 'Who is this that cometh from Edom, with dyed garments from Bozrah?'[303] Likewise, the angels said, 'Wherefore art thou red in thine apparel?'[304]

43. It is also asked whether men will be naked after the Day of Judgment or whether they will be clothed, for angels are always attired. Christ, after His Resurrection, appeared clothed, and it was the same in His Transfiguration, since, 'his raiment white as snow.'[305] It appears, on the contrary, that men will be naked, and it is an authoritative feeling that we will be in the same form and condition as Adam was before sinning, and in a better state. Adam was naked then, so we will be naked. This is resolved in that we do not define anything about the garments,[306] but we content ourselves with saying that there will be no deformity, no adversity, and that we will be clothed and adorned with the ornaments of virtues. But who is to be buried and in what place? Does the place of burial confer something or provide any benefit? We dealt with this in Book One, in the chapter *Cemeteries and Other Sacred and Religious Places*. Now, note that, as it is written in Leviticus, the high priest shall not, 'go in to any dead body, nor defile himself

---

[302] Acts 1:10-11
[303] Isaiah 63:1
[304] Isaiah 63:2
[305] Matthew 28:3
[306] In spiritual terms one does think in terms of physical clothes

for his father, or for his mother; Neither shall he go out of the sanctuary.'[307] It is for this reason that the Roman pontiff does not enter the house of any deceased person. Likewise, as it is said that priests, 'shall not make baldness upon their head, neither shall they shave off the corner of their beard, nor make any cuttings in their flesh.'[308] That is why those who are afflicted by the death of those who are dear to them let their beards grow, do not shave their hair and also wear black clothes, so that, by the black colour and their pain, they appear to be buried with the dead whom they mourn.

44. We can also ask here if the dead speak and have a voice, and it seems that they do, according to this word of the Prophet, 'Let the high praises of God be in their mouth.'[309] Pope Hormisdas[310] says that those for whom we have had a false indulgence will accuse us before the tribunal of Christ and blessed Augustine says that the deceased who do not know what is happening on the earth at the moment when things are happening, then learn from those who, in dying, go away from this land. But the Apostle seems to say the opposite, when he says that, 'whether there be tongues, they shall cease,'[311] and the Psalmist, that, 'The dead praise not the Lord.'[312] And note, according to St Augustine, that during the time that is between the death of man and the last resurrection, souls inhabit hidden places, that is, hidden from our eyes. Finally note, according to Master John Beletho, the ancients used to say that when the souls of men are enclosed in their bodies, they are called souls; in hell, *manes*; in the heavens, spirits. When the dead were newly buried, or when the spirit wandered about the burials, they are called shadows. Hence the Psalmist says, 'Yea, though I walk through the valley of the shadow of death, I will fear no evil.'[313] This is why they placed bread and wine on the tombs of the dead, as was said in the chapter *The Chair of Saint Peter*.

---

[307] Leviticus 21:11-12
[308] Leviticus 21:5
[309] Psalm 149:6
[310] In office from 514-523
[311] 1 Corinthians 13:8
[312] Psalm 115:17
[313] Psalm 23:4

45. At the Mass of the Dead, the Epistle that is sometimes said is, 'But the most valiant Judas exhorted the people, etc.,'[314] sometimes also, 'But I would not have you to be ignorant, brethren, etc.,'[315] at other times, 'And I heard a voice from heaven saying unto me, etc.,'[316] at other times, 'Behold, I shew you a mystery; We shall not all sleep, etc.'[317] The Gospel which is sometimes said is, 'Verily, verily, I say unto you, The hour is coming, etc.,'[318] and sometimes, 'Then said Martha unto Jesus, etc.'[319] At other times it is, 'For as the Father raiseth up the dead, etc.,'[320] and other times again, 'All that the Father giveth me shall come to me, etc.,'[321] and sometimes also, 'I am the living bread which came down from heaven, etc.'[322]

---

[314] 2 Maccabees 12:42-48
[315] 1 Thessalonians 4:13-18
[316] Revelation 14:13
[317] 1 Corinthians 15:61-57
[318] John 5:25-20
[319] John 11:21-27
[320] John 5:21-23
[321] John 6:37-40
[322] John 6:51-55

36 THE FOUR-CROWNED, MARTYRS

1. What is remarkable about the Four-Crowned, is that it was five who had come to build a temple. Diocletian[323] having learned that they were Christians, crowned them with martyrdom; and as their names were known, that is why they are placed in the Collect. Two years later, four others received martyrdom, and their bodies were buried near those of the five martyrs mentioned above and as their names were unknown, Pope Melchiades[324] decreed that their feast should be celebrated under the names of the five martyrs above. This is how their festivity came to be called the Four-Crowned Feast.

2. Later on their names were revealed to a certain religious. They were called Severus, Severinus, Carpophorus, and Victorinus. Yet the name of their feast was not changed for that and this day is not recorded in the Calendar either.

---

[323] Emperor from 284-305
[324] In office from 311-314

37 THE BLESSED MARTIN, BISHOP AND CONFESSOR

1. Of Blessed Martin one must know that he is said to be equal to the Apostles, not because he raised up some who were dead, as some think, since many other martyrs and confessors have done the same thing. Nor because of the multitude of his miracles, but especially because of a single miracle. For when he was Archbishop of Tours, a poor man came to him who asked him for a tunic. Martin granted him his request, and ordered his steward to buy one. He went to the market and, without hurrying, he came back, carrying with him a bad tunic that looked like a *penula* [325] (penula), and that one could call almost of no importance. The holy man asked to see it. Now it was short and came only to his knees and the sleeves only came to his elbows. Martin took off his, gave it to the poor man, and dressed himself in the said penula. Shortly afterwards he prepared to celebrate Mass, and, standing before the altar, as is the custom at the Preface, he raised his hands to the Lord, his wide sleeves falling back, for his arms were not fat or fleshy, and as this penula only came to his elbow, his arms remained naked. Then gold bracelets came miraculously to cover them decently, and a globe of fire appeared over his head, by which we saw that the Holy Spirit had descended on him to give him strength, as he had descended on the Apostles at Pentecost. That is why he was rightly named the equal of the Apostles. He is equal to them in his office.

---

[325] A Roman cloak similar to a poncho

2. It must be considered that he alone, among the confessors, has an octave of institution, like Blessed Lawrence among the martyrs, for the latter said, 'Thou hast tested me by fire, and iniquity has not been found in me.' Also Martin, on his part, about to die, said to the demon who was standing near him, 'You will find nothing in me, cruel beast.' Here is the relationship between these two saints. One, an eminent martyr, who has, in preference to all the others, both an octave and a vigil. The other, an excellent confessor, which is why, above all other confessors, he has an octave. The kings of the French are accustomed to wear their copes in combat, as was said in Book Two, in the chapter *The Priest*. The poet Fortunatus, a man remarkable for his life and his genius, having come from Italy to Tours, wrote the deeds of the Blessed Martin, at the time of Pope John III.[326]

---

[326] In office from 561-574

38 THE BLESSED ANDREW, APOSTLE

1. St Andrew was brown in colour, his beard was long, his height small. This is said so that we know how he is to be represented in the church, which is something one would wish to know for each of the Apostles and for other saints of great name.

2. He preached in Achaea and Athens and in the surrounding countries. He possessed merit and excellent virtues and it is appropriate that Blessed Gregory had so much devotion to him, that he composed special Office for him and that he founded a monastery in his honour and became a monk there. This feast has no fast of institution, because it is during the time of fasts, therefore it was not necessary to institute a vigil. The same thing is practiced for Blessed Thomas, an Apostle. Now, the bones of this saint and those of the blessed Luke the Evangelist were, in the time of the emperor Constantine II,[327] transported to Constantinople.

3. On this day they say the Epistle, 'For with the heart man believeth unto righteousness, etc.,'[328] the Gospel is, 'And Jesus, walking by the sea of Galilee, etc.'[329] and the Post Communion is, 'Follow me, and I will make you fishers of men, etc.'[330] At the vigil, the Introit is, 'And Jesus, walking by the sea of Galilee, saw two brethren, etc.,'[331] the Gospel is, 'Again the next day after John

---

[327] Emperor from 337-340
[328] Romans 10:10-18
[329] Matthew 4:18-22
[330] Matthew 4:19-20
[331] Matthew 4:18-19 Psalm 19:1

stood, etc.,'³³² and the Post Communion is, 'He first findeth his own brother Simon, etc.'³³³

---

³³² John 1:35-51
³³³ John 1:41-42

39 THE BLESSED NICHOLAS

1. We read that in a church called Holy Cross, dependent on the monastery of Blessed Mary of Charity, the new narrative[334] of Blessed Nicholas, had not yet been sung. The brothers of this monastery urged their prior to allow them to sing it but he rejected it positively, saying that it would be an unseemly thing to change old usages to substitute new ones. And as they redoubled their insistence he answered with anger, 'Leave me, I do not want to sing new songs, I say more, songs that are pure fun, in my church.' However, the great annual feast of St Nicholas was approaching and the brethren finished the Matins of the vigil with sad souls. When all had returned to their beds, Blessed Nicholas appeared to the prior with a terrible face, and pulling him by the hair out of bed, laid him on the slabs of the dormitory. He then began intoning the antiphon, *O pastor*, and at each note, with the rods with which he was armed, he increased the most terrible blows on the back of the groaning prior. In this way he slowly chanted the antiphon to the end. The monks, awakened with a start by the cries of the culprit, carried him half-dead to his bed, and when he was finally back to himself, he said to them, 'Go and sing in great chorus the new history of St Nicholas.'

2. At the time of the Emperor Henry IV[335] the bones of Blessed Nicholas were transported to Benevento.

---

[334] Or the new Office
[335] King of the Germans from 1056-1105

40 THE VENERABLE BEDE, PRIEST

1. The Venerable Bede, priest and monk, illustrator, flourished in England around the year of Lord six hundred and sixty-six. Although he is included in the Catalogue of Saints, yet the Church does not call him a saint, but Venerable, for two reasons. First, because being blind, and because of his extreme old age, he was led by the countryside and towns and everywhere preached the word of God. As one day he passed through a valley covered and strewn with great stones, one of his guides mockingly told him that there was a great people gathered there, waiting silently and eagerly. Then Bede began to preach with ardour; which he concluded by saying, 'For ever and ever,' and it is said that all the stones then began to exclaim, 'Amen, venerable father.' That is why he is called the Venerable.

2. Others affirm that the angels replied, 'You have spoken well, venerable father.' The second reason is that after his death a certain clerk, who had a lot of devotion to him, wanted to make a verse that he intended to have engraved on his tomb. This line began thus, 'In this pit,' and he wished to end it with, 'the bones of Saint Bede.' But as such an end of verse was not in accord with prosody, so he racked his mind ardently and did not find a suitable end. One night, after much reflection, he rushed in the morning towards the saint's tomb, and found his verse written in the hand of the angels, and finished, which said, 'these are the bones of the venerable Bede in a ditch.'[336] It is said that his body is honoured in Genoa with proper devotion.

---

[336] *Hac sunt in fossa Bedae venerabilis ossa*

41 SAINT THOMAS, APOSTLE

1. The history or legend of St Thomas, an Apostle, with the extracts that can be found in the responsories or antiphons, is considered apocryphal. On this feast we read at Mass the Gospel for Thomas, 'But Thomas, one of the twelve, called Didymus, etc.'[337]

---

[337] John 20:24-29

42 SAINTS STEPHEN, JOHN THE EVANGELIST, AND THE HOLY INNOCENTS

1. The day following the Nativity of the Lord, we celebrate the feast of the death of Blessed Stephen, first martyr, although he suffered martyrdom in the month of August. We have said, in the chapter *The Finding of Saint Stephen's Relics*, why we celebrate this feast of his Finding. One asks why these three feasts, namely of St Stephen, St John, and the Holy Innocents, are arranged immediately after the feast of the Nativity of the Lord? The reasons are, first, that all his companions may be gathered to Christ, the head and the bridegroom. For Christ, spouse of the Church, when He came to this world, to his birth, added three companions, of whom it is said in the Song of Songs, 'My beloved is white and ruddy, the chiefest among ten thousand.'[338] He is white in the person of John, a virgin and confessor, rose in the person of Stephen who was the first martyr and chosen from a thousand, in the person of the innumerable crowd of Innocents. Secondly, so that the Church may bring together all kinds of martyrs, of whose martyrdom the Nativity of Christ was the cause.

2. For there are three kinds of martyrs. The first is the martyrdom of will and of work, such was the martyrdom of Blessed Stephen, and it is the kind of the most worthy and most meritorious martyr. Now, we say this, that there are certain circumstances that may lead to confessors having more merit than some martyrs. This is why the feast of Stephen precedes that of the other martyrs and

---

[338] Song of Songs 5:10

SAINTS STEPHEN, JOHN THE EVANGELIST, AND THE HOLY INNOCENTS

follows the feast of the Nativity of the Lord. Which why in this feast it is said that the death which the Saviour deigned to suffer for all, Stephen, the first above all, has restored it to the Saviour and, moreover, Christ was born yesterday on earth, so that Stephen would be born today in heaven.

3. On the feast of Blessed Stephen, the Introit says, 'Princes also did sit and speak against me, etc.,'[339] by which one shows the treachery of the princes of the Jews who were lying in wait for Blessed Stephen. The Epistle is, 'Stephen, full of faith and power, etc.,'[340] and this Epistle, as Blessed Augustine says in his sermon for that day, is no less admirable and worthy in terms of form than of mystery. The passion of the martyr is told of as well as the cause of this passion, and its merits or its reward, which is also insinuated and represented in the responsory, which is, 'Princes also did sit and speak against me, etc.,'[341] and in this one, 'And said, Behold, I see the heavens opened, etc.,'[342] which is also in the Offertory and Post Communion. The same thing is repeated in the Night Office, as it needs to be pointed out often and frequently that the princes of the priests consulted to put him to death.

4. The Gospel is, 'Wherefore, behold, I send unto you prophets, etc.,'[343] and it we see these words, 'O Jerusalem, Jerusalem, thou that killest the prophets, and stonest them which are sent unto thee, etc.;' and Stephen was stoned. One also reads, 'from the blood of righteous Abel,' For as Abel was the first martyr of the Old Testament, so was Stephen in the New Testament.

5. Alcuin,[344] teacher of Charlemagne[345] and his chaplain, composed the Office of St Stephen.[346] He took the Night Office

---

[339] Psalm 119:23, 86, 23, 1
[340] Acts 6:8-10, Acts 7:54-59
[341] Psalm 119:23, 86, Psalm 6:4, Acts 7:56
[342] Acts 7:56
[343] Matthew 23:34-39
[344] Flaccus Albinus Alcuinus, English scholar, clergyman, poet and teacher from York, c. 735–804
[345] King of the Franks from 768, King of the Lombards from 774, and Holy Roman Emperor from 800
[346] Or perhaps composed a service for St Stephen

antiphons from the psalms and gave them titles and the rest is taken from the Acts of the Apostles. The antiphons of Lauds are also preceded by verses, as was said in Book Six, in the chapter *Holy Trinity Sunday*. Alleluias are also frequently heard in the short verses, either because of the solemnity of the Lord's Nativity, or to express our joy that St Stephen shares the society of angels. Now we say the capitula, 'And Stephen, full of faith and power, etc.,'[347] and this one, 'Then there arose certain of the synagogue, etc.,'[348] and this other, 'But he, being full of the Holy Ghost, etc.'[349]

6. The second martyrdom is voluntary or wilful martyrdom, and not by work, as was the martyrdom of St John the Evangelist, who was martyred, as it evidently appears by this antiphon, 'The blessed Apostle John was cast into a vessel of boiling oil,'[350] which he came out of intact. Protected by divine grace, he did not feel the sting of the flesh. Because he was virgin and in relation to the soul and the body, he did not feel the most ardent boiling of the oil. Now, on the day of his birth, in certain churches, Mass is sung at daybreak, to show that, having received the light of this world, he has always offered to God the sacrifice of his virginity. Furthermore, as he could not have two vigils, because of the feast of Blessed Stephen, it was decreed that he should have two Masses.

7. In the Mass of Blessed John the Epistle is, 'He that feareth God, will do good, etc.'[351] The Gospel is, 'And when he had spoken this, he saith unto him, Follow me. Then Peter, turning about, etc.,'[352] and we sing the Alleluia, 'Right worthy of honour is the blessed Apostle John, etc.,'[353] where it is said that John, at the Last Supper, rested on the breast of the Lord. It is taken from John 21. The Introit is, 'And in the midst of the church she shall

---

[347] Acts 6:8
[348] Acts 6:9
[349] Acts 7:55
[350] The blessed Apostle John was cast into a vessel of boiling oil, but by the favour and protection of God, he came out unharmed. Alleluia.
[351] Ecclesiasticus 15:1-6
[352] John 21:10-24
[353] Right worthy of honour is the blessed Apostle John, who leaned on the Lord's bosom at the Last Supper

SAINTS STEPHEN, JOHN THE EVANGELIST, AND THE HOLY INNOCENTS

open his mouth, etc.,'[354] and the responsory is, 'Then went this saying abroad among the brethren, etc.'[355] The Alleluia is, 'This is the disciple, etc.,'[356] and the Communion is, 'Then went this saying abroad among the brethren, etc.'[357] The capitulum, 'With the bread of life and understanding, etc.,'[358] is also said at the Hours and this one, 'Blessed be the God and Father of our Lord Jesus Christ, etc.,'[359] and this one, 'He that feareth God, will do good, etc.[360]

8. And note that Blessed John the Baptist died on the feast day of Blessed John the Evangelist. However, as it was impossible to celebrate his feast, it was transferred to three days after the birth, or the third day of the birth, of the Lord so that the Spouse might have all His companions with Him, as has been said above. And the feast of Blessed John the Baptist remained on his day and it is no wonder, because this day was announced or appointed by the authority of an angel, to indulge in the joy of the Nativity of the Precursor. We must not dogmatize nor pretend that John the Evangelist gave way to John the Baptist as the greatest and most worthy, and deduce this opinion from what we read, 'Among them that are born of women there hath not risen a greater than John the Baptist.'[361] For it has been revealed in a divine way that one should not argue over their pre-eminence. Two masters, one of whom preferred John the Baptist and the other John the Evangelist, having appointed a day for a solemn discussion on this subject, both sought with the greatest care the authorities and the best reasons for doing so, so that the John they preferred to prevail. Finally, on the day of the discussion, each of the two saints appeared to his partisan or zealot, saying, 'We are well united in heaven; do not argue about us on the earth.' Then the two adversaries mutually shared this vision, which they then

---

[354] Ecclesiasticus 15:5 Psalm 92:1
[355] John 21:23, 19
[356] John 21:24
[357] John 21:23
[358] Ecclesiasticus 15:3
[359] Ephesians 1:3
[360] Ecclesiasticus 15:1
[361] Matthew 11:11

announced to the people, and they blessed the Lord. Or else, this feast was transferred to the third day after the Nativity of the Lord, perhaps because it was on that day that a basilica was dedicated to St John the Evangelist, or because, perhaps, it was on that day that he returned from the island of Patmos, or that he received the mitre, for he was patriarch of Ephesus.

9. There are some who say that Blessed John, having descended to the tomb after the celebration of the Mass, disappeared in the eyes of the assistants. Now as the water gushes from the earth in this place they add that John lives under this earth and that it is his breath that forms this spring that comes out of the land. Others claim that he was taken up into heaven. So the Office of this day is composed, partly from the Gospel and partly from the tribulations that St John had to endure. In this last responsory, namely, 'In the midst of the Church he opened his mouth, etc.,'[362] taken from the book of Wisdom, and which is concerned with the of spirit of understanding, we end with a neume, because it was by the spirit of understanding that he spoke of the ineffable Word, that is, of the true God.

10. The third martyrdom is actual and non-voluntary martyrdom, for example that of the Innocents, which ranks third in dignity and among the martyrs' feasts. But why is the feast of the Innocents celebrated before the feast of the Star, that is to say, Epiphany, since they were put to death after the appearance of the star, namely when Herod saw that he had been fooled by the Magi? To this it is replied that Herod, having heard the rumours which were spreading concerning Christ, was greatly troubled, fearing to lose his crown. This suggested to him the thought of putting all the children to death, so that Christ might not escape. However he was prevented from doing so because Caesar Augustus commanded him to come and find him, with Aristobulus and Alexander his son, to justify himself before him. Now because he did not dare to disobey, he went there. When he returned one year after the birth of the Lord, he had all the children put to death from the age of two and below. Now *dietia*

---

[362] In the midst of the Church he opened his mouth, and the Lord filled him with his spirit, the spirit of wisdom and understanding: He clothed him with a robe of glory. He has stored up joy and exultation for him

in Greek is called a *biennium* in Latin, which means, 'a period of two years.'

11. One asks why, on the festival of the Innocents, at the Mass, one does not sing the *Gloria in excelsis*, nor an Alleluia, nor other songs of joy? The masters say that it is because the Innocents died before the Passion of Christ, and thus they descended into limbo. However for a similar reason, they should also suppress them at the feast of Blessed John the Baptist. We must say that this happens because the author of the Office wanted us to unite in this festivity to the souls of devout women moaning and lamenting the death of the Innocents. It is because of their sadness that we remove the hymns of joy. This is why we read Jeremiah's prophecy concerning the Innocents, 'In Rama was there a voice heard, lamentation, and weeping, etc.'[363] These words are understood in the literal sense to relate to the Benjamites who were exterminated because of the Levite woman whom they had outraged, and Rachel was Benjamin's mother. Or by Rachel, which by interpretation means, *ovis*, 'sheep,' or *videns*, 'seeing,' we hear the Church crying for its three kinds of children. The first are the martyrs. In considering that they have been torn from her, she will not console herself in the present time but keeps all her consolations for the future. The second children whom the Church cries for are those who die in their mother's womb before seeing the light, or who come before their time.[364] The third are those who, after being regenerated in baptism, retreat or walk backward through sin. The Church mourns both because they are no longer, that is, because they are damned.[365] This is why the Church groans, and removes the hymns of joy. One can also bring another reason. For the songs of joy must be sung after the victory, regarding which it was said to Ezekiel, 'Set thine house in order: for thou shalt die, and not live,'[366] for not singing the songs of joy after the victory. However the Innocents have not won a victory because where there is no fight, there is

---

[363] Matthew 2:18 See also Jeremiah 31:15
[364] Which is why the Church does not permit abortion.
[365] Confined to a state of spiritual death
[366] Isaiah 38:1

no victory. The second reason is the best. Some, however, instead of an Alleluia, sing at Mass, 'Praise be to Christ,' others, 'Let us sing.'

12. The Epistle is, 'And I looked, and, lo, a Lamb, etc.'[367] and the Gospel is, 'And when they were departed, behold, the angel of the Lord, etc.'[368] If this festival falls on a Sunday, no song of joy is suppressed because of the joy of the Resurrection. In the octave also we sing the songs of joy, to mark the joy they will be filled with in the octave, that is to say, the resurrection, because, although they descended into limbo, however, they will rise with us in glory. Indeed, the octaves of the festivities are celebrated in memory of the general resurrection they designate. On this day again, as the sadness of women has been represented, the deacons, in a great number of churches, do not wear the dalmatic, nor the subdeacons the stole or tunic, to mark that the Innocents, immediately after their death, did not receive the first dress, but descended into limbo. We talked about this in Book Three, in the chapter *The Four Colours of Church Vestments*.

13. On this feast, we say that capitulum, 'And I looked, and, lo, a Lamb stood on the mount Sion, etc.,'[369] and this one, 'These are they which were not defiled, etc.,'[370] and also, 'These were redeemed from among men, etc.'[371] Notice that the anthems for the Night Offices are taken from the psalms, otherwise from the Epistle and the Gospel. When one speaks of this number one hundred and forty-four thousand, one speaks of the finite for the infinite, because God understands all the elect under a certain number. What is also said is, 'I saw under the altar of God the souls of those who had been slain,'[372] must be taken in the sense that John saw under the altar the souls of those who had been put to death, that is to say, who inclined their heads, or because he

---

[367] Revelation 14:1-5
[368] Matthew 2:13-18
[369] Revelation 14:1
[370] Revelation 14:4
[371] Revelation 14:4
[372] From a responsory following the reading from Jeremiah 31:18-20

SAINTS STEPHEN, JOHN THE EVANGELIST, AND THE HOLY INNOCENTS

saw this in the concealed,[373] because no one here below can penetrate it.[374]

14. But why does the Church solemnise the death of the Innocents, who have not had the will to suffer? For it seems, for the same reason, that if a tyrant put to death such a number of children, the Church should also celebrate a solemnity for them, which is not true. One can answer that this festival must be celebrated for three reasons, although the Innocents did not have the will to suffer. First, because it was Christ who was sought and later put to death in their person. Secondly, because in them Christ was hidden from the devil and from Herod. Third, because they confessed the name of the Lord, not by speaking, but by dying, because they were put to death for Christ and in the place of Christ. They were innocent because they had been circumcised, because circumcision was then the remedy for original sin, although it did not have the same efficiency that baptism now has.

15. Now, it must be known that in certain churches, on the day of the Nativity of the Lord, the deacons, when Vespers are finished, form a religious dance and while dancing they sing the antiphon of St Stephen, who was the most excellent of the deacons, and a priest says the Collect. They celebrate the Night Office until the next day and they give the blessings to the lessons, which however they must not do. The priests do the same at the feast of Blessed Stephen, at Vespers, in honour of Blessed John, because he was a priest. On the evening of St John's Day, the children do the same in honour of the Holy Innocents. The subdeacons, in certain churches, celebrate the day of the circumcision, as has been said in this place. Others celebrate at Epiphany, others at the octave of Epiphany, which is called the Feast of Fools. But as, since antiquity the appearance of this order is very uncertain, for in the ancient canons many call this a sacred order, while many say the opposite. That is why the subdeacons have no particular day and stopped celebrating it. The service of their feast is very confused.

---

[373] Through spiritual discernment, in the hiddenness of the mystery
[374] Because ordinary mundane awareness cannot perceive such things

43 THE APOSTLES

1. The Greek word *apostolos*[375] is *missus*, 'sent,' in Latin. This is where the name of the Apostles came from, because Christ sent them to evangelize through the whole world. It is certain that the Church celebrates the Apostles together and sings in Matins, 'Behold, I send my messenger before thy face, etc.,'[376] because all twelve were elected at the same time by the Lord, after the sermon He gave them on the mountain, as we see it in St Matthew and St Mark. However, the Church has given some of their own Office, for example for St Peter, because of the privilege of his dignity. For St Paul, although he is not one of the twelve, because of the privilege of preaching. For the blessed John, because of the privilege of love or virginity, and for Blessed Andrew, because of the privilege of the cross which he preached, which he so ardently desired, and which he obtained.
2. During the Hours, one says this capitulum, 'Now therefore ye are no more strangers and foreigners, etc.,'[377] and this one, 'Ye have not chosen me, but I have chosen you, etc.,'[378] and this one, 'Blessed is the man that endureth temptation, etc.,'[379] and this one, 'Magnified him in the fear of his enemies, etc.'[380] Also, 'He made an everlasting covenant with him, etc.,'[381] and this other, 'He

---

[375] 'one sent forth' or 'apostle'
[376] Matthew 11:10
[377] Ephesians 2:19
[378] John 15:16
[379] James 1:12
[380] Ecclesiasticus 45:2
[381] Ecclesiasticus 45:8

THE APOSTLES

sanctified him in his faith, and meekness, etc.,'[382] and this one, 'And they departed from the presence of the council, etc.,'[383] and this, 'For whom he did foreknow, he also did predestinate to be conformed, etc.,'[384] and this other, 'Their bodies are buried in peace, etc.,'[385] and this one. 'They shall hunger no more, neither thirst any more, etc.,'[386] and, 'We fools esteemed their life madness, etc.,'[387] and this one, 'Jesus Christ himself being the chief corner stone.'[388]

3. Now, they have vigils and octaves because if we suffer with them we will reign with them.[389] We have spoken of this in Book Four, in the chapter *The Wednesday and Fasts of the Ember Days*. An exception, however, is the example of the feast of St John the Evangelist, for the purpose of the fast which is obligatory, not only because, as some say, he was not a martyr by intent, but also because of the feast of Blessed Stephen, which is at the vigil of the vigil-fast of St John.

4. At the vigil of the Apostles, one says the Epistle, 'The Lord gave him the blessing of all nations, etc.,'[390] and this, 'And by the hands of the apostles were many signs and wonders wrought, etc.'[391] and the Gospel is, 'I am the true vine, and my Father is the husbandman, etc.'[392]

5. At the Feast of the Apostles, the Epistle is, 'Now therefore ye are no more strangers and foreigners, etc.,'[393] and this one, 'But these were men of mercy, etc.,'[394] this also, 'And we know that all things work together for good to them that love God, etc.,'[395]

---

[382] Ecclesiasticus 45:4
[383] Acts 5:41 The capitulum changes 'they' to 'Apostles'
[384] Romans 8:29
[385] Ecclesiasticus 44:14
[386] Revelation 7:16
[387] Wisdom 5:4
[388] Ephesians 2:20
[389] Reflecting Romans 8:17 'if so be that we suffer with him, that we may be also glorified together'
[390] Ecclesiasticus 44:25-27, 2-4, 6-9
[391] Acts 5:12-16
[392] John 15:1-7
[393] Ephesians 2:19-22
[394] Ecclesiasticus 44:10-15
[395] Romans 8:28-30

then this one, 'Blessed be God, even the Father of our Lord Jesus Christ, etc.,'[396] also this one, 'For we are made a spectacle unto the world, and to angels, etc.,'[397] and this one, 'But unto every one of us is given grace, etc.'[398] Likewise the Alleluia is, 'Ye have not chosen me, but I have chosen you, etc.,'[399] and this one, 'Come unto me, all ye that labour and are heavy laden, etc.'[400] The Gospel is, 'This is my commandment, That ye love one another, etc.,'[401] and this one, 'These things I command you, that ye love one another, etc.,'[402] and this other, 'Behold, I send you forth as sheep, etc.,'[403] and this one, 'And there was also a strife among them, etc.,'[404] then this one, 'After these things the Lord appointed other seventy, etc.,'[405] and this one, 'I am the true vine, and my Father is the husbandman, etc.,'[406] and this other, 'Then answered Peter and said unto him, etc.'[407] The Post Communion is, 'Verily I say unto you, That ye which have followed me, etc.,'[408] and this one, 'Amen I say to you, that you, who have left all things, etc.,'[409] which is from the same place.

6. And note that we read that there were only three Apostles who lived in Rome, namely, Peter, Paul, and John, and the three Evangelists John, Mark, and Luke. It should also be noted that the Apostles or disciples of Christ not only suffered because they preached Christ but also because they said He was God, without Roman authority to say so, which was forbidden. The Church once ordained that a common feast be celebrated for all the

---

[396] 2 Corinthians 1:3-7
[397] 1 Corinthians 4:9-14
[398] Ephesians 4:7-13
[399] John 15:16
[400] Matthew 11:28-30
[401] John 15:12-17
[402] John 16:17-25
[403] Matthew 10:16-22
[404] Luke 22:24-30
[405] Luke 10:1-9
[406] John 15:1-7
[407] Matthew 19 27-29
[408] Matthew 19:28 'Ye which have followed me shall sit upon twelve thrones, judging the twelve tribes of Israel'
[409] Matthew 19:28-29 'Amen I say to you, that you, who have left all things and followed Me, shall receive an hundredfold, and shall possess life everlasting'

THE APOSTLES

Apostles, by the calends of May, as has been said in this book, at the feast of the Apostles Philip and James.

44 THE EVANGELISTS

1. After the Apostles, the Church also venerates the Evangelists, who not only preached but also wrote the Gospels. We read in Genesis, 'And a river went out of Eden to water the garden; and from thence it was parted, and became into four heads,' namely, the Pishon, the Gihon, the Tigris and the Euphrates. It is certain that, in the allegorical sense, this river is the evangelical preaching, which proceeds from Christ, from whom all sweetness flows. 'Come,' He said, 'unto me, all ye that labour and are heavy laden, and I will give you rest. Take my yoke upon you, and learn of me; for I am meek and lowly in heart: and ye shall find rest unto your souls. For my yoke is easy, and my burden is light.'[410] 'O taste and see that the Lord is good: blessed is the man that trusteth in him.'[411]

2. Now, it is with reason that this preaching is compared to a river, not only because it restores, purifies, and fertilizes, but also because a river is called running water and, as Solomon says, 'The words of a man's mouth are as deep waters, and the wellspring of wisdom as a flowing brook.'[412] Such words have spread so far and wide that they have filled the whole world, according to this saying, 'Go ye into all the world, and preach the gospel, etc.'[413] That is why, 'Their line is gone out through all the earth, and their words to the end of the world.'[414] This is the river that waters

---

[410] Matthew 11:28-30
[411] Psalm 34:8
[412] Proverbs 18:4
[413] Mark 16:15
[414] Psalm 19:4

THE EVANGELISTS

paradise, which fertilizes the Church, according to what the Apostle says, 'I have planted, Apollos watered; but God gave the increase.'[415] This is, 'A fountain of gardens, a well of living waters, and streams from Lebanon.'[416] Now this river is divided into four main branches, because the preaching of Jesus Christ fills the four Gospels. For although a great number have written gospels, since, in the testimony of St Luke, 'Forasmuch as many have taken in hand to set forth in order a declaration of those things which are most surely believed among us,'[417] the Church has received only four, namely, those of St Matthew, St Mark, St Luke, and St John.
3. But it did so for four reasons. First, to show the agreement of the two Testaments. For in the Old Testament there was only one legislator, namely Moses, and four great prophets, namely, Isaiah, Jeremiah, Ezekiel, and Daniel, and twelve lesser prophets, and a great number of sages, namely, Job, David, Solomon and Jesus-Syrach. So in the New Testament there was Christ, four Evangelists, twelve Apostles, and many other teachers like Jerome, Augustine, Ambrose, and Gregory. Which shows that all is, 'a wheel in the middle of a wheel,'[418] and the two cherubim, facing each other, look at each other, their faces turned toward the mercy seat. Secondly, to lead the chariot of Amminadib, whose bride says in the Song of Songs, 'my soul made me like the chariots of Amminadib.'[419] For Amminadib, by interpretation, means, 'will of the Lord,' or the 'spontaneity of the Lord,' and it was Christ who became man, who offered Himself because He wanted to. The evangelical doctrine is His *quadriga*,[420] where his fame goes around the world. The four wheels of this chariot are the four Evangelists; by this chariot, the bride, that is to say, the Church, is disturbed by a salutary pain to penance. Thirdly, to designate the deliverance of the human race from the four kinds of death, that is, the four transgressions. The first transgression

---

[415] 1 Corinthians 3:6
[416] Song of Songs 4:15
[417] Luke 1:1
[418] Ezekiel 1:16
[419] Song of Songs 6:12 'chariots' translates from *quadriga*, a four horse team used in chariot racing, also the four horse team used to draw the chariot of the sun
[420] A chariot drawn by four horses abreast

was disobedience to the precept of God in paradise, the second is that of natural law, the third that of written law, the fourth that of the Gospel. In other word, the sin of frailty by impotence, the sin of simplicity by ignorance, the sin of safety by negligence, and the sin of malice out of envy. For it is through these four kinds of sins that the soul dies and is separated from God. Fourth, for the *quadriga* shape of the Ministry. For just as the square form is the strongest and firmest of all, so of all the doctrines it is the Evangelical doctrine which perseveres and lasts in the most unshakeable and stable manner, for it reigns and dominates everywhere. And this is why it is read in Revelation, 'And the city lieth foursquare.'[421] Now this evangelical doctrine, because of its stability, is called eternal, and it is this which makes man square, unshakable in morals, and which strengthens him in virtues. Moreover, the Gospels of the four Evangelists were received in preference to those of others, both because they wrote the evangelical history with greater care and clarity and also because, although their writings present variety between them, yet they are never contradictory or opposed, because they have been prefigured by the figures of the four animals, which John and Ezekiel saw in a vision.

4. Matthew has the figure of a man, because his intention and his main purpose was to describe the humanity of Christ. This is why his book begins at the human birth of Christ, and he says, 'The book of the generation of Jesus Christ.'[422] Mark is represented by a lion roaring in the desert, because he proposes above all to describe the Resurrection of Christ. This is why his Gospel, because it relates to it, is read on the day of the Resurrection. Now it is said that the lion, with a long and loud roar, raises its young on the third day, thus God the Father, by His immense power, raised His Son on the third day. Therefore Mark begins with a cry, that is, with that of John, 'The voice of one crying in the wilderness.'[423] And it should be known that Mark had a long nose, frowning brows, beautiful eyes, his head was bald, and he had a long beard which was in excellent condition and, due to middle

---

[421] Revelation 21:16
[422] Matthew 1:1
[423] Mark 3:3

age, was sprinkled with grey. Luke is represented by a bullock, because his main purpose is to describe the Passion, where Christ, both a priest and a victim, offered himself as a sacrifice to God His Father. The bullock was the sacerdotal victim and this is why St Luke begins with the priesthood, saying, 'There was in the days of Herod, the king of Judaea, a certain priest, etc.'[424] St John is represented by the eagle, because while the other Evangelists walked with the Lord, without leaving the earth so to speak, he took his flight to the heavens, to describe the divinity of Christ, saying, 'In the beginning was the Word.'[425] We have spoken of this in Book One, in the chapter *Pictures, Curtains, and Church Ornaments*. The four main intentions of the Evangelists are therefore designated by the figures of the four animals. Now each of these animals, according to the vision of Ezekiel, had four faces, that is, with his own face he had those of the three others. Because all the Evangelists, although some treat special points in their writings, they all return to a single theme, especially when all speak of Christ, to whom the four figures concur. For He was a man at birth, a bullock in dying, a lion in rising, and an eagle in ascending to heaven. In order that you may understand better, imagine an animal with a square head, and on each surface imagine a figure, namely, in the front, the figure of a man; on the right, that of a lion; on the left, that of a bullock, and that of an eagle on the back and slightly above. Now, as the figure of the eagle seemed to dominate the others because of the length of the neck, that is why it is said that it was above the others. Each of these animals had four wings, because you figure each animal, so to speak, as square. In a square there are four angles, and at each corner was a wing.

5. Now, these four Evangelists have been designated by the four abovementioned rivers. The Phishon designates John, the Gihon Mathew, the Tigris Mark, and the Euphrates Luke. This is clearly shown in a sermon by Pope Innocent III[426] on the Evangelists.

6. They are also designated by the four rings of the Ark, which were golden and round. In gold is the brightness and the

---

[424] Luke 1:5
[425] John 1:1
[426] In office from 1198-1216

roundness, which has no beginning or end, and this refers to eternity, for the Evangelists portray eternal splendour and splendid eternity. The two rings on the left indicate the two Evangelists, namely Matthew and John, who were instructed by Christ Himself. There are some, however, who designates Matthew and John by the two rings of the left, because they adhered to or believed in the Christ still passible and mortal. By the two on the right, one hears Mark and Luke, who, after the Ascension, adhered to or believed in Christ who has become impassible and immortal. For the left marks mortality, and the right immortality, according to these words, 'His left hand is under my head, and his right hand doth embrace me.'[427] Therefore, in the paintings of churches, Paul is placed on the right and Peter on the left of the Saviour. Also, on the pope's bull,'[428] Paul's head is on the right, and Peter's on the left of the Cross.

7. Now, in some churches, the antiphon to the Magnificat, in their Office, is, 'After this I looked, and, behold, a door was opened in heaven, etc.'[429] During the Hours one says the capitulum, 'And in the midst of the church she shall open his mouth, etc.,'[430] and this one, 'With the bread of life and understanding, she shall feed him, etc.,'[431] and this other, 'She shall heap upon him a treasure of joy and gladness, etc.'[432] All the responsories are from Ezekiel. Prime relates to the vision of God, namely, 'I saw men standing together, etc.'[433] At Lauds, there is talk of the ministry of their preaching, 'Moses was beloved of God, and men, etc.'[434] The Introit of the Mass is properly, 'The mouth of the righteous speaketh wisdom, etc.'[435]

8. However, John the Evangelist has his own Introit, because of the privilege of love and dignity, namely, 'And in the midst of the

---

[427] Song of Songs 2:6
[428] Or pope's seal used on a bull
[429] Revelation 4:1-2, 6, 9
[430] Ecclesiasticus 15:5
[431] Ecclesiasticus 15:3
[432] Ecclesiasticus 15:6
[433] I saw men standing together, clad in shining raiment, and the Angel of the Lord spoke unto me, saying: These men are holy, for they are the friends of God
[434] Ecclesiasticus 45:1
[435] Psalm 37:31-32

church, etc.'[436] because he was not only an Evangelist, but a prophet. This becomes evident at the beginning of the book of Revelation, where it is said, 'Blessed is he that readeth, and they that hear the words of this prophecy, etc.'[437] However, it must be noted that this Introit, because of the privilege of preaching, is also secondarily suited to the blessed Augustine, Gregory, and other doctors.

9. In some churches the Epistle refers to the figure of the four animals, 'After this I looked, and, behold, a door was opened in heaven, etc.'[438] Other churches say, 'As for the likeness of their faces, etc.'[439] The responsory is, 'Blessed is the man that feareth the Lord, etc.'[440] The verse is, 'His seed shall be mighty upon earth, etc.,' which is to be understood of the seed of the word of God, and the works of the righteous. Then follows, 'the generation of the upright shall be blessed,' because the Evangelists create children of God, who are blessed. The Alleluia in some churches is, 'The first shall say to Zion, Behold, behold them: and I will give to Jerusalem one that bringeth good tidings.'[441] In other churches, we say the Alleluia, 'Blessed is the man that feareth the Lord, etc.' The Gospel is, 'After these things the Lord appointed other seventy also, etc.'[442] These words follow, 'The harvest truly is great, but the labourers are few.' The Offertory is, 'Thou settest a crown of pure gold on his head,'[443] and the Post Communion is, 'His glory is great in thy salvation, etc.'[444]

---

[436] Ecclesiasticus 15:5
[437] Revelation 1:3
[438] Revelation 4:1-9
[439] Ezekiel 1:10-14
[440] Psalm 112:1-2
[441] Isaiah 41:27
[442] Luke 10:1-9
[443] Psalm 21:3
[444] Psalm 21:5

45 THE MARTYRS

1. The Greek word *martur* means *testis* in Latin, 'one who testifies,' or a 'witness.' For the martyrs are witnesses that Christ suffered for all, and they suffered for Him. Now, only the blessed Lawrence, among the martyrs, has a vigil and an octave, as has been said in the chapter of his feast. Indeed all the particular martyrs have common Offices, except Blessed Stephen, Lawrence, John the Baptist, and some others.

2. The Introit of the Mass is, 'For thou hast made him a little lower than the angels, etc.'[445] or, 'Let the people shew forth their wisdom, etc.,'[446] or, 'They shall judge nations, etc.,'[447] or, 'O ye priests of the Lord, bless the Lord, etc.,'[448] or, 'The righteous shall be glad in the Lord, etc.'[449] Yet these, during Easter time, have another Office, because at this time it is necessary to repeat the Alleluia, because of the joy of the Resurrection; and then the Introit is, 'Hide me from the secret counsel of the wicked, etc.'[450] And, as the crown is due to those who win, that is why frequent mention is made of their crown. Hence, 'Stephen,' is interpreted as, 'crowned.' Sometimes the Epistle for a martyr is, 'He will give his heart to resort early to the Lord, etc.'[451] sometimes this one, 'Happy is the man that findeth wisdom, etc.,'[452] sometimes, 'But

---

[445] Psalm 8:5 Psalm 148:2
[446] Ecclesiasticus 44:15, 14
[447] Wisdom 3:8
[448] Daniel 3:84, 87 (Vulgate)
[449] Psalm 64:10, 1
[450] Psalm 64:2, 1
[451] Ecclesiasticus 39:6-14 Psalm 33:1
[452] Proverbs 3:13-23

THE MARTYRS

the souls of the just are in the hand of God, etc.,'[453] sometimes this one, 'But the just man, if he be prevented with death, etc.,'[454] by the same author. Sometimes this one, 'Blessed is the man that hath not slipped by a word out of his mouth, etc.,'[455] is said and sometimes this one, 'Blessed be God, even the Father of our Lord Jesus Christ, etc.'[456] At other times, 'Remember that Jesus Christ of the seed of David was raised from the dead, etc.'[457] or this one, 'Thou therefore, my son, be strong in the grace that is in Christ Jesus, etc.,'[458] or, 'Blessed is the rich man that is found without blemish, etc.,'[459] or, 'The Lord gave him the blessing of all nations, etc.,'[460] or, 'Then shall the just stand with great constancy, etc.'[461] Sometimes the Gospel which is said is, 'Then said Jesus unto his disciples, If any man will come after me, etc.,'[462] or, 'If any man come to me, and hate not his father, etc.,'[463] sometimes, 'Verily, verily, I say unto you, Except a corn of wheat fall into the ground and die, etc.,'[464] or else, 'Think not that I am come to send peace on earth, etc.,'[465] or, "Think not that I am come to send peace on earth, etc.,'[466] or, 'If any man come to me, and hate not his father, etc.'[467]

3. Now, for several martyrs, the Epistle, 'The tongue of the wise, etc.,'[468] sometimes this one, 'Blessed be the God and Father of our Lord Jesus Christ, etc.,'[469] or else, 'But the souls of the just are in the hand of God, etc.,'[470] or, 'But call to remembrance the

---

[453] Wisdom 3:1-9
[454] Wisdom 4:7-10
[455] Ecclesiasticus 14:1-11
[456] 2 Corinthians 1:3-7
[457] 2 Timothy 2:8-10, 2 Timothy 3:10-12
[458] 2 Timothy 2:1-7
[459] Ecclesiasticus 31:8-11
[460] Ecclesiasticus 44:25-27, 2-4, 6-9
[461] Wisdom 5:1-5
[462] Matthew 16:24-27
[463] Luke 14:26-33
[464] John 12:24-26
[465] Matthew 10:34-42
[466] Matthew 10:26-32
[467] Luke 14:26-33
[468] Proverbs 15:2-7
[469] 1 Peter 1:3-7
[470] Wisdom 3:1-7

former days, etc.'[471] At other times, 'Who through faith subdued kingdoms, etc.,'[472] at other times, 'The hope of the righteous shall be gladness, etc.,'[473] sometimes, 'These were men of mercy, etc.,'[474] at other times, 'And I saw a new heaven and a new earth, etc.,'[475] and at other times, 'And she rendered to the just a reward of their labours, etc.,'[476] or else, 'But the just shall live for evermore, etc.,'[477] or 'Who shall separate us from the love of Christ? etc.,'[478] The Alleluia is, 'These are the two olive trees, etc.'[479] The Gospel is sometimes, 'But when ye shall hear of wars and commotions, etc.,'[480] or, 'And he came down with them, and stood in the plain, etc.,'[481] or, 'And seeing the multitudes, he went up into a mountain, etc.,'[482] sometimes, 'And as he went out of the temple, one of his disciples saith unto him, etc.,'[483] or, 'In the mean time, when there were gathered together an innumerable multitude of people, etc.,'[484] or this one, 'And as he sat upon the mount of Olives, etc.,'[485] sometimes, 'Woe unto you! for ye build the sepulchres of the prophets, etc.'[486] or else, 'He that heareth

---

[471] Hebrews 10:32-38
[472] Hebrews 11:33-39
[473] Proverbs 10:28-32
[474] First part from, Ecclesiasticus 44:10 'These were men of mercy whose godly deeds have not been forgotten, O Lord, and of them with the good things continue as they were; to obtain the glory of eternal life, and in their time, each illustrious in his day'
[475] Revelation 21:2-5
[476] Wisdom 10:17 The alternative translation often used is, 'God pays back the wages of their labours, He will guide them in a wonderful way.' In a number if texts, 'the Lord.' Is substituted when Wisdom is referred to the Bible. This indicates the profound Wisdom of God
[477] Wisdom 5:16-20
[478] Romans 8:35-39
[479] See Revelation 11:4 The antiphon is, 'These are two olive trees and two candlesticks, giving light in the presence of the Lord these have power to shut heaven with clouds, and have power again to open the gates thereof, for their tongues are become keys of heaven
[480] Luke 21:9-19
[481] Luke 6:17-23
[482] Matthew 5:1-12
[483] Mark 13:1-13
[484] Luke 12:1-8
[485] Matthew 24:3-13
[486] Luke 11:47-51

THE MARTYRS

you heareth me, etc.,'[487] or else, 'I thank thee, O Father, Lord of heaven and earth, etc.'[488] The Post Communion said is, 'For verily I say unto you, Till heaven and earth pass, etc.,'[489] sometimes, 'And though in the sight of men they suffered torments, etc.,'[490] or again, 'For whosoever shall do the will of my Father, etc.,'[491] or else, 'Verily I say unto you, It shall be more tolerable, etc.,'[492] or, 'And these signs shall follow them that believe, etc.'[493] and again, 'And the whole multitude sought to touch him, etc.'[494]

4. In the Night Office the first responsory is, 'This saint fought, even unto death, for the law of his God, etc.'[495] And it is of the fifth tone, because in them was repressed and sacrificed the petulance of the five senses. In paschal time, the first responsory is, 'Blessed is the man that feareth the Lord, etc.,'[496] and it is of the eighth tone, because of the octave, which designates the glory of the Resurrection. Now, as the holy martyrs have shown an invincible constancy in suffering torments, and constancy comes from God alone, that is why we sing in their honour this responsory, 'O revered martyrs' of glorious struggles, etc.,'[497] and it is of the fifth tone, because the martyrs have sacrificed to God their five senses. In honour of the martyrs, one also sings the responsory, 'The just shall shine, and shall run to and fro like sparks among the reeds. They shall judge nations, and rule over people, and their Lord shall reign for ever.'[498] Here is the meaning.

5. The righteous will shine in the future age and will enjoy various beatitudes but before that they will run their race in this age, that

---

[487] Luke 10:15-20
[488] Matthew 11:25-30
[489] Matthew 5:18
[490] Wisdom 3:4-6
[491] Matthew 12:50
[492] Matthew 10:15
[493] Mark 16:17
[494] Luke 6:19
[495] This Saint fought, even unto death, for the law of his God, and feared not the words of the wicked; for he was set upon a firm rock
[496] Psalm 112:1
[497] O revered martyrs' of glorious struggles who, for Christ, bore enormous pain and suffering in their bodies, therefore deserve the crown of eternal glory
[498] Wisdom 3:7-8

is to say, travelling here and there to the different parts of the world, they will announce to others the divine word. They act in the manner of the sparks that roam here and there in a place where reeds grow. For just as sparks or embers reduce to ashes and destroy the fragile matter of reeds, so the saints, by their burning preaching, that is to say, burned by the divine fire, will destroy vices, which are fragile in relation to the strength of virtues. They will judge, that is to say, they will rule the nations, that is, those who have persisted in their sins, and they will reign eternally, that is, in eternity, with God; they will receive immortality, impassibility and other virtues.

6. These words also express the dress of the flesh which the saints will receive, and this dress consists of four qualities, namely, clarity, discernment, agility and impassibility. For they will shine gloriously, and as light sparks in a place strewn with reeds, they will fly and move with agility from one place to another. Their Lord will reign forever, and they themselves will be impassible with God; for God will wipe away every tear from the eyes of the saints.[499] Moreover, they will rejoice in glory, and they will leap with joy in the place of their rest. As for the dress of the spirit, it is said that the saints will receive it also.

7. And note that a reed bed is a place planted with many reeds and canes, as are marshes, and when the south wind comes to blow these reeds are inflamed by a continual friction, the sparks flutter on all sides, and the reed bed is engulfed. This happens in an allegorical way in the saints.

8. We also sing for the martyrs, 'they wandered about in sheepskins and goatskins; being destitute, afflicted, tormented.'[500] The sheepskin is a garment made of the hair or skin of some animal and is a necessary garment for work.

9. During the Hours, we say the capitula, 'Blessed is the man that endureth temptation, etc.,'[501] and this one, 'Blessed is the rich man that is found without blemish, etc.,'[502] and this one, 'Blessed is the man that shall continue in wisdom, etc.,'[503] and that one, 'But the

---

[499] See Isaiah 25:8 Revelation 7:17 Revelation 21:4
[500] Hebrews 11:37
[501] James 1:12
[502] Ecclesiasticus 31:8-9
[503] Ecclesiasticus 14:22

souls of the just are in the hand of God, etc.,'[504] and this other, 'But the just shall live for evermore, etc.,'[505] and this other again, 'Who through faith subdued kingdoms, etc.,'[506] and this one, 'He that could have transgressed, and hath not transgressed, etc.,'[507] and this one, 'A gold crown on his head, a symbol of holiness, glory and honour.'[508] Or, they, 'clothed him with a robe of glory, and crowned him with majestic attire.'[509] Or again, 'They were stoned, they were sawn asunder, etc.,'[510] or again, 'As gold in the furnace, he hath proved them, etc.,'[511] or this, 'These are they who are come out of great tribulation, etc.,'[512] and that one, 'They shall no more hunger nor thirst, etc.,'[513] and this other, 'Therefore the just took the spoils of the wicked, etc.,'[514] or, 'When it goeth well with the righteous, etc.'[515] It must be known that the Church celebrates the feast of some Old Testament martyrs, as was stated in the chapter of the Maccabees.

---

[504] Wisdom 3:1-22
[505] Wisdom 5:16-17
[506] Hebrews 11:33-34
[507] Ecclesiasticus 31:10
[508] Derived from Matthew 27:37 and John 19:19 and is similar to Ecclesiasticus 45:9
[509] Ecclesiasticus 45:9
[510] Hebrews 11:33
[511] Wisdom 3:6
[512] Revelation 7:14
[513] Revelation 7:16
[514] Wisdom 10:19-20
[515] Proverbs 11:10

46 THE CONFESSORS

1. Those who praise the Lord and celebrate His glory are called confessors, because both the martyrs and the virgins, like all the saints, are the true confessors of Christ. However, the martyrs, who win the victory against the irascible, have a transcendent rank, surpassing that of confessors to acquire that special name of martyrs. They surpass the virgins, because they gain a triumph over the lustful desires and they acquire, in addition, the name of virgins. They surpass the doctors, because they prevail over others by reasoning and also acquire the name of doctors. Hence the martyrs, virgins, and doctors will be adorned with the halo.

2. It is certain that the confessors are distinguished by having been bishops or priests. For the bishops they say the Introit, 'He made an everlasting covenant with him, etc.,'[516] and the Epistle is, 'Behold a high priest, who in his days pleased God.'[517] For they themselves are high priests, and it is said of the bishops, 'I have found David my servant; with my holy oil have I anointed him, etc.'[518] For not only were they anointed in baptism and confirmation, but also in their priestly ordination and, moreover, in episcopal consecration, to have an overabundant mercy. These Offices, which priests begin, are properly suited to the bishops, the rest is common and there are several responsories of the eighth tone, (because they macerated and crucified their flesh from vices and lustful desires), for the octave of the resurrection.

---

[516] Ecclesiasticus 45:8 Psalm 132:1
[517] See Ecclesiasticus 44:16
[518] Psalm 89:20-21

THE CONFESSORS

3. Sometimes, for the confessors, the Epistle, 'Moses was beloved of God, and men, etc.,'[519] is said, sometimes, 'I charge thee therefore before God, etc.,'[520] sometimes, 'And they truly were many priests, etc.,'[521] at other times, 'In all his works he gave thanks to the holy one, etc.'[522] Or else, 'He will give his heart to resort early to the Lord, etc.,'[523] or 'Wisdom shall praise her own self, and shall be honoured in God, etc.,'[524] or, 'She conducted the just, etc.,'[525] or again, 'Be not carried about with divers and strange doctrines, etc.,'[526] and sometimes, 'For I am now ready to be offered, etc.'[527] The Alleluia is, 'The just will spring forth, etc.'[528] Now, the Gospel, 'Let your loins be girded about, etc.,'[529] is sometimes said, sometimes, 'Watch therefore, etc.,'[530] sometimes again, 'For the kingdom of heaven is as a man travelling into a far country, etc.,'[531] at other times, 'Take ye heed, watch and pray, etc.,'[532] at other times, 'He said therefore, A certain nobleman went into a far country, etc.,'[533] at other times, 'No man, when he hath lighted a candle, etc.,'[534] or else, 'Ye are the salt of the earth, etc.,'[535] or, 'Fear not, little flock, etc.'[536] The Post Communion is, 'Lord, thou deliveredst unto me five talents, etc.,'[537] and sometimes, 'Who then is a faithful and wise servant, etc.'[538]

---

[519] Ecclesiasticus 45:1-6 The word, 'Moses,' is usually omitted
[520] 2 Timothy 4:1-8
[521] Hebrews 7:23-27
[522] Ecclesiasticus 47:9-13
[523] Ecclesiasticus 39:6-14
[524] Ecclesiasticus 24:1-4; 12-16
[525] Wisdom 10:10-14
[526] Hebrews 13:9-17
[527] 2 Timothy 4:4-8
[528] See Isaiah 35:2
[529] Luke 12:35-40
[530] Matthew 24:42-47
[531] Matthew 25:14-30
[532] Mark 13:33-37
[533] Luke 19:12-26
[534] Luke 11:33-36
[535] Matthew 5:13-19
[536] Luke 12:32-34
[537] Matthew 25:20
[538] Matthew 24:45

4. During the Hours, one says the capitula, 'Behold a high priest, who in his days pleased God, etc.,'[539] and this one, 'The Lord gave him the blessing of all nations, etc.,'[540] and this one, 'He acknowledged him in his blessings, etc.,'[541] and this one, 'She conducted the just, etc.,'[542] and this one, "He will give his heart to resort early to the Lord, etc.,'[543] and this other, 'He glorified him in the sight of kings, etc.'[544] However here we say, 'glorify,' and elsewhere, 'magnify.' Also this one, 'For the priest's lips should keep knowledge, etc.,'[545] and that one, 'There was not found the like to him, etc.,'[546] and, 'To execute the office of the priesthood, etc.,'[547] and this other, 'For it was fitting that we should have such a high priest, etc.,'[548] and this other one, 'Many shall praise his wisdom, and it shall never be forgotten.'[549] Also this, she, 'made him honourable in his labours, and accomplished his labours,'[550] and this one, 'She kept him safe from his enemies, etc.'[551]

5. It must be remarked that if several feasts fall on the same day, the Office of the one of greatest eminence is celebrated. We have spoken of this in the *Preface* of this book.

---

[539] See Ecclesiasticus 44:16
[540] Ecclesiasticus 44:25
[541] Ecclesiasticus 44:26
[542] Wisdom 10:10
[543] Ecclesiasticus 39:6
[544] Ecclesiasticus 45:3
[545] Malachi 2:7
[546] Ecclesiasticus 44:20
[547] Ecclesiasticus 45:19
[548] Hebrews 7:26
[549] Ecclesiasticus 39:12
[550] Wisdom 10:10
[551] Wisdom 10:12

47 THE VIRGINS

1. The Office of Matins, for the virgins, is drawn largely from the epithalamic[552] psalm, 'My heart is inditing a good matter, etc.,'[553] where the praises of the bridegroom and bride are treated. For virgins are the wives of Christ; 'These are they which follow the Lamb whithersoever he goeth,'[554] in body and soul, because of the integrity of their bodies and their souls. It must be remarked that this responsory, which relates to the bridegroom, is, 'And I heard a loud voice saying in heaven, etc.,'[555] is said in some churches. It is of the first tone, because Christ is the only bridegroom of souls. This other, which relates to contempt for the world, namely, 'I despised the kingdom of the world, etc.,'[556] is of the fifth tone, because it shows the mortification of the five senses trampled underfoot.

2. Now, for the virgins we sing, 'Stay me up with flowers,'[557] which was explained in Book Five, in the chapter *Sext*. In some churches they say this verset for the virgins, 'God chose her and set her apart, etc.'[558] But others, considering, with more reason,

---

[552] Of a song or poem celebrating a marriage
[553] Psalm 45
[554] Revelation 14:4
[555] Revelation 12:19, Revelation 14:6
[556] I despised the kingdom of the world, and all the beauty of the world, for love of the Lord Jesus Christ: whom I saw, whom I loved, in whom I have believed, in whom I have delighted
[557] Song of Songs 1-5, 12, 15 Known as, *Fulcite me floribus*, 'Stay me up with flowers.' which is taken from verse 5
[558] V. God chose her and set her apart. R. He made her dwell in His tabernacle

that the blessed Virgin Mary alone has been pre-elected, say this verse only in her honour. For other virgins they recite, 'God chose her and enriches her. At times, we say the capitula, 'He that glorieth, etc.,'[559] and this one, 'For I am jealous over you with godly jealousy, etc.,'[560] and this one, 'For after this cometh night, etc.,'[561] and this one, 'I remembered thy mercy, O Lord, etc.,'[562] and this other, 'And hast preserved my body from destruction, etc.,'[563] and this other one, 'She girdeth her loins with strength, etc.'[564]

3. In the Office of the Mass, if it is a virgin and martyr, the Office proper is, 'I will speak of thy testimonies also before kings, etc.'[565]

4. The rest is common, except for the Introit, which is said for Blessed Agatha, 'Let us all rejoice in the Lord, etc.,'[566] for she, filled with joy, suffered in an excellent way, as it was said of her, 'Agatha went to the prison with the greatest joy, and as in triumph.' Therefore let us mingle our joy with his joy, and rejoice with her in the Lord. For Blessed Agnes, the service of the Mass is, 'The wicked have waited for me to destroy me, etc.,'[567] and we can see the reason in her legend.

5. Note that for the virgins they sometimes say the Epistle, 'I will give glory to thee, O Lord, O King, etc.,'[568] sometimes also, 'But he that glorieth, let him glory in the Lord, etc.,'[569] other times, 'Thou hast exalted my dwelling place, etc.,'[570] sometimes, 'Wisdom shall praise her own self, etc.,'[571] else, 'For after this

---

[559] 1 Corinthians 1:31
[560] 2 Corinthians 11:2
[561] Wisdom 7:30
[562] Ecclesiasticus 51:11
[563] Ecclesiasticus 51:3
[564] Proverbs 31:17 To which is added, 'and therefore the strength of the lamp shall not be put out for ever'
[565] Psalm 110:46-47 Psalm 92:1
[566] Let us all rejoice in the Lord, celebrating a festival in honour of blessed Agatha, virgin and martyr; at whose passion the Angels rejoice, and give praise to the Son of God. Psalm 45:1
[567] Psalm 119: 95, 1 A Mass often takes its name from the first words of the Introit
[568] Ecclesiasticus 51:1-12
[569] 2 Corinthians 10:17-19, 2 Corinthians 11:1-2
[570] Ecclesiasticus 51:13-17
[571] Ecclesiasticus 24:1-6

cometh night, but no evil can overcome wisdom, etc.,'[572] or else, 'Now concerning virgins, etc.,' [573] sometimes, 'The Lord possessed me in the beginning of his way, etc.'[574] The Alleluia and the Post Communion are, 'But the wise took oil in their vessels, etc.'[575] Sometimes one reads the Gospel, 'Again, the kingdom of heaven is like unto treasure hid in a field, etc.,'[576] and at other times, 'Then shall the kingdom of heaven be likened unto ten virgins, etc.'[577]

---

[572] Wisdom 7:30, Wisdom 8:1-2
[573] 1 Corinthians 7:25-28
[574] Proverbs 8:22-24, 32-35
[575] Matthew 25:4-6
[576] Matthew 13:44-52
[577] Matthew 25:1-13

48 THE FESTIVAL AND OFFICE OF THE DEDICATION OF A CHURCH

1. Since we said, in the first book, how to consecrate a church, we have to add here something about the Office that is said at the Dedication of the Churches. This feast, therefore, is solemnly celebrated by the Church. On this subject it is said in St John, 'And it was at Jerusalem the feast of the dedication,' that is to say, the feast of the Dedication was celebrated in Jerusalem, 'And Jesus walked in the temple in Solomon's porch'[578] in confirmation of that festival. This is called Solomon's porch, because Solomon used to pray there, and prayed on the day of the dedication of the temple.

2. This feast was also celebrated in the Old Testament, regarding which it is read in the first book of the Maccabees, 'And he[579] chose priests without blemish,' and, 'they cleansed the holy places.'[580] For the Church Militant can be purified but not the Church Triumphant, as St Augustine says in a homily on the above-mentioned words, 'the feast of the dedication.' The Jews solemnly celebrated this day when the temple was consecrated.

3. Now the Jews celebrated the dedication for eight days, from which it appears that we must also solemnize the Feast of Dedication for eight days, as we have seen in the earlier chapter *The Maccabees*. Yet it is surprising that the Jews celebrated with incense for eight days, since they solemnized Passover and the Feast of the Tabernacles for only seven days. To this we answer

---

[578] John 10:22-23
[579] Judah Maccabee
[580] 1 Maccabees 4:42-43

THE FESTIVAL AND OFFICE OF THE DEDICATION OF A CHURCH

that this festival particularly designates the eternal dedication, in which the Church, namely the holy soul, will be so dedicated, that is to say united to God, that is, bound more tightly to, so as not to be able to be transferred for other purposes, which will happen in the octave of the resurrection. That is why in the New Testament this festival has an octave. This church is built by baptism, doctrine and penance. It is here that one hears the axe and every kind of tool of iron, that is to say, all kinds of scrouges and all the disciplines, namely, in the Church Militant, which is represented by the tent of Moses, because the tents are for the soldiers. Now, this temple of Solomon designates the Church Triumphant, in which we do not hear these noises.

4. In the Office of Matins they say the psalms where gates are mentioned, which pertain especially to fear and love, as we see in the Psalm, 'The earth is the Lord's,'[581] at these words, 'Lift up your heads, O ye gate, etc.'[582] Also those in which the altar is mentioned, as in this psalm, 'Judge me, O God, and plead my cause, etc.,'[583] likewise those in which a city is mentioned, such as these, 'God is our refuge and strength, etc.,'[584] and, 'Great is the Lord, etc.'[585] Likewise those in which vestibules and doors are mentioned, such as these, 'How amiable are thy tabernacles, etc.,'[586] and, 'His foundation is in the holy mountains, etc.'[587] But we ask why then we say the psalm, 'O Lord God of my salvation, etc.'[588] To this, some reply that it is because there is mention of sepulchres but this reason is not valid, because there is no mention of the sepulchres in which the bodies of the faithful, who once lived and are now buried near the church. Rather reference is made to the sepulchres of the wicked, which is what we claim this psalm speaks of because it is a penitential psalm, and it is especially a question here of the prayer to be made in the Church,

---

[581] Psalm 24
[582] The Vulgate has, 'Lift up your gates, O ye princes, etc.' (v. 7)
[583] Psalm 43
[584] Psalm 46
[585] Psalm 48
[586] Psalm 84
[587] Psalm 87
[588] Psalm 88

for it says here, 'Let my prayer come before thee.' Now the Lord says, regarding the Church, 'My house shall be called the house of prayer.'[589] The eighth psalm is, 'He that dwelleth in the secret place of the most High, etc.,'[590] that is, in the Church, because it says, 'which is my refuge, even the most High, thy habitation,' since the church is founded on the highest mountain.

5. Now, the last antiphon at Vespers, that is to say, that of the Magnificat, is, 'Peace eternal from the Eternal, etc.,'[591] because we celebrate the Dedication so that we are dedicated or consecrated and we have this eternal peace. Now, during the Hours one says the capitula, 'And I John saw the holy city, New Jerusalem, etc.,'[592] and this one, 'Behold, the tabernacle of God is with men, etc.,'[593] and this one, 'Every man shall receive his own reward, etc.,'[594] and this one, 'I have laid the foundation, and another buildeth thereon, etc.'[595] Certainly, it is right to compare this festival to what Jacob saw, namely, 'a ladder set up on the earth, and the top of it reached to heaven: and behold the angels of God ascending and descending on it.'[596] That is to say, he saw the whole Church in a vision, and erected a stone, that is to say, Christ, who is the stone placed at the foundations, and He is the cornerstone and the foundation that supports the whole building. He raised it, I say, as a pillar, as a triumphal memorial, spreading oil on it. Indeed, Jacob, that is to say, the prelate, poured oil on the stone, which is Christ, to show his chrism or his anointing. Jacob prophesied the same thing, saying, 'How dreadful *is* this place! this *is* none other but the house of God, and this *is* the gate of heaven.'[597]

6. For the Church is terrible to demons, because of the resemblance she has with God, whom she possesses. That is why,

---

[589] Matthew 21:13

[590] Psalm 91

[591] Peace eternal from the Eternal be to this house! May the unending Peace, the Word of the Father, be peace to this house! Peace may the loving Consoler grant unto this house!

[592] Revelation 21:2

[593] Revelation 21:3

[594] 1 Corinthians 3:8

[595] 1 Corinthians 3:10

[596] Genesis 28:12

[597] Genesis 28:17

THE FESTIVAL AND OFFICE OF THE DEDICATION OF A CHURCH

at Mass, the Introit is, 'How dreadful is this place, etc.,'[598] then follow these words, 'it shall be called the Court of God.' It was blessed Gregory who added this, because here God is ready to answer, as the Lord said to Solomon, 'I have heard thy prayer, etc.'[599] Now, why is it terrible? It is shown in the little verse, 'The Lord reigneth, he is clothed with majesty,'[600] that is, with His members, and that is why the Church is terrible to demons. Now, in the consecration of the altar the Introit is, 'My words which I have put in thy mouth, shall not depart out of thy mouth, etc.'[601] The Epistle is, 'And I John saw the holy city, new Jerusalem, etc.'[602] The responsory is, 'This place was made by God, etc.'[603] 'This place,' that is, the material church, 'is holy,' because it has been sanctified, that the Lord may hear the prayers, and that is why he recommends holiness to those who pray. For Solomon prayed that the Lord might hear those who prayed to him, and the Lord said to him, 'Your prayer has been answered.' Now this was expressed when Solomon, after consecrating the temple, says, 'Hearken therefore unto the supplications of thy servant, and of thy people Israel, which they shall make toward this place: hear thou from thy dwelling place, even from heaven; and when thou hearest, forgive.'[604] The Alleluia in some churches is, 'How dreadful is this place, etc.,'[605] and the Gospel is, 'And Jesus entered and passed through Jericho, etc.,'[606] because it says, 'This day is salvation come to this house.' In some churches, however, we read the Gospel of St Matthew, where it says that they could not overthrow this house, 'for it was founded upon a rock.'[607] Then follows the Offertory, taken from David's words, or, according to others, from Solomon's words, 'As for me, in the

---

[598] Genesis 28:17, Psalm 84:1-2
[599] 1 Kings 9:3
[600] Psalm 93:1
[601] Isaiah 59:21, Isaiah 56:7, Psalm 112:1
[602] Revelation 21:2-5
[603] This place was made by God, a priceless mystery; it is without reproach
[604] 2 Chronicles 6:21
[605] Genesis 28:17
[606] Luke 19:1-10
[607] Matthew 7:25

uprightness of mine heart I have willingly offered all these things, etc.'[608] For he had offered inestimable sacrifices, which designate good works or good desires, which are priceless both in number and in price. Then follows the Post Communion, 'My house shall be called the house of prayer.'

7. Note that if the feast of the Church's dedication arrives in the Lord's Passion, it is celebrated during the following week. If it is at Ascension, this is the Office used, and that of the Dedication is deferred; for Solomon dedicated the temple on the twelfth day of the month, and the Feast of the Tabernacles was on the tenth day of the month. He celebrated the dedication of the temple for seven days; he extended the Fast of the Tabernacles until after the dedication.

END OF BOOK SEVEN

---

[608] 1 Chronicles 29:17-18

BOOK EIGHT

1 COMPUTATION, THE CALENDAR, AND WHAT RELATES TO THEM

1. Priests, as the Blessed Augustine says, are obliged to know the compute, otherwise they would hardly deserve the name of priests. Under this word 'compute' we understand the knowledge of the course of time, the moon and the calendar.
2. Now the compute is a science whose object is to make time known according to the course and the march of the sun and the moon. That is why, in this eighth and last book we shall say, in a clear and concise abstract, a few words of the compute, as we know it is in use in the Church, for the instruction of those priests who are ignorant.
3. The word, 'compute,' comes from 'computations', 'calculating', 'counting', not that in the compute we learn the art of calculating and counting, but because in the compute we proceed by calculating, by the knowledge of arithmetic, which is then both useful and necessary. There are two kinds of computes, namely, the astronomical or philosophical compute, and the vulgar or ecclesiastical compute, but nothing is said now of the astronomical compute. The vulgar compute is the knowledge whose object is to distinguish, or to divide time in a fixed or certain way, or the knowledge which divides time according to the use of the Church.
4. Time here is taken, according to Cicero, for a certain portion or quantity of the year, the month, the day, or some other period. Or again, it is the time or interval that variable things take to execute their movement and to provide their course. Time is divided into ten parts, which are the year, the month, the week,

the day, the quarter, the hour, the point, the moment, the ounce, and the atom. The year contains twelve months, fifty-two weeks and one day, or three hundred and sixty-five days and six hours. The month consists of four weeks or a little more. The week is a seven day period. The day has four periods of six hours or quarters. An hour is a sixth part of a quarter. The point is a quarter of an hour. The moment is the tenth part of a point, and has twelve ounces. An ounce consists of forty-seven atoms. Finally there is the atom which is indivisible, because the Greek word *atomos* means *indivisio*; what cannot be divided, hence *atomos* in Greek is *indivisio* in Latin or 'indivision'. So the month is about the twelfth part of the solar year; the week is about a quarter of the month; the natural day is the seventh part of the week; the quarter, the fourth part of the natural day; the hour, the sixth of the quarter; the point, quarter of an hour; the moment, the tenth of the point; the ounce, the twelfth of the moment; the atom, the forty-seventh of an ounce. There are even further divisions of time, that is, eternity, where the period of time is indeterminate and more considerable than the century; the age, the century, then lustre, the Olympiad and the indiction. We will discuss these various divisions below.

5. There are three times of years or three kinds of years, namely, the solar year, the lunar year, and the great year, which we intend to treat in this eighth book, which contains two main parts. In the first part, we deal with the solar year and the great year and, in the second, of the lunar year.

2 PART ONE, THE SOLAR YEAR

1. The first part of this work deals with the solar year. This part is subdivided into four sections. In the first section we examine what the solar year is. It deals with the beginning of the year, the various kinds of years, the twelve signs of the zodiac, the leap year, the four times of the year, the fasts of the four times,[609] the solstices, the equinoxes, the great year, the era, the Olympiad, the lustre, the age, the century, and the indefinite age or eternity.

2. In the second part we deal with the month, the calends, the nones, the ides; where they come from, and what is the denomination of days; the Egyptian days and the dog days.

3. In the third we deal with the week. We explain what the letter of the calends is of each month, on what day of the week each month begins; we treat of Sunday letters, regular or invariable solar numbers, competing numbers and the indiction.

4. In the fourth we deal with the day, the moment and the hour. When discussing the hour, we will speak of the quantity of daylight hours and of the night.

---

[609] The ember days

3 WHAT THE SOLAR YEAR IS

1. The year is the course or circuit of the sun, which, at the end of three hundred and sixty-five days, returns to the same place in the sky from which it had departed. We say year, because, the months turning on themselves, the year turns, *volvitur*, around a circle, (*volvitur*, from *am*, which is synonymous with, *circum*, 'around', and *eo is*, 'returning circularly'). The year rolls from one point of the circuit, does like a turn, and returns to the point from which it left, in a somewhat circular way. Which is why we also say 'year', as one would say a 'ring', a 'circle', because it returns to itself, like a circle. That is why Virgil said:

> *And the year comes rolling back on itself, following the road through which it passed previously.*

This is why, before the invention of letters, the Egyptians marked or designated the year as follows. They represented it with a dragon biting its tail, because the year is bent and returns to itself and that is how some still represent it. Others derive the word, *annum*, 'year', from, *innovation*, 'renewal', because the year is constantly renewed.

2. The year, according to various people, has various beginnings. For the Arabs and the Egyptians it begins after the summer solstice, that is to say, from September, because one reads that at the beginning of the world the trees bore fruit, and the trees carry fruit in September. They think that the world was created at that time, so that is when they start the year. However, Numa

WHAT THE SOLAR YEAR IS

Pompilius[610] and the Romans began the year in January, because then, or a little earlier, the sun began to come closer to us. The Jews began it in March, because the world was created in this month, and that is why it is said that its eighteenth day is the first day of the century. Those who deal with the compute, the calculators, imitate all these peoples in a few points. For they begin the regular lunar numbers, the embolisms, the epacts and all the lunar years from the month of September. Starting in January, they begin with the Golden Number and some Sunday letters and then from March, the regular solar numbers, competing numbers and some Sunday letters, as will be seen in the second part. It is certain that some moderns, out of respect for the Saviour, begin the year from His Nativity, others from His Incarnation, that is to say from the Conception of Blessed Mary, when she says to the Angel, 'Behold the handmaid of the Lord, etc.,'[611] for immediately Christ was man and full of the Holy Spirit.

3. There are different years, namely, the natural year, the usual year, the legitimate year, the emerging year, the solar year, the great year, the year of the Olympiad, the lustral year, the year of indiction, the jubilee year, the year of goodness, and the year of eternity and glory. The natural year is when the moon is in place in front of the sun, so that the sun is eclipsed. The usual or temporal year is that which begins with the use of men, for example from January to the following January. The legitimate or ceremonial year is that which is calculated according to lunations, from April to April, because April is the first month among the Hebrews. The emergent year is when some great event happened to the Jews or other peoples. In memory of this event, they start counting the year from this fact, or from any day.

4. The solar year is the period in which the sun makes its circuit around the twelve signs of the zodiac. It makes this circuit in the space of three hundred and sixty-five days and almost six hours, as has already been said. I said, 'almost', because of certain moments that are added, as will be said below. Now these six hours, four in four years, form a natural leap day. This year is common to all nations and it begins on some day, and ends on a

---

[610] The legendary second king of Rome, succeeding Romulus
[611] Luke 1:38

certain day, when the aforesaid days are accomplished; this day can also be called natural.

5. The above signs are, Aries, Taurus, Gemini, Cancer, Leo, Virgo, Libra, Scorpio, Sagittarius, Capricorn, Aquarius and Pisces; hence these verses:

> *Here are the celestial signs that are always the road that the sun travels:*
> *Aries, Taurus, Gemini, Cancer, Leo, Virgo,*
> *Libra, Scorpio, Chiron,*[612] *Capricorn, Urn (Aquarius), Pisces.*

Note that the heavenly habitation or the vault of heaven is separated or divided into zones or belts of circles. There are five zones, which are called zones or circles, because they are in the circumference of the sphere. The zodiac is a circle that consists of five line angles and one line. The Greek word, *zodiacos* means 'animal', because of the image of animals or signs of the zodiac. Or, in Latin, *zodiacos*, is called, *signum*, 'sign', from which zodiac is called a 'living creature', or a circle that bears signs, because in the middle of the firmament there are twelve signs placed across or flank, which are also cut off or separated by the circle, and which are designated by the figure and the name of animals. For the sun, entering into these signs, enjoys in some way the properties of these animals, or else because the stars are arranged in these signs in the shape of animals. A sign is the twelfth part of the zodiac. The sun enters into one of these signs every month, on the fifteen before the calends, according to the Church. Thus, in March the sun enters Aries on the fifteenth before the calends of April, then in April it enters Taurus, on the fifteenth before the calends of May, and so on in the order of months and signs.

6. The first sign is Aries, in which it is said that the sun was created. The sun enters this sign towards the beginning of spring. This sign is so called because the ram is weak in its posterior part and has some force in its anterior part. Likewise, at this time, the posterior part of the sun has a feeble heat, and the cold weakens the force of its rays; but the anterior part, which looks at the summer, or which is turned towards the summer, has some force,

---

[612] An old, wise centaur who served as Achilles' mentor and teacher

that is, some heat. Or else, just as the ram, in winter, lies on the left side and begins in the spring to lie down on the right side, so the sun, before that time, remains on the left side of the firmament, that is, to the south, but then it enters the right side, that is towards the aquilon[613] or the north. The ancients called this sign Jupiter, because of his loves, and those who make statue images of this god represent it with ram's horns on the head.

7. The second sign is Taurus and is called this because, just as the bull is stronger than the ram, so at this time the sun has more ardour in its anterior than posterior part and in this is like the bull. Or perhaps the sun is more ardent when it ascends into the sky than when it descends. The ancients placed the bull among the stars, to honour Jupiter, because the fable has imagined that this god changed into a bull when he took Europe. 8. Gemini is the third sign, which is so named because at this time the heat of the sun is doubled because it actually begins to be hot and to dry up the earth. Or else because it is then is the mating season when everything is reproduced or multiplied in nature, because birds and animals make their young. Or because of the double degree or the two degrees of elevation of the earth, which the sun has more under this sign than under the preceding one. The ancients called this sign Gemini, because of Castor and Pollux, which they placed, after their death, among the most famous stars.

9. The fourth sign is Cancer or the crayfish, so called because the crayfish walks backwards, and the sun also retrogrades and moves away from us after having first approached us.

10. The fifth is Leo, the lion, so called because the lion is a cruel animal and always has fever and, in the same way, this time is unhealthy and causes fevers. Moreover, because Hercules, in Greece, put the strongest lion to death, that is why the Greeks, because of its courage, placed it among the twelve signs of the zodiac.

11. The sixth is Virgo, the virgin, who produces nothing. In the same way, this time is sterile and produces nothing; but it matures what has been produced before, because it is the time of the heat of days.

---

[613] North wind

12. The seventh sign is Libra. It is so called from the equality of this month, because then the sun balances the days and the nights, because it is the autumnal equinox.

13. The eighth is Scorpio and, just as the scorpion is venomous and pique, so is this time morbid because of the irregularity of the temperature; for in the morning it is cold, and at noon a devouring heat.

14. The ninth is Sagittarius, because it is almost always then that the archers engage in the practice of hunting. Or because of the lightning which often falls then, and which the Italians call *sagittas*, 'arrows,' or 'bolts.'

15. The tenth is Capricorn.[614] For just as the capricorn grazes on the steep mountains and the high banks of the precipices, so the sun is at its highest degree towards the south. Or, just as the capricorn is accustomed to climb the mountains, so the sun begins to rise in relation to us. Moreover, the ancients placed the figure of Capricorn among the signs of the zodiac, because of the feeding goat of Jupiter, and they represented the posterior part of the capricorn in the form of a fish, to designate the rains, that almost always the same month usually brings to an end.

16. The eleventh is Aquarius. This sign is so designated, because this weather is very rainy, and windy.

17. Pisces are the twelfth sign. For, just as the fish is an aquatic animal, so is the time of abundant with water, because of the great quantity of rain. Or because then, when the waters are cleared of ice, comes the time of fishing. But although, as it is evident from the above-mentioned things, the signs are equal according to astronomers, the Church, however, does not consider them, nor does it see them as equals. For sometimes one sign contains more days than another, since there are months which contain more days than others, which is why there are some signs which contain more degrees than others. The degree is the space in which the sun, through its movement, passes into the zodiac on the natural day. From what we have already said, one can know in what degree of any sign the sun is on a given day.

18. Now, the bissextile or leap day, of which it has been spoken, is called, 'leap,' by philosophers, as if it were said that it is the

---

[614] *Capricornus*, from *capra*, 'goat', and *cornu*, 'horn'

product of the meeting of two-thirds of moments, which may well be understand. For the sun remains in each sign for thirty days, and the third of thirty hours, which is two-thirds of thirty moments.[615] Now, the third is the third part of a whole, which is composed of three parts; two-thirds are two parts of this whole; but, multiplying thirty days by twelve, we have three hundred and sixty days. The third of thirty hours is ten hours, which, multiplied by twelve, make five days. Two-thirds of thirty moments are twenty moments (here we must suppose that thirty has been divided by twenty-four) and consequently two points (since the point consists of ten moments). But multiplying two points by twelve, we have six hours, of the meeting of two-thirds of the moments, which of four in four years constitute a day which is called a leap.[616]

19. Moreover, according to St Isidore, every year the quarter value increases and in the fourth year it disappears because it has taken one leap, and therefore is one over the four years, and a leap day is added. According to the same St Isidore, the bissextile comes from leaps or increments of six hours, which is the value added each year, which gives the extra day. Now where in the calendar should this day be placed? This is stated in the following two verse:

Bissextum sextae Martis tenuere Calendae,
Posteriore die celebrantur festa Mathiae:

That is to say, on the sixth day of the calends of March we stand or we remain on this date for two days,[617] and that it should be celebrated with a feast of St Mathias, but this feast is postponed to the next day, so that, between the feast and the vigil, there is no interval. However, it does not matter whether the person celebrates the first or the second of the aforementioned days, but in this we must preserve the use of each country. St Isidore says

---

[615] A third of 30 is 10 hours, two-thirds of 30 moments = ¾ hour = 20 moments = 2 points = ½ an hour. So the sun remains in each sign of the zodiac for 30 days, and 1/2 hours

[616] 12 months x 30 days = 360 days + 12 x ½ hour = 6 hours, 6 hours over 4 years = 1 (leap) day

[617] 24 February usually, but 25 February in leap years

that the leap day comes and drifts from the course of the moon, from the six of the nones of March until the day of the calends of January.

20. But if we want to know when the leap year is, we must divide the Lord's year by four, as many times as we can and if there is no remainder then we are in the leap year. If there is a reminder, we are not in one, hence the following verse:

Anni divisi Domini per quattuor aeque.
Monstrat Bissextum qua ratione scias.

Now this is true for those who divide the Lord's years beginning from the Nativity, or from January, but not from those who start from the Incarnation. There is yet another way to find the leap year, which will be discussed below when dealing with competitive numbers.

21. The times or parts of the solar year are four, namely, spring, summer, autumn, and winter, as was said in Book Six, in the chapter, *The Wednesday and Fasts of the Ember Days*. Now, it is called, 'time,' or 'season,' because of the action which these various epochs have on temperament, by humidity, drought, heat, and cold. They are also called, *curricula*, 'chariots,' because they do not remain motionless, but walk and run incessantly. Spring is so called, because it is at this time that the sap develops and everything is green. The summer, *aestas*, is so called from, *aestu*, 'hot,' from which it is said *aestas*, 'summer,' as if it were said, *usta* (burnt), and, *arida*, 'arid.' Autumn, *Autumnus*, is thus named from, *tempestate*, a 'time,' or, 'season,' of storm. Or *tempestas*, is also said of something that arrives in time, in a timely manner, at maturity, because then leaves fall and everything matures. Winter, *hyems*, is thus called in relation to the hemisphere, because then the sun revolves around a much narrower circle. Hence this time is called, *bruma*, 'winter solstice,' like the Greek *brachus*,[618] for the days are short. Or else, winter comes from, *cibo*, 'nourish,' because then one is endowed with a greater appetite; because 'greediness', as is

---

[618] 'short'

WHAT THE SOLAR YEAR IS

said in Greek is, *bruma*, 'winter.'[619] The seasons of the year, according to the system of the Church, are enclosed in this verse:

Festum Clementis, Hyems caput est Orientis.
Cedit Hyems retro cathedrato Simone Petro.
Ver fugat Urbanus, Aestatem Symphorianus.
Id tibi quod restat Autumni tempora praestat:

Which means that the feast of St Clement, which is the eighth of the calends of December, is the beginning of winter. This lasts until the feast of the Chair of St Peter, which is the beginning of spring, and this last feast is on the eighth of the calends of March, and the spring is prolonged until the feast of St Urban,[620] which is the eighth of the calends of June. Then summer begins, which lasts until the feast of St Symphorian, which is the eighth of the calends of September. Autumn then begins, and lasts until the feast of St Clement, which begins the winter.[621]

22. At each of these four seasons we observe a fast of three days, what are called the fasts of the ember days. The fast of the spring is in the first week of Lent, namely on the Thursday after Ash Wednesday. The summer fast is the first Wednesday after Pentecost. The autumn fast is the third Wednesday of September, namely, on the Wednesday after the feast of the Holy Cross. The winter fast is the Wednesday after Blessed Luke's feast; hence this verse:

Vult Crux, Lucia, Cineres, Charismata dia,
Ut det vota pia, quarta sequens feria.[622]

---

[619] Durandus appears to be relating this to *brevis dies*, shortest days
[620] In office from 222 to 230
[621] Pope Clement I, died in the year 99, His feast day is November 23. The feast of the Chair of St Peter is on February 22, Pope Urban I, was in office from 223-230, saint and martyr, his feast day is on April 2. Symphorian was an early martyr who was executed in 178 on August 22, which is his feast day
[622] In other words, the Wednesdays following the feasts of the Holy Cross (September 14), the feast of the Blessed Lucy (December 13), Pentecost (the day of the giving of charismata or spiritual gifts), and also Ash Wednesday, require that one to render to God many vows full of piety

23. Now, these fasts take place on Wednesdays, because it was on the fourth day of the week (Wednesday) that Christ was betrayed and sold by Judas. On the sixth day of the week (Friday), because it was on that day that He was crucified; and on Saturday, because then we represent the sadness of the Apostles, in pain at the death of the Saviour, 'If we suffer, we shall also reign with him.'[623] We said in Book Six, in the chapter *The Time of Advent*.

24. In the solar year there are two solstices and two equinoxes. Solstices arrive in summer and winter, and the equinoxes in spring and autumn. The solstice is a considerable inequality between day and night, or the entrance of the sun into the signs of Capricorn and Cancer. One says, *solstitium*, solstice, as one would call a *solis statio*, a 'station', 'state of rest', 'immobility', a 'halt of the sun', because then the sun stops in its retrograde march and the days or the nights start to become longer.

25. The equinox is the greatest equality of the day and the night, because then the sun into enters into the sign of Aries or Libra and day and night have an equal number of hours. Where should the solstices and the equinoxes be placed? This will be seen in the following verse:

Solstitium decimo Christum praeit, atque Joannem.
Aqua Crucis festum dat tempora Martis et Idus.

Which means that the winter solstice is ten days before the Nativity of Christ, namely the eighteenth of the calends of January, the time in which the sun begins to describe higher circles, and the summer solstice is found as many days before the Nativity of St John the Baptist, namely, the eighteenth of the calends of July, the time in which the sun begins to describe lower circuits. From which we find that the longest day of the year is that of the summer solstice, and the shortest day that of the winter solstice. However according to the Egyptians the winter solstice is on the twelfth of the calends of January, and the ninth according to the Greeks. According to the Egyptians the summer solstice is the twelfth of the calends of June, and the ninth according to the Greeks. Likewise at the feast of the Cross, where

---

[623] 2 Timothy 2:12

WHAT THE SOLAR YEAR IS

according to others, the equinox of autumn is the twelfth of the calends of October. Also, when one uses the expression, 'in the calends,' the equinox of the spring is at the ides of March, or, according to others, on the twelfth of the calends of April. For formerly the year was divided into only two parts, namely the summer solstice and the winter solstice, and into two hemispheres.

26. As for the great year, it is fulfilled when all the planets return to the place of their creation, which does not take place in less than five hundred and thirty years. Now, the mundane year of the world will take place when all the stars will have returned to their original position, a revolution that will take place after fifteen thousand years. The master of ideas says in the story of Genesis, in the passage in which he deals with the intoxication of Noah, that the great year is accomplished in the course of six hundred years.

27. The era used by the Spaniards consists of a year, and was established by Caesar Augustus when he made the first census of the world. Now, the word, *aera*, 'era', comes from *aere*, 'money', because the whole world professed to render tribute to the Roman republic. First came the indictions, then the eras.

28. The year of the Olympiad was established among the Greeks in the city of Elis where the Gentiles would establish games and competitions every five years. The games were separated by four years, or there were four years between these games, which took place in the fifth year. That is why the time of the games of Elis was called the Olympiad, and there was a space of four years for a single Olympiad, that is to say from one Olympiad to the next Olympiad, which took place in the fifth year.

29. The lustral year comes from the Greek, *penteteris*,[624] which is a period of five years. The lustral was completed in the fifth year, and it was instituted by the Romans, in imitation of the Olympiad of the Greeks; for then, in Rome, neither consuls nor eras were known. Now this time has been named, 'five years,' because, after having completed the five-year census in the republic, the city of Rome was surveyed (*lustrabatur*).

---

[624] 'consisting of five', (in this case, five years)

30. Among the Romans, there is the year of indiction, which contains fifteen years, as will be said below, and as we have already said.

31. The Hebrews have the jubilee year or year of redemption,[625] which is completed and celebrated after seven weeks of years. We talked about it in Book Six, in the chapter *Of Quinquagesima*.

32. Among Christians, there is the year of goodness and grace, in which Christ came and redeemed us by His kindness alone. For the saints who enjoy the presence of God, who understand God, exists the year of eternity and glory, where the saints will rejoice in a glory that will have no end. Moreover, the ages are formed of generations that follow each other; for as men die, others follow them continually. Some call this time the fiftieth year, which the Hebrews call the jubilee year, as has already been said. It is for this reason that the Hebrew loving his master because of his wife and children, pierced his ear, and was reduced to servitude and forced to remain a slave for an age, that is to say until the fiftieth year arrived.

33. An *aetus*, 'age', for the most part, is taken for a year, for seven years, for a hundred years, and for an indefinite time; hence the *aetas*, 'age,' is composed of a number of generations. Therefore, *aevum*, 'age' is the perpetual *aetas*, or 'period of time' which does not start and of which the end is not known. The word *aevum* is derived from the Greek aeon,[626] which sometimes has the meaning of century and sometimes of eternity. 'Age', *aetas*, is properly understood in two ways, namely, the age of a man, such as in infancy, youth, and old age; or to an age of the world. The first age of the world extends from Adam to Noah; the second, from Noah to Abraham; the third from Abraham to David; the fourth from David to the captivity of Judah in Babylon; the fifth, from the captivity of Judah to the coming of the Saviour into the flesh; the sixth is now to the end of this world. We have said, in Book Six, in the chapter *The Sunday of Septuagesima*, how many years since the origin of the world.

---

[625] See Leviticus 25:23-38
[626] 'age', 'eon', Durandus has *aiuon*

4 PART TWO, BEGINNING WITH THE MONTH

1. After having spoken of the year it remains to speak of the month. Now the month is a space of time when the moon, moving away from the sun, comes to meet it after completing its circle or completing its course. One says, *mensis*, 'month', from *mensurando*, 'to measure', because the month serves to measure the year, or from menis[627] which means, 'lack', deficiency', or 'eclipse'; because every month the moon is eclipsed or rather disappears from our eyes. Or, according to St Isidore, 'month' comes from *mene*, a Greek word meaning, 'moon,' or *luna* in Latin. Among the Greeks, the legitimate months are not counted by the circle of the sun but by the course of the moon, which takes place from the hour of None[628] to the hour of None.

2. Now, the year is divided in twelve months, because the sun, while traversing the zodiac, passes through twelve regions of signs, where it remains for the space of twelve months. However, Romulus wanted only ten months in the year, starting with the month of March, which he consecrated to Mars, god of war, whom he believed to be his father. This made Ovid say in the first book *Fasts*:

> He lived when the founder of the city established that the year would have twice five months.

3. But Numa Pompilius, seeing that the year was incomplete by this number of ten months, added two, in the beginning, namely,

---

[627] This probably comes from *mene*, 'moon'
[628] The ninth hour

January and February. January, *januarius*, is called this from *janua*, 'door,' because, just as it is by the door that we enter a house, so it is by the month of January that we enter the year, for it is the threshold or the beginning of the year. Or January, *januarius*, is named from the god Janus, who the ancients said was the principle and the end of all things. Indeed, this month was consecrated to him by the Gentiles. This is why this same Janus is represented with a double face, to designate that he is the beginning and the end of the year. We have spoken of this in Book Six, in the chapter *The Feast of the Circumcision*.

4. February, *februarius*, is named from *febribus*, 'fevers,' which are then easily contracted, or *februis*, that is, 'purifications.' Now, *februae*, are offerings made for the dead. The Romans, in this month, made remembrance of the souls and purified them, by celebrating funeral rites of the dead. Hence, according to St Isidore, February comes from *febru*, that is to say, from Pluto, who was sacrificed in that month.

5. March, *martius*, is so named from the god Mars, father of Romulus. Or else, because it is at this time that all the animals, *aguntur ad marem*, that is to say it is at this time that the females seek the males, and are driven by the need to mate. It is also sometimes called month of the new year, because it is the beginning of the year. Or else, of the new spring, because it is at this time that the fruits are becoming green, which proves that the old ones have fallen from the tree.

6. The month of April, *aprilis*, is thus named as if it were called *aperilis*, which means, 'opens,' because then the earth opens its bosom to let the germs of the seeds which have been entrusted to it pass. The flowers also open, and the trees begin to sprout. Now April is taken in the sense of Venus, as if we said *Aphrilis*, deriving from the Greek *Aphrodite*, which in Latin is Venus.

7. *Majus*, May, is said to have received its name from, *majoribus natu*, the elders, or ancients, who were the princes of the republic, or from *Maja*, mother of Mercury.

8. *Junius*, June, said to have come from, *junioribus*, 'the youngest,' because formerly, in the city of Rome, the *majores*, the elders, that is to say the oldest, who were called fathers, remained in the city and provided its government, while the younger ones were fighting for the defence of the republic. That is why May received

its name from the elders, June from the young men, and these two months were established in their honour. Or again, *Junius*, June, comes from, Juno, (*Junone*).

9. *Julius*, 'July,' receives its name from, *Julio Caesar*, 'Julius Caesar,' who was born in that month, or because it was then that he triumphed over his enemies. Indeed he conquered Cleopatra, Queen of Egypt, with Mark Antony, her husband, in a naval combat in that month.[629] Previously, the month of July was called, *quintilis*, because it is the fifth, *quintus*, month from March, which, according to Romulus, was the first month of the year.

10. *Augustus*, 'August,' is thus called from Octavio Augustus, who was born then, or because it was then that he defeated his enemies. Previously it was called *sextilis* because it is the sixth month from March.

11. September, is so called from the rank it occupies in the series of months, of which it is the, *septimus*, 'seventh,' from March, and, *imbres*, rain, because it is rainy.

12. In the same way the months of October, November, December, have received their name from the order they keep in the number of months and the rains to which they are subject. December is placed last of all, because the number ten finishes the number of previous months, from March. We can see in the following verse the number of days that each month contains:

June, April, September and November have thirty days;
The other months are thirty-one; but February
Is only twenty-eight, and twenty-nine in leap years.

13. Now, it must be known that originally each month had thirty days, which, multiplied by twelve, give three hundred and sixty. Of the remaining five days one is given to January because it is the beginning of the year. Also because of the number itself, because the odd number is pure or simple, and God rejoices in the odd number. The second was granted to March, because of this same lack of equality; the third to May, the fourth to July, and the fifth to October. Caesar Augustus, wishing that the month

---

[629] Here the author, or rather his copyists, attribute by mistake to Caesar what should be to Octavian, that is to say, the victor of the battle of Actium

devoted to him was equal in number of days to the month of July, cut off a day in February, a month of sadness and mourning, and added it to the month of August. So February was only twenty-nine days long and August thirty-one. Finally, the Roman astrologers cut off another day in February and postponed it until December, so that the end would correspond to the beginning of the year. In this way February was only twenty-eight days long and December was thirty-one. However, to make up for the month of February one day, that is, a leap day, was returned to this month once in every four years. We will say, in the chapter *Of the Week*, in what day or at what fair the month begins.

14. In each month there are three days of note, which alone have special names, and the others derive their names from them. These principal days are the calends, the nones and the ides, which the Romans established because of the days of celebration and the offices of the magistrates, because on those days we gathered in the cities.

15. The first day of each month is called the calends, as if it were said *colendae*, days to be honoured, respected; because the festival of Juno always took place then, hence this verse of Ovid:

> *Juno daughter of Saturn claims the Italian calends.*

Or because then the beginnings of the months were celebrated by the Roman people, as the Hebrews do, which is why Ovid says:

> *Welcome festive day, always to return better, worthy to be honoured by the people, lord of things.*

Or else, 'calends,' comes from the Greek *kalo*, which in Latin is *voca*, 'I call,'[630] because, on the first day of the month, a herald used to call the people to the *nundinas*, 'nundines', markets which took place every nine days. They cried as many times as there were days until the nones. This is why we say 'calends' in the plural, because of the various names that we made then. Or else, calends comes from *kalon*,[631] which is a good omen, an auspicious one that

---

[630] *Kalo* is a form of *kalos* or *kallos* which means 'good' or 'beautiful'
[631] Also from *kalos*

should last for the whole month. For then we were extending to each other prosperity for the new month.

16. The nones are on the fourth or sixth days after the calends of each month,[632] and we say, from *nundinis*, as, *nundinae*,[633] markets that took place every nine days, because the Romans observed the *nundines*. Now, in certain months, the beginning of the nundines was sometimes the fifth day, sometimes the seventh day of the month, in order not to leave thieves advanced knowledge of a fixed time, so they could wait for the merchants. Or else, we say, 'nones,' from, *nonis*, ninths, because that day was the ninth before the ides. Or else, *a non*, 'a negation of none,' because then no festival was celebrated, which is why Ovid said:

The guardianship of the nones is missing a divinity.

17. The ides are eight days after the nones, therefore they are always on the thirteenth or fifteenth day, according to where the nones which precede them are placed. In fact, if the month has nones on the fourth day, the ides are the fifteenth day; if it is on the sixth, the ides are on the thirteenth day.[634] When the Council of Antioch said that the ides are on the tenth day it was considering the ides in another relation. It was taken in the sense of division, because then the *nundines* were parted or divided, or because at the ides the division of the month takes place. We say, 'ides,' from *iduo, iduas*,[635] that is *separo, separas*, 'I separate,' 'you separate.' It is from this that an unmarried woman[636] is called *vidua* that is, *divisa*, 'divided,' or, 'separated,' that is to say, divided or shared. Most Romans think that *idus*, ides, is from *edendo*, 'to be eaten', because these days, among the elders, were devoted to feasts. Now the next days are called immediately after the calends.

---

[632] i.e. the fifth or seventh
[633] *nundinis* means, 'ninth-day,' from which comes, *nundinae*, a 'holy day,' 'festival,' or, 'fair'
[634] This appears to be an error for eight days from fourth or sixth day from the calends (the 5th or 7th of the month) would be the twelfth or fourteenth day after the calends (the 13th or 15th of the month). The ides were on the 15th in March, May, July, and October and on the 13th in other months
[635] Think of *iduo* as, 'i-duo,' 'in two'
[636] or unmarried woman

If it is a month that has nones on the fourth day, we must say in the calendar, '*quarto nonas*,' 'the fourth before the nones'; on the third day we shall say, 'third before the nones'; the fourth, 'the day before the nones'; on the fifth, we shall say, 'the nones,' as it evidently appears in January, and in similar months. But if the month has nones on the sixth, we must say, immediately after the calends, 'the sixth before the nones'; the third day, 'the fifth before the nones'; the fourth day, 'the fourth before the nuns'; the fifth day, 'the third before the nones'; the sixth day, 'the day before the nones'; and on the seventh day, 'the nones,' as it evidently appears in March, and in similar months.

18. Now the days that follow after the nones are thus named in each month, namely, the eighth before the ides; the seventh before the ides; the sixth, the fifth, the fourth, the third before the ides; the day before the ides; and the ides, as this obviously appears in the calendar. The following days after the ides take their name from the calends of the following month, in the following manner. January has thirty-one-days, so subtract one of these days for the calends, eight for the ides, four for the nones; and then only eighteen days remain. Now, add to these eighteen days the day of the calends of the following month, and you will have nineteen days. Therefore, in the month of January we must, immediately after the ides, say: The nineteenth of the calends or before the calends of February; the next day is the eighteenth, and so on in order until the end of the month, in descending order. Note, however, that what is said is: The day before, the day before the nones, the day before the calends, and not *secundo*, for the second day, because *secundus*, 'second', comes from *sequor*, 'I follow'; but this day does not follow the calends, but it precedes it. And the preposition *prae* means 'before', that is, *ante* 'in front', *prius*, 'previous'; which is where *pridie*, 'the day before', comes from. That is to say, *priori die*, 'the first day', or rather, 'the day before'; because of *prae*, that is, 'before the day of'; and when we say *quarto nonas*, we understand the fourth day before the nones, and so on for the others.

19. We can see, by the following verses, the number of days that are given their name from the nones, how many from ides, and how many from the calends of every month:

PART TWO, BEGINNING WITH THE MONTH

Sex nonas Majus, October, Julius, et Mars.
Quattuor at reliqui: tenet Idus quilibet octo.
Janus et Augustus, denas nonas que December.
Julius, October, Mars, Majus, hepta decemque.
Junius, Aprilis, September, et ipse November
Ter senas retinent; Februsque bis octo Calendas.

Which means that the months of May, October, July and March have six days for the nones, but that the other months have only four; and each month has eight days for the ides. Also January, August, and December have nineteen days for the calends; but July, October, March, and May have seventeen. June, April, September and November have eighteen. February is sixteen, and seventeen if the year is a leap year.

20. Now, it must be remarked that every month there are two Egyptian days, that is to say, taken from the Egyptians. The reason for this is that in Egypt there were astronomers who, in those days, found that there were certain constellations harmful or contrary to the actions of men, and that is why they wished that they should be known to men. However, we cannot know or understand the points of these constellations, because of the errors of our compute or calendar. Perhaps they also found that these days were well starred, benevolent, or better starred than the others, and that is why they indicated them in the calendar, so that on these days, rather than on others we apply and give ourselves to our business. The Church is careful of this system, so as not to appear to follow them and fall into their error. Or again, these days are called Egyptian days, according to some, because it was on those days that the Lord struck and afflicted the Egyptians with nine plagues. We can see in the following verses which the Egyptian days are, supposing at the beginning or at the end of the month:

Augurior decies, audito lumine clangor:
Liquit olens abies, coluit colus, excute gallum.

In these verses, there are twelve words that serve for the twelve months or that correspond to the twelve months. The first word is used for the first month, the second word for the second month, and so on in order starting from January. So that the day that will correspond with the first letter of the first syllable of any one of these words, in the alphabet, will be a whole Egyptian day, in the word to which this word corresponds by calculating from the beginning of the month and heading towards the end. In the same way, the whole day will be Egyptian, which will correspond to the numerical order in the alphabet, of the first letter of the second syllable, in the month to which this word corresponds, by calculating from the end to the beginning of the month. For example, *Augurior*, is the first word, and it corresponds to the first month, that is, in the month of January. 'Au,' is the first syllable, and, 'a' is the first letter of the same syllable and is the first letter of the alphabet. So the first day of January is an Egyptian day. In the same way, 'gu,' is the second syllable, and, 'g,' is the first letter of this same syllable and the seventh of the alphabet. Therefore the seventh day of January is Egyptian, counting from the end of the month and heading towards the beginning, and so on for the other words. It should be observed that 'H', in this place, is not placed as a letter. Now, each of these days is called Egyptian, because of its unique time. We talk about this at the end of this book.

21. As for the happy or unhappy days that some astronomers have noticed, there is no mention of them in the present book, because the Church forbids us to believe such superstitions. In some months also, there are certain days that are called, *caniculares*, 'dog days,' from the star, Canicula,[637] located at the front of the Lion and in front of the knees of the Bull.[638] In the summer months she is in the centre of the sky, and when the sun has come up to her, she meets him, keeps close, and doubles her heat, which is such that bodies become irritated, weakened and parched. This why it she is called, *canis*, 'dog,' because at this time bodies are very susceptible to diseases; and for seventy-two days, because of the heat of the sun, it is dangerous to bleed and take medicinal potions. We can see, in the following verses, when these days begin and end:

---

[637] Sirius or the dog star, in the constellation Canis Major
[638] The constellations Leo and Taurus

PART TWO, BEGINNING WITH THE MONTH

*The scorching days (*caniculares*) begin the day before the ides of July, and end the day before the nones of September.*

According to some, they begin the fourteenth before the calends of August.

5 OF THE WEEK

1. Let us talk about the week now. The week contains seven natural days, the repetition of which forms months, years and centuries. Among the Greeks, week is called, *hebdomada*, and among the Hebrews, *Sabbatum*, Sabbath. *Septimana* is another word for 'week' and it is called this from, *septem*, 'seven,' and *mane*, 'morning,' so we take the part for the whole, namely the morning, *mane*, for the whole day. Or week comes from, *septem* and, *mantel*, 'to remain,' 'to last,' because it lasts for seven days. Or we say week, *septimana*, as if we said, *septem luces*, 'seven lights,' from the morning light, according to St Isidore. The same period is also called weekly, week, from *hepta*, a Greek word which means seven, and *tropus*,[639] which means 'day', or *modus*, which means, 'measure;' and, according to it, *hebdomada* is a more common word or has a wider acceptation than *septimana*. Thus it is said in Daniel, *Septuaginta hebdomades*, etc., 'Seventy weeks, etc.'[640] Here one takes, 'week,' in the sense of weeks of years, that is to say for seventy times seven years. Now weeks cannot have fixed names because they have no positive, certain and fixed beginning. In fact, each year they differ or vary by one or two days, and years sometimes have surplus weeks.

2. All the days of the weeks are written following the first seven letters of the alphabet. In the same way, the days, according to the Gentiles, receive their name from the planets. The first day receives its name from the sun, which is the prince of all the stars. Also this same day is at the head of all the other days. The second

---

[639] 'way' or 'manner'
[640] Daniel 9:24

day borrows its name from the moon, which, for brilliancy and grandeur, is the star which comes closest to the sun and borrows its light from that star. The third takes its name from the star of Mars, which is called Vesper. The fourth, from the star of Mercury, which some call, *candid circulum* 'white circle.' The fifth, from the star of Jupiter, which is called, Phaeton.[641] The sixth, from the star of Venus, which is called Lucifer,[642] because among all the stars it is the most brilliant. The seventh, from the star of Saturn, which, placed in the sixth heaven, takes thirty years, it is said, to complete its course. We talked about it in the *Preface* of Book Eight.

3. Yet we ask why the days are not arranged in the week in the same order as the planets are in the sky? For in the sky they are placed in the order indicated by this verse:

The Sun, Venus, Mercury, Moon, Saturn, Jupiter and Mars.

Or by this one:

Saturn, Jupiter, Mars, the Sun, and Venus, Mercury, the Moon.

Here is the reason: We say that the days in the week are not placed according to the order of the planets, but according to their influence or their reign on each day. Therefore, as the philosophers have remarked, the sun reigned (or had its greatest influence) at the first hour of Sunday, that is why they named this day, *a sole*, 'by the sun.' Likewise, as they perceived that the moon reigned or had its greatest influence in the first hour of the second day of the week, that is why they named this day, *a luna*, 'by the moon,' and so on for others, as it appears obviously by the distinction of the hours of the day, made in successive order. Moreover, the philosophers borrowed names from the said planets because they wanted each of these planets to be something in man or to have relation to the good or bad passions

---

[641] In Greek mythology he was the son of Helios and Clymene. He received permission from his father to drive the sun's chariot for a day. However, he lost control of the horses and was struck down by a thunderbolt of Zeus, to prevent his setting the earth on fire
[642] Light bearer

of man. They borrowed from Saturn, candour; from Jupiter, temperance; from Mars, ardour; from the Sun, the spirit; Venus, voluptuousness; from Mercury, eloquence; from the Moon, the heart. And as the order of the planets does not exceed the number seven, but by a convolution then returns to the first number, that is why the sages have placed only seven days in the week.

4. Now you have to see which day of the week each month starts with. There are two ways to know this. The first is contained in the following verse:

Alta domat Dominus, gratis beat aequa gerentes.
Contemnit fictos, augebit dona fideli.

In these verses there are twelve words which relate to the twelve months; the first word, to the first month; the second, to the second; and so on in order, beginning with January; so that, whatever may be the initial letter of some of these words, the same letter will be that of the calends of the month to which this word relates. For example, *Alta* is the first word, and A is the first letter of that word *Alta*; so, 'A,' is the first letter of January; in the same way, *damat* is the second word, which serves for the second month, namely for the month of February, and 'd,' is the first letter of that word; so, 'd,' is the first letter of February, and so of the others. So when one has the letter of the calends, one can easily know on which day each month begins. In effect, proceed by the Sunday letter of this year, calculating by the subsequent letters to the letter which is to the calends of the month of which you wish to know on what day it begins. Then the day which accompanies this letter will be the one from the beginning of the month. The second way of knowing on which day the month begins is by means of regular and competing numbers. Now, note that in the solar year is fifty-two weeks and a day, or two, if the year is leap year, and it is because of the leap day that the beginnings of the months vary each year. For, if in this year January begins with a Sunday, during all this year, 'A,' which is the first letter of January, will be a Sunday. However, when we reach the end of the year, the final, 'A,' of the calendar, which is entered before the day which is in surplus of whole weeks, will represent the Sunday. Thus the, 'A,' following, which is also the initial letter of January will represent Monday; and thus this variation will remain throughout this year. It is in the same way that each year the beginnings of the months are variable and arrive at various days. If the year is a leap year, there will be a double variation; the first to the calends of January, the second to the feast of St Matthias. Now in order to know on which day of each year each month began, the calculators found two numbers: An invariable, which is called the regular solar, festive; the other variable, named the competitor, of which we will say a few words.

5. First, we must see what the solar regular number is from what it derives its name, its origin, and how many each month has regular numbers. The solar regular number is an invariable number given to the month, which number, joined to the competing number, marks on which day of the week each month begins of which it is the regular number. Now, we say *regularis,* 'regular,' from, *regula,* 'rule,' because it is invariable as the rule. It is called, *solaris,* 'of the sun,' to distinguish it from, *lunaris,* 'of the moon,' which will be discussed below. The regular numbers have their origin in March, because in the month of March there are five regular numbers or five numbers to serve as a rule, *pro regulari*. Indeed, March began in the first year of the world or the centuries. Moreover, it is said that the world was created in this month, on the day when it is said, or where is marked, the fifteenth of the calends of April. Or, according to others, the eighth of the calends (or before the calends). For, if we count the days of the week in a reverse order until the calends of March, we will find that the world began on the fifth day of the week, only if it began before March, and that is the reason why March had the number five for regular. The regular numbers of the other months are formed in the following way. Add up the regular numbers with the days of the same month and subtract from the sum of the number seven as many times as you can, and the rest will show you the regular number of the following month. For example, March has five days for a regular number and thirty-one days; add up all, and you will have thirty-six; subtract seven as many times as you can, and there is one day left for the next month for a regular number. In the same way, April has thirty days and one day for a regular number, which is thirty-one days; subtract seven as many times as you can, and there will be three,

which is given in the month of May, for a regular number; and so for the others until March. We can also know the regular numbers of the months, by the following verse:

Est astris clara fulgentibus ara Deorum,
Grata bonis extat, gratissima cuique fideli.

In this verse there are twelve words that serve for the twelve months. The first word for the first month, the second for the second, and so on in order, starting from March; so that the month has as many regular days as the first letter of the corresponding word has numbers or degrees in the order it occupies in the alphabet. For example, *est* is the first word that is used for the first month, which is March, and, 'E,' is the first letter of that word and the fifth letter of the alphabet; so March has five days for a regular number. In the same way, *astris* is the second word and serves for the second month, that is to say for the month of April. 'A' is the first letter of this word and the first letter of the alphabet; so April has only one day for regular number, and so for the others.

6. Now let us talk about competing numbers. They are called competitors, because they meet, compete, or relate to each other, as it appears in their formation, or because they compete with regular numbers to demonstrate the initial day of the month, each year. Now, the competing number is the excess of one or more days of the fifty-two weeks of the solar year. I said, 'or more,' because in the leap year there is an excess of two days. In the other years there is only one surplus of a single day, and it is this excess which is the origin of the competing numbers. The other competing numbers that follow after the first are formed by adding a day or unit to each term or year, so that they do not exceed the number seven, because there are only seven days in the week. Whenever the seventh day is a competitor in that year, the months have the same beginning as they had in the first year of the world, for every day or every day of the week is far from it, even by an interval of seven days, or returns every seven days.

7. The competing numbers are designated in this line:

1. 2. 3. 4. 6. 7. 1. 2. 4. 5. 6. 7. 2. 3. 4. 5. 7. 1. 2. 3. 5. 6. 7. 2. 3. 4. 5. 6.

For the first year of the solar cycle has a competing number, the second has two, the third three, the fourth four, the fifth six, because it is leap; the sixth has seven, the seventh has one, because we do not go beyond the number seven, but we return to the number one. Then we must go as far as twenty-eight years, then we go back to the first year of the cycle, and we proceed as before. The course or space of twenty-eight years is called the solar cycle or competing numbers, and we say 'cycle', as if we said 'circle', by similarity. But if we want to know what the year of the solar cycle is we must divide the years of the Lord by twenty-eight as many times as we can, and add nine before the division. The reason is because at the birth of Christ this cycle had arrived at this point, and the years that remained of the division formed the whole cycle of years. The number of years remaining after the division will be that of the cycle, and if there is no remainder, it is because we are in the last year of the solar cycle. Hence this verse:

Add nine years to the nine years of the Lord, divide everything by twenty-eight; that is how you will know the cycle.

8. We can therefore know the competing numbers of each year by the Sunday letter of this year, as indicated by the following small verse:

A, six; B, five; C, four; E, two; D, three.
First competing f. G is the seventh letter.

And so on for others. Which means that when A is the Sunday letter, in that year, there are six competing numbers; when it is B, there are five; when it is C, four; when it is E, two; when it is D, three; when it is F, one; when it is G, seven. When we have found the competing number, we must join it to the regular numbers of the month of which we wish to know the day of the calends, that is to say the beginning. Then, if the sum is not more than seven, the month will begin on the day of the week marked by the result of that total sum; but if the sum exceeds seven, the month will begin the day of the week obtained in the excess of the sum. However Sunday letters vary like competing numbers. Indeed, in the first year of the solar cycle the Sunday letter is F; in the second, E; in the third, D; in the fourth, C; in the fifth, A; for then, because of the leap year, we pass off the letter B; this is what is written in these verse:

Fert ea dux, cor amet, gens, fautor, eum coluit bis.
Ars genus est de corde bono, gignit ferus ensis.
Dicta beant aqua gens, fons dat cunctis bonus auctor.

In these verses there are twenty-eight words, corresponding to the twenty-eight years of the solar cycle. The first to the first, the second to the second, and so on in order, starting from the first year of the cycle; so that the initial letter of each of these words will be the Sunday letter in the year to which this word corresponds. For example, *Fert* is the first word and is used in the first year of the solar cycle, and, 'F,' is the first letter; hence, 'F', is the Sunday letter in the first year of the solar cycle, and so on for the others. Notice that the year to which a word terminates in, 't,' like *Fert*, is leap; and so the first year of the cycle is always leap, since it refers to a word finishing with, 't', namely *Fert*. That is why the first letter of the word finishing with 't', will not be a Sunday letter for the year this word is used for, if not later, from the leap location, because the Sunday letter changes together with leap year, or day, or month. Now, from the calends of the preceding January to the place of the leap day, the Sunday letter will be the one immediately following in the calendar after the one which should be the Sunday letter. That is why, in the first year of the cycle, 'F,' is the Sunday letter from the leap position until the next January. Since from the calends of January preceding to the place of the leap, 'G,' is the Sunday letter, and so for the others. However, the year in which this word is used can be known by the means exposed above regarding the solar cycle. The system of the Sunday letter then current begins and ends in the same way.

9. Let us now say a few words about the indiction which is a lapse of time that the Roman emperors marked for the nations to pay their tribute. If we want to know the date of the indiction we must

add three years to the years of the Lord and then divide the years of the Lord by fifteen, as many times as we can. The remaining years after the division will all be indiction. If there is no remainder we are in the last year of the Indiction and then we return to the first indiction, because the indiction does not exceed fifteen years. Hence this verse:

> *If, after adding three to the years of the Lord, you divide them by five, you will obtain the starting of the indiction.*

We have dealt more fully with indiction in the *Speculum Judiciale*,[643] in the treatise, *de Instrumentorum edictione*. We will talk about it even further when dealing with cycles. We spoke earlier of the Era.

---

[643] An extensive work by Durandus on civil law

6 OF THE DAY

1. Although we have already said a few words of the day in a large number of places above, nevertheless we will speak more particularly here. It is therefore necessary to know that there are two days, namely, the natural day and the artificial or ordinary day. The natural day is the lapse of time during which the sun makes its revolution around the earth from east to west, that is to say the time of day and night, which always contains twenty-four hours. The word, 'day,' comes from *diis*, 'gods', whose names the Romans gave to some stars. This is why each day was called by the name of some god, for example, Jupiter, and others, as it was said in the chapter *The Week*. Now *dies*, 'day,' comes from the Greek *dua*, which means 'two', because the day contains two distinct times, namely the night and the usual day. It was said when the day begins, in the *Preface* of Book Seven. The artificial day is the space of time that the sun dwells on our hemisphere, from sunrise to sunset; and the day, accordingly as the sun goes up and down, grows and decreases as well. The day is also called 'brightness.' Then it is said to be ordinary or artificial, because this time alone is suitable for work and the exercise of the various professions. The other part is the night is *nox*, 'night,' from, *noceo*, 'I hurt,' because it harms the view and is unfavourable for the various forms of work. It is called, 'day', because of the best part, and without mention of the night, according to these words, 'And the evening and the morning were the first day.'[644]

2. In addition, there are three parts of the day, according to St Isidore, namely the morning, noon and the last part of the day.

---

[644] Genesis 1:5

The morning is when the light is full and twilight no longer exists. They say, *meridies*, is at noon, as if they say, *medi dies*, half of the day, or because then the day is purer. *Suprema*, 'final,' is the last part of the day. The night is divided into seven parts, *vesperae* in the evening; *crepusculum*, dusk; *conticinium*, the calmest time of the night; *intempestum*, the time when the night is deep; *gallicinium*, the moment when the cock sings; *matutinum*, morning or daybreak; and *diluculum*, which is dawn. The evening is named from *Vespere*, Vesper, a western star which precedes the darkness that comes after it. We say darkness, as if we said, *tenentes umbram*, 'holding the shadow.' Twilight is called, *dubia lux*, 'doubtful light', that is, between light and darkness. The, *conticinium* takes place when all nature is immersed in silence. The *intempestum* takes place at midnight, when nothing can be done and all remains silent; it is as if it were called *importunum*, an unseasonable time. The next is called *gallicinium*, because of the roosters, the heralds of light. In the morning, *matutinum*, lies between the retreat of darkness and the appearance of dawn. The point of the day, *diluculum*, is said in the sense of a weak light that begins with the dawn that precedes the sun. For the dawn is the beginning of the effective and brilliant day.

3. Notice that among the days, some are sidereal, *siderales* (which concern the stars), and these are those in which the stars make their revolution or movement and which prevent men from sailing. Then the *praeliares* concern combats, or are favourable for war, they are mentioned in the book of Kings, and these are those in which kings are accustomed to go to war. Others are, *intercalares*, 'interleaves,' or 'added;' they are the ones we know to be in surplus to the twelve months. Others are, *caniculares*, others *solstitiales*, others *aequinoctiales*, and we have already spoken of them. Some are, *fasti*, 'splendid,' where favour blows, the favourable days; others are, *nefasti*, 'bad ones,' which are all contrary to them. Others are the, *festis*, feast days, or festivities, like the days of unleavened bread, others are, *profestis*, far from the feasts, such as, *feriales*, weekdays. Others are called bad days, because men experience more evil and affliction than usual in those days; it is from there that the Apostle says, 'Redeeming the

BOOK EIGHT

time, because the days are evil."[645] Good days are just the opposite. Others are Egyptian days which we talked about earlier. There is also the day of salvation, which is the one on which the Lord came to save us. There is also the Day of Judgment, on which the Lord will come to judge men. For the good it will be a day of joy, and for the wicked a day of calamity and misery.

4. The moment is a very short and very small time, so called from the movement of the stars. It is the last, or one of the last fractions of the hour, divided into short intervals. It is what happens when one moment comes after another and succeeds it. According to St Isidore, *ara*[646] is a Greek word, and yet has the same Latin sound,[647] and it is a division of time,[648] namely, *finis temporis*, 'the end of time.' It has been said, in the beginning of this book, how many hours the natural day contains.

---

[645] Ephesians 5:16
[646] It seems Durandus means *hora*, which is the same in both Greek and Latin. They both mean 'hour', but not as a definite period of time; rather as a particular time, such as 'the hour has come for us to act'
[647] Or is also a Latin word
[648] Or a term that expresses time

7 WHAT THE LUNAR YEAR IS AND THE DAYS IT CONTAINS

The second part deals with the lunar year and the number of days it contains. Secondly, we speak of regular lunar numbers; thirdly, of the epact; fourthly, the embolism; fifth, the Golden Number; sixthly, the Paschal term and other mobile festivities; seventh, cycles.

1. The lunar year is so called in three senses. First, it is the space during which the moon travels around the entire zodiac, a revolution that it accomplishes in the space of twenty-seven days and twelve hours. Secondly, the lunar year is the space of time during which the moon revolves around the sun, from one elevation to another, from one ascension to another; and it accomplishes this in twenty-nine days and twelve hours. For when the moon separates from the sun to traverse the zodiac and then returns to the same point from which it had separated from itself, it no longer finds it in the same place. This is because the sun has advanced and moved away by its own motion, and the moon tries to reach it, without being able to, for two days and three hours. Thirdly, the lunar year is the space of time of the twelve lunations in the common year, and thirteen in the year of embolism, which will be discussed below. As each moon consists of twenty-nine days and twelve hours, because the Church does not take into account the minutes, the twelve hours of the previous moon and the twelve of the next one form a natural day, which is always attributed to the previous lunation. This means that the lunation of the preceding month is always thirty days, and

that of the next twenty-nine days, unless it is otherwise, because of the leap, the embolism, or the jump of the moon. Hence the following verse:

The moon of an even month will never have thirty days;
That of an odd month has thirty, it will never fail.
When February is leap, the moon has thirty days,
In fact in July moon is twenty-nine.

We say even month, because by counting from January, in order, we meet even numbers, as in February, April, June, August, October and December, whose lunation is also twenty-nine days, except February whose lunation is thirty days, when it is a leap. The month is odd when it meets an odd number, such as in January, March, May, July, September and November, when the lunar month is always thirty days, except July, which, in the last year of the solar cycle, is only twenty-nine days long, because of the leap of the moon. These twelve lunations form three hundred and fifty-four days in the lunar year and so the solar year exceeds it by eleven days. It is from this excess that comes the whole variation of the age of the moon; so that the moon takes the same place in the first year, then it always takes that place eleven days later in the second. It is because of this variation that we have invented two kinds of numbers, namely regular numbers and epacts, which we will discuss in a few words.

8 THE REGULAR LUNAR NUMBERS

1. Now let us talk about the regular numbers. The regular lunar number is an invariable number given to find the moon of that month on the calends of each month. These regular numbers have their origin in the five days which, in the solar year, exceed three hundred and sixty days. That is why five regular numbers were given in September, which is the month when the lunar year begins. The following is way in which we form the regular numbers of the other months. Add up the regular numbers of the month with its days, then from this sum subtract the lunation of this month, and the rest will be the regular number of this month. For example, September has five regular numbers and consists of thirty days which, when combined to the regular numbers, form thirty-five days. The lunar month of September is thirty days, subtract it, and the remainder is five, which are the numbers the following month, that is, October, and so on for the others, returning to September. Because the Egyptians start their year from September, and that is why we start our lunar year from this month.

2. We give the following verse for regular numbers:

Day E, G twice, I, K twice: and after continue in this order

As if saying, repeat E twice, which is the fifth letter of the alphabet, that is, for the first two months of the lunar year, one gives each month five regular numbers. Similarly, say G twice, which is the seventh letter of the alphabet, that is, the third and fourth months each have seven regular numbers. Say I twice, which is the ninth letter of the alphabet, that is, the fifth and seventh months have nine regular numbers. Similarly, say K, twice, which is the tenth letter of the alphabet, that is, the sixth and eighth months have ten for regular numbers. Now notice that here we go from five to seven and from ten to eight, as it obviously appears by forming the regular numbers, because January and March have nine days, February and April ten. But afterwards, order is restored, that is to say that May has eleven, June twelve, July thirteen and August fourteen.

9 THE EPACT

1. Next, of the epact.[649] The epact is a variable number given to the year to find the moon on the calends of each month. We say 'epact' from the Greek *epi*, 'on' or 'upon', and *aucta*, 'augmented,' because it is an increase of the lunar year, furnished by the excess of the solar year. That is why the first year of the lunar cycle has no epact, because there was no previous year from which it could draw the number eleven. The second year has eleven for the epact, because the epact comes from eleven days whose solar year exceeds the lunar year. The third year has twenty-two days, because we always add eleven days, if they do not exceed thirty, but if they exceed thirty, the excess of thirty will be the epact of that year. That is why, in the fourth year, as the sum with eleven added amounts to thirty-three, we neglect the number thirty, and it is the excess three which is the day of the epact. The Greek word, *epact* means in Latin the annual lunar additions which, by the number eleven, roll on themselves up to the number thirty. The Egyptians make these additions so that the lunar measurement becomes equal to that of the sun. For the moon makes her revolution in the space of twenty-nine and a half days, when she gives us her light, which makes the lunar year three hundred and fifty-four days. This is eleven days less than the course of the solar year, so the Egyptians add these extra days to the lunar year. Otherwise you would not be able to find the moon's date in the year, month, and day. The epacts of all the

---

[649] The medieval computists described the epact as the age of the moon in days on 22 March. However, in the newer Gregorian calendar the epact is reckoned as the age of the ecclesiastical moon on January 1st

years of the lunar cycle are indicated by the following table, in which the word, 'zero,' indicates the absence of the epact, and this corresponds to the first year. Each following year corresponds to each year of the cycle, up to twenty-nine.

Zero. 11. 22. 3. 14. 25. 6. 17. 9. 21. 12. 13. 5. 16. 27. 8. 19. 30.

2. This is further indicated by the following verse:

Annis adde monon Domini, partire per unde
Viginti Lunae cyclis, et inde patet.

Which means that if we want to know if a year will be epactal year, or the cycle, we must divide the years of the Lord by nineteen, as many times as we can, and add one. The reason is because this cycle would only then have appeared when Christ was born. The sum that remains will be the year of the epactal cycle. For instance, we are in the year of the Lord one thousand two hundred and eighty-six, of which one thousand two hundred and seventy-three are exactly divided by nineteen and leaves a remainder of thirteen on the first number. Let us add one, so we have fourteen and therefore this year is the fourteenth year of the lunar cycle. The next year will be the fifteenth, and so on until the nineteenth, after which we come back to one. Now this is true, according to those who begin to guess the years of the Lord since the birth of Christ, or the calends of January, but not for those who change or count them in the calends of September, and make the division there, because then you have to add two years.

3. One can also find the epact in another way. The sum of the remainder of the division is counted by means of the three articulations of the thumb. If the number ends at the first joint, we must subtract 1 from the number itself. If it is the second, we must add 9. If it is in the third, we must add 19. The sum from these numbers is the epact, if it does not exceed 30, otherwise, we neglect the 30, and the rest is the epact; hence this verse:

Take one away, then add nine; then nineteen.

THE EPACT

When the epact is found, we must join it to the regular numbers of the month of which we want to find the moon, and the sum which will come from it will be the moon in the calends of this month, provided that it is not more than thirty. If it exceeds thirty, the excess from thirty will be the age of the moon. If the sum is thirty in the calends of the month, thirty will be the age of the moon. If there are no epacts, for example in the first year of the lunar cycle then to find the moon the regular number suffices. However as the Epact system sometimes deceives, because of embolism or leap of the moon, that is why we will speak briefly of the embolism.

10 THE EMBOLISM

1. In the case of embolism or leap of the moon, it should be noted that in Greek, *embolismos*,[650] which is in Latin, *super augmentum*, 'super augmenting,' or *super excrescentia*, 'over exceeding,' and refers to the solar year being longer than the lunar year. As, therefore, the solar year exceeds the lunar year by eleven days, it is this surplus which forms the seven lunar months in the nineteen years of the lunar cycle; from multiplying by these eleven days. They are called 'embolismal lunations'. Each of them is thirty days, and they are attributed to seven embolismal years, so that at each lunar cycle there are seven embolismal years and twelve common years.

2. Now, it is called an embolismal year because the embolism year, from the fourteenth moon preceding Easter to the fourteenth moon following Easter, has thirteen lunar months or fourteen lunar months. That is to say three hundred and eighty-four twenty-four days; and this year was revealed in a divine way to the holy man Moses. The common year has only twelve lunations, that is to say three hundred and fifty-four days, which this verse indicates the nature of:

Cur fles has lacrimas, odiosum quare tyrannum.

In this verse there are seven words which serve for the seven embolismal years. The first for the first, the second for the second, and so on in order; so that the year of the epactal cycle, corresponding to the numeral order in any one's alphabet of those

---
[650] 'insertion' or 'addition'

words, will be an embolism year. For example, *Cur*, is the first word and is used for the first embolismal year. This is the first letter of this word and the third of the alphabet. Therefore the third year of the lunar cycle is embolismal, and so for the others, observing that the word, *has* is written with an 'h'.

3. It is called the 'common year', because often two years run together, so that they follow each other in the Easter solemnity; because the embolismal year is always alone. The order of these common and embolismal years is evident in the following lines:

common, common, embolismal, common, common, embolismal, common, embolismal, common, common, embolismal, common, common, embolismal, common, embolismal, common, common, embolismal.

When we have the embolismal year we can know in which month the embolismal lunation takes place, from this next verse:

Mobilis et Christum mudo liber habeto coevum.

In this verse there are seven words which serve for the seven months in which the embolismal lunations arrive. The first serves the first, the second the second, and so on in order. So the embolismal lunation will correspond to the number occupied in the alphabet by the first letter of any one of these words and will arrive in any month of the year to which this word serves or corresponds. Similarly, in the numerical order of the first letter of the second syllable, in the alphabet the embolismal lunation begins on any day of the month corresponding to this letter. For example, *Mobilis* is the first word and serves for the first lunation that arrives in the third year of the lunar cycle. 'M' is the first letter of this word and the twelfth of the alphabet, so the embolismal lunation arrives in the twelfth month. Similarly, 'B' is the first letter of the second syllable and the second of the alphabet; so this lunation begins on the second day of this month, and so on for the others. If you want to ascertain in a more complete way the truth of this, use the epact, and so you will find the regular numbers of the year which you want to know about.

4. Let us now see how the epact, when joined to the regular numbers, misleads us because of the embolism or the jump of the moon. On this subject note that although in the lunar cycle there are seven embolismal years, as has been said above, however the epact deceives only in three years, namely the eighth, the eleventh, and the nineteenth; hence this verse:

Octavo, undecimo, postremo fallit epacta.

We can see in the following verses in which place or what months, or in which places the epact is with regular numbers:

Julius undenis ter, Majus octo vicenis:
Bissextus nisi sit, Mars peccat in undetricenis:
in totidem Majus, Augustus vero duobus.

That is to say that, the eighth year of the solar cycle, the epact with the regular numbers is misleading in May and in July, since in the calends of May, when the moon should be the on the 28th, according to the Epact, it is only found on the 27th, because of the embolism. Likewise, it deceives in the calends of July of the same year, because then the moon should be on the 30th, according to the epact, and yet it is only found on the 29th, because of the embolism. So then you have to rely on the embolism and not on the epact. In the same way, the epact deceives in the eleventh year, because, in the calends of March, according to the epact, the moon should be on the 29th; but, because of the embolism, it is only on the 28th. However, if the leap takes place in this year, the error disappears, because of the leap a day is added. Similarly, in the nineteenth year, the epact deceives in two places; for, according to the epact, the moon should be the 29th in the calends of May; but, because of the embolism, it is found only on the 28th. In the same year again, it deceives in the calends of August. According to the epact, the moon in this month should be on the 2nd, but it is only the 3rd, due to the jump of the moon. The lunation of July, which should be the 30th is only on the 29th for that year, because of the error of our computation, and then the year is exceeded by two days by the solar year.

THE EMBOLISM

5. Here is a sure verse for the leap of the moon:

The moon makes a leap on the last day of the fifth month (quintilis).[651]

In fact, the moon delays by one day, as we have said, because of the error of our compute, so that, the following year, the moon returns, as it should, on the calends of September. If we did not bring together the leaps of the moon, the following error would occur. In fourteen cycles it looks like the first moon, when we are in the full moon. Now one day is formed in the following manner; for each lunation, (in order for the lunations to be equal), there would be 29 and a half days, minus four moments, then an ounce and an atom. Now in a cycle there are 235 lunations; so there will be four times as many moments, which are in total 940, which, divided by 40, give 23 hours and half an hour. Then 235 ounces make nineteen moments, with a remainder of 7 ounces and 335 atoms are 5 ounces. These ounces, united to the preceding seven, are twelve ounces or a moment. These, united at the 19 moments obtained above, forms a half-hour which, united with the other 23 hours, is more than the other half an hour, so forms a day, which, in the last year, is cut off from the lunation of July, and called a lunar leap. We can also deduce it more easily today, in the following way. The lunar year consists of 354 days less an hour, a quarter of an hour, and the 76th of an hour, or the 76th fourth part of a single hour, or the 76th part of a quarter of an hour. So, in nineteen years, this gives us 19 hours, 19 quarters of an hour and an hour, and 19.86 quarters of an hour, which make up 19 years, a quarter of an hour. So there will be 20 and a quarter hours, which make up 5 hours, which joins the 23 hours noted above, make up one day.

6. The leap of the moon thus forms a day in the space of nineteen years from the excess which is given by the lunations. We say 'leap of the moon' not that the moon leaps on that day rather than another, but because we, calculating the moon, jump over this day. Or we omit this day on which, in the other years, the lunar month of July is called *trigesima*, 'thirtieth', because, in the last year of the nineteen year cycle, we only skip the nineteenth year and

---

[651] *Quintilis* is the Roman month following June, renamed Iūlius in 44 BC

we do not take into account the moon in the last year of the cycle of nineteen years of the moon. Now, this day is taken from the lunar month of July in the last year of the nineteen year cycle, because July is the last in the epactal year among the months having thirty days in the lunation; which is why in the last year the lunar month of July is only twenty-nine days instead of thirty. That is why the Golden Number for this year, that is to say, although it increases, follows the smaller number without interval and consequently in the other following months until the 1st of January, as will be explained below. So the leap of the moon means that there are also two lunations of twenty-nine days. Now, in order to more easily correct the aforementioned errors, we have invented the Golden Number, which we must speak about in a few words.

11 THE GOLDEN NUMBER

1. The Golden Number is a number placed in the calendar to indicate in each month the first moon and it was invented to more easily correct particular errors. Golden Numbers are called this because, just as gold outweighs all metals, so this number outweighs all the other means used to know the moon. It was Julius Caesar who, it is said, found it with the greatest care, beginning with each year of the lunar cycle. Where he found the first moon in the first year of the cycle, he placed 1 on the calendar, on the outer side near the letters, namely in every month. In the second year when he found the first moon, he placed 2 for every month; and in the third, 3; and so for others. Now on the calends of January, the number is three, because it is there that one finds the moon in the third year, on the first day. We must not place any number other than the number 3, because the moon is on the first day of the calends of January that the third year of the cycle of nineteen years.

2. However, in certain calendars, the numbers themselves are designated by the letters of the alphabet; because, for the number 1, the letter A is interposed there. Then for 2, B; for 3, C; and so on for the other numbers and other letters, successively up to the letter T, which is the nineteenth in alphabetical order. The Golden Number of the ternary number which is placed on the calendar of January is formed. To these 3 we add 8, which makes 11, and this number must be placed in the third letter of January; likewise, to these 11 we add 8 = 19; this number must be placed, with an interval, at the fifth letter of January; to these 19 we add 8 = 27. However as the Golden Number does not exceed 19, subtract 19, and the number 8 must be placed immediately after 19; and so on

for all the calendar. It is evident, therefore, that when the larger number follows the smaller, then the two numbers must be separated by a letter; when it is the opposite, we must not interpose any letter; hence this verse:

De tribu octo canens superet et dena novemque;
Major sit ternus, minor aureus esto secundus.

3. However, this formation deceives in any month whose lunation is twenty-nine days, as in February, April, June, August, October, and December, in which the greatest number, placed after the smallest, immediately follow it towards the beginning of the month. Which seems evident in this verse:

Mense brevis Lunae Februs est ars dat cito ganger

In this verse there are six words which serve for the six months whose lunation is twenty-nine days, beginning in the middle of the verse, at the word *Februs*. Therefore, whatever the initial letter of some one of these words on the same letter in the calendar, the greater number follows the smaller one without interval, that is to say that no letter is lowered or interposed in the month in which this word is served. For example, *Februs* is the first word and is used in the first month of which the first letter is F and the lunation of twenty-nine days, namely February. Therefore, on the first F of February, the largest number immediately follows the smaller one. It is the same on the first E of April, and so of the others. On the first G of December, of May, the number 23 immediately follows the smaller, which is 2, and on the same letter, because there are two Golden Numbers; which is what is meant by the doubling of the letter G. In the word *ganger* likewise, this formation deceives in July and the other months until January, in which, towards the end, the number 19 immediately follows the number 11. Hence this verse:

Juliut et reliqui, qui restant dena novemqu»
Jungunt undeno: sic est ratus aureus ordo.

THE GOLDEN NUMBER

It should be known that when the number 19 immediately follows the number 11, then the eighth which follows must be put in third place; hence this verse:

Quando continuant undenis dena novemque,
Majori trinus tunc octonarius esto.

12 THE EASTER TERM

1. The Easter term is determined in three ways. The first is by the keys of Moses, the second by the age of the moon, and the third by manual tables. We will examine each of these. Let us talk first about the keys. We will see what the key is, where it gets its name from, its origin, and why it was invented.

2 The key is a variable number given to the year to find the beginning of the five moving feasts, which are the Septuagesimas, Lent, Easter, the Rogations and Pentecost. That is why there are five keys, and each of these festivals has thirty-five days during which it is always celebrated. From the starting point of each key until the beginning of these same 35 days we count 11 days, as will be seen later. We say 'key' because of similarity, for just as keys serve to open doors, so this number indicates the beginning of the festivities. Now these keys derive from the 19 years in terms of the lunar cycle and the 7 days of the week. Hence the first key is 26. The keys of the other years are formed as follows. Always add 19 to the key of the previous year and the sum will give us the key of the following year, if it does not surpass 40. If the sum surpasses 40 subtract 30 and the rest will be the key of the following year. For example, the key of the first year is 26, let us add 19 and we will have 45. Deduct 30, and the remainder will be 15, which is the number of the key of the following year. In this way they are formed in order until the nineteenth year, because we do not exceed the number 19 but come back to unity. So the cycle of the keys, the Golden Number and the epacts do not differ in quantity. However they differ initially, because the cycle of epacts begins in September, while that of the Golden Number and the keys begins in January. Therefore, if we want to

THE EASTER TERM

know the calendar for the year, the cycle, the Golden Number and the keys, we can know them by the division of the years of the Lord, made above, in the chapter of *The Epact*. After finding the year of the keys, we can know that it is the key of this year by this other method. The remaining number of the division of the years of the Lord must be counted on the end of the five fingers starting with the thumb. If the number ends at the thumb, we must add 25, and the sum that will result will be the key of this year. But if the number ends at the index, we must add 13. Again, if it is on the middle finger add 13, if it is on the ring finger add 19, and if it is to the little finger add 7. If the sum from there is 40, we will subtract 30, and the rest will be the key. This addition is contained in this verse:

Vigintiquinque tredecim, plus esse tricenos,
Undevicena, epia, digitis pro clavibus apta.

3. The seat of the keys is never found in the calendar except on the letter G. So the first letter G, of January, is the key of Septuagesima. The last letter G, of the same month, is the key of Lent; the second letter G, of March, is the Paschal key; the third letter G, of April, is the key to the Rogations; the last letter G, of April, is the key of Pentecost; hence this verse:

Ultima g, prima Jani, Marlisque secunda,
Aprilis terna tibi signat, et ultima clavem.

So, having obtained the key of the year, begin to calculate from the place of the key, and complete it by proceeding in order and following the calendar days, and where it ends will be the end of the solemnity. So the beginning of the solemnity of which it is the key will be the nearest Sunday following. However the Rogations begin the next day of the moon (the second day); and if one is in a leap year, one must add one day to each key.

4. We can also know the Easter terms by the age of the moon by using a method we follow according to the custom of the Jews. Here is the rule that is given on this subject. Take the moon at the point where it is at the feast of the Epiphany and complete it, following in order the calendar days up to forty, and up to forty-

one if the year is a leap year. The next Sunday will be the beginning of Septuagesima. Hence this verse:

A festo stellae numerando perfice Lunam:
Quadraginta dies post Septuagesima fiet.
Bissextus quando fuerit, superadditur unus
Si cadit in lucem Domini, tunc sume sequentem:
Si cadit in feriam septenam, sitque Bissextus,
Linque diem Domini primum, sumasque secundum.

However, once we know the Septuagesima, we can easily find the terms of the moveable holidays since from the Septuagesima to the Quadragesima there are three whole weeks. From Lent or Quadragesima until Easter, there are six whole weeks. From Easter to the Monday of the Rogations, five weeks and a day. From Easter to Pentecost, five times ten days or fifty days.

5. You can also know the Easter term by this verse:

After the March nones, find out where the new moon is.
Easter will be the third Sunday following.

Moreover, when we meet the fourteenth of the moon after the twelfth of the calends of April we celebrate Easter on the Sunday which is nearest. In the same way, at the feast of St Benedict, or the twelfth of the calends of April, take the moon, as it was on the calends of January, count until it completes the twenty-fourth day, and there will be the Passover of the Hebrews.

6. Furthermore, from the ides of March until the nones of April there are twenty-nine days. Now in the days of the first moon it is necessary to bring it to its thirteenth day, and there will be the Passover of the Hebrews. There is yet another way to find Easter by the age of the moon, in that if the moon is one day old, Easter will be the first Sunday after the nones of April. If the moon is two days old, Easter will be the first Sunday after the eighth of the calends of April. If the moon is three days old, Easter will be the first Sunday after the April ides. If it is four days old, it will be the first Sunday after the April nones. If it is five, it will be the first Sunday after the eleventh of the calends of April. If it is six, the Sunday after the four of the ides of April. If it is seven, it will

THE EASTER TERM

be the Sunday after the third of the calends of April. If it is eight, it will be the first Sunday after the fourteenth of the calends of May. If it is nine, it will be the first Sunday after the seventh of the April ides. If it is ten, it will be the first Sunday after the sixth of the calends of April. If it is eleven, it will be the first Sunday after the seventeenth of the calends of May. If it is twelve, it will be the first Sunday after the eve of the April nones. When it is thirteen, Easter is the first Sunday after the ninth of the calends of April. If it is fourteen, it is the first Sunday after the second of the April ides. If it is the fifteenth, it will be the first Sunday after the calends of April. If it is the sixteenth, it will be the first Sunday after the twelfth of the calends of April. If it is the seventeenth, it will be the first Sunday after the fifth of the April ides. When it is the nineteen, Easter will be after the fifteenth of the calends of May.

7. Some, like Denys[652], Isidore and others, make manual tables to find the Paschal terms. We do not think it is appropriate to give them now, lest the difficulty becomes too strong and too heavy. The following verses that we have written or composed will suffice for the present:

Esse gravem nobis bello karmen kaveamus.
Bellum saepe gerens, etiam puto dejicit hostem.
Mox animae lucrum invenies cum religiosis.

In these verses there are nineteen words for the nineteen years of the lunar cycle. The first for the first, the second for the second, and so on in order, starting with the first year of the cycle. Every April day corresponding to all the first letters, in the order of the alphabet, which do not end in M, by calculating from the beginning of the month until the end, will be the end of the Passover of the Hebrews, that is, the fourteenth of the moon; and the next Sunday will be the day of our Easter. This has been said in detail in Book Six, where we have dealt with the Passover. Here again it is evident why the Resurrection of the Lord is inscribed in the calendar on the fifth of the calends of April. Now, if the word ends in M, all the days of March, by calculating from the

---

[652] Pseudo-Dionysius

end of the month going to the beginning, which will correspond to the numerical order of the first letter in the alphabet, will be the Paschal term of the Jews. The first Sunday which will be met next, coming down towards the end, will be our Easter, observing with the greatest care that *carmen* and *caveamus*, in the above verses, must be written with a K, and *hostem*, with an H, which in this place is considered as one letter. One can also, in another way, find Easter with ease, which is, place at the margin of your calendar the next Golden Number, that is to say, with the 12 of the calends of April, place 16. At the 11 of the calends, place 5. At the 9 of the calends, place 13. Near the 8 of the calends, 2; at the 6 of the calends, 10; at the 4 of the calends, 18; and at the 3 of the calends, 7. In the same way, at the calends of April, 15. At the 4 of the nones of April, 4; near the 2 of the nones, 12; and at the nones, 1. At the 6 of the ides, 19; at the 5 of the ides, 17; at the 4 of the ides, 6; at 2 of the ides, 14; and at the ides, 3. At 17 calends May, 11; at the 15 calends 19; and at the 14 calends, 8.

8. If you want to find the Easter term, add one to the common years of the Lord, then divide it as many times as you can by 19, so that there is no remainder. Or have recourse to your calendar, and the day on which you will find 19 will be the Passover of the Hebrews, which they always celebrate on the fourteenth of the moon, and the following Sunday will be our Easter. But if there is a remainder to the last member of the division by 19, for example 5, 10 or 15, then the Passover of the Hebrews will be the day with which you will find written five, ten or fifteen, and so for others numbers and days mentioned above. The following Sunday will be our Easter, which cannot be celebrated before the eleventh of the calends of April, nor after the seventh of the calends of March. For example, we are in the year of the Lord 1286 of which 1273 are exactly divided by 19 and there remains 13 from the aforementioned number, and adding 1 gives 14. Now, where you find this number in your calendar, there will be in this year the Passover of the Jews; but, the following year, it will be at the place where you will find written the number 15, and so on up to 19. Then we return to the first year of the cycle and it will be so on indefinitely.

9. It is also in the same way that you will be able to find the term of the Septuagesima. Indeed, place at the margin of your calendar,

next to the 16 of the calends of February, the number 18. Next, on the same line, place 19 near the 15 of the calends of February; place 5 with the 13 of the calends, 13 with the 12, 2 with the 10, 10 with the 8, and 8 with the 7. Then at the 5, 15; at the 4, 4; and near the 2, 12. In the same way, near the calends of February, place 19; at the 3 of the nones of February, 6; at the 6 of the ides, 3; at the 5, place 3; at the 3, place 11; and at the ides, 19. Then, dividing the years of the Lord by 19, as has been said before, see the number that remains on nineteen; and when you find it in the calendar there will be the end of the Septuagesima, which is always at the eleventh moon. Then on the following Sunday we celebrate the Septuagesima, which cannot be before the 15 of the calends of February, nor after the 9 of the calendars of March. Thus Lent cannot be before the 6 of the ides of February, nor after the 2 of the ides of March.

10. The term of Pentecost can be found in the same way. Place at the margin of your calendar, near the 7 of the ides of May, 16; at the 5 of the ides, 5; at the 4 of the ides, 13; near to the 3 of ides, 2; and at the ides, 10. In the same way, at the 17 of the calends of June, 18; near the 15 of the calends of June, 7; at the 13 of the calends, place 15; at the 10 of the calends, 4; near the 12 of the calends, 12; near the 9 of the calends, 1; near the 7 of the calends, 19; near the 5 of the calends, 12; near the of the 4 calends, 6; and near the 2 of the calends, 14. In the in same way, at the calends of June, 3; at the 3 of the nuns, 11; with the nuns, 18; and at the 8 of the ides, 8. After having divided the years of the Lord by 19, seek in the abovementioned places of the calendar the number that remains from the 10, and where you find it will be the Pentecost of the Hebrews, which is always in the fourth Moon. The following Sunday will be our Pentecost, which cannot be before the 6 of the May ides, nor after the ides of June, as the Rogations cannot be before the 7 of the calends of May, nor after the 3 of the calends of June.

11. The Passover can also be found by this table:

BOOK EIGHT

5, 15, 13, 2, 20, 2, 10, 30, 10, 8: 7, 27, 15, 4, 24, 12, 1, 21, 9, 29, 10, 7[653]

These numbers represent certain days of April and March in which the Passover of the Hebrews arrives, counting these days from the beginning of those months; so that the numbers below twenty correspond to April, and the numbers above twenty correspond to March. This table means that in the first year of the lunar cycle, the Passover of the Hebrews is in the fifth day from the beginning of April. In the second year of the same cycle, it is the fifteenth day from the beginning of March beginning; and so on for the others, until the numbers of this table are completed and then we come back to the first year of the cycle. We have said above, in the chapter *The Epact*, how one finds the years of the cycle. We said in Book Six, in the chapter *The Christmas Office*, why the feasts of the Saviour, except that of Christmas or the Nativity, are moveable. Finally, according to St Isidore, we must know that among the Romans and the Greeks, there is, regarding the Paschal term, a divergence that comes from the fact that the Romans seek the moon from the three of the nones from March to the three of the nones of the first month of April. Also, if the fifteenth of the moon happens to be a Sunday, they put Easter back to another Sunday, as has been said above. However, the Greeks count the first moon from the eighth of March until the ninth day of April.

---

[653] Three of these numbers vary in different Latin sources, 17 instead of 27, 23 instead of 24, and 19 instead of 29

13 THE CYCLE

1. As we have mentioned the cycle on almost every page of this book, we will say a few words regarding it. It should be noted that the cycle lasts for a period of several years before returning to its beginning, according to some numbers; and it is thus said to be a double syncope,[654] as if *circulas*, circular; for it is called a cycle, because it forms an ellipse and is counted by a circle of years arranged successively and uniformly.

2. The cycles are six in number. The first is the solar and begins the six of the calends of March, at the feast of St Matthew. It consists of twenty-eight years, contains concurrent and regular solar numbers, sundials, leap years and common years.

3. The second cycle is the *decemnovenalis* and contains nineteen years. It begins in January and contains the Golden Number and the keys of the terms.

4. The third is the lunar cycle, which also begins in January. It contains nineteen years and begins in the fourth year of the *decemnovenalis* cycle. It was the Romans who invented it in order to know at what time the moon borrows its light from the sun. But as, in the course of time this discovery has been altered, we do not use this cycle.

5. The fourth is the epactal cycle, beginning the fifth of the calends of September. It simply encloses nineteen years, lunar and regular numbers, epacts, common and embolismal years.

6. The fifth is the great cycle, composed of five hundred and thirty-two years, or, according to others, five hundred and thirty years. It is from this cycle that the table of Dionysius is formed.

---

[654] From the ancient Greek *sunkopé*, 'a cutting up'

7. The sixth is the indicative cycle, composed of fifteen years. It contains the indictions. As it was difficult, from the farthest ends of the world, to come to Rome each year to pay the taxes established in each province, the Romans decided that they should be paid at least every five years. Thus, after the first five-year indiction, they were brought iron to make weapons. After the second, money was brought to pay the troops. After the third, gold to make statues; and so on continually, after the gold was brought. At the end of fifteen years, the space of five years or the five-year indiction, where the tribute consisting of iron was again brought, was recommenced. It was like a circle of time and as it was the Romans who commanded this to be in this way, which is why these years were called indictions, as has been said above. This space of five years was named *lustrum*, 'to make bright', because when the couriers of the provinces arrived with the tribute, they traversed the city with candles and formed a magnificent procession, (*urbem lustrabant*).

14 THE CONCLUSION OF THE WORK

Let no one imagine that the various Offices have been sufficiently explained in this work, in case sometimes, by elevating or by praising the work of man, the sacrament or the divine mystery becomes swallowed up. For in the divine Offices of the Mass there are so many great hidden mysteries that no one, unless enlightened by the anointing of the Holy Spirit, is able to explain them. Indeed, who is the one who knows the order of the heavens and can expose that system on this earth? For he who scrutinizes majesty will be crushed by glory. For myself, who does not pretend with stupid eyes to contemplate the sun in its rotational movement, I thought I saw, as in enigma and as in a mirror, the majesty of such a great mystery. Without going into the heart of the cenacle, but happy to stay at the door and in the vestibule, I did what I could (in a way that leaves much to be desired), and not what I have wanted. For I was hindered on account of the innumerable ties of the unavoidable affairs of business of the Apostolic See, which I am obliged to attend to and which, like waves, overwhelm the mind of those who study and who wishes to rush towards the higher spheres. Not knowing what to do, so to speak, and embraced in various and inevitable bonds, I could not give myself entirely to this work as I would have liked. Even more, I was hardly able to dictate what I had meditated, far more of conceiving what I had to meditate on, or of indulging in deep meditation. Now, the mind of man, when he is distracted by various occupations, obviously becomes less capable of filling each of them in particular. That is why, not only do I hasten to implore the benevolence of the reader, but, moreover, I desire to be the object of an independent criticism; for I cannot deny that many assertions of this pamphlet cannot be very justly criticized and blamed without any temerity. If there be anything to praise there, let it be attributed entirely to divine grace; for every high favour and every perfect gift comes to us from above, coming down from the Father of lights.[655] If one finds something reprehensible and incomplete and which marks the insufficiency, let it be blamed on human weakness. For the body, which is corrupted, overwhelms the soul, and this earthen envelope which has many concerns crushes the spirit. This book contains, sometimes of my own thoughts, or perhaps for the most part, rather by way of narration, things which are known to me. I have carefully collected this work, like the diligent bee, both contradictory writings and commentaries of others, and those whom divine grace has suggested to me. Leaning on the protection of God, I have presented this doctrine which contains a sweet nectar, like a honeycomb, to those who wish to devote themselves to the study of the Divine Offices; and, for this considerable work, I expect men of no other reward than the help of their devout prayers, to obtain the forgiveness of my sins from the most merciful of judges.

END OF BOOK EIGHT

---

[655] See James 1:17

SCRIPTURE INDEX

Genesis
1	6
1:5, 8	202
1:21	65
2:2	6
18:24, 26	111
28:12	166
28:17	105, 166, 167
50:1-12	109

Exodus
3:17-18	121
16:5	5

Leviticus
12:2	36
21:5	124
21:11-12	124
23:32	8
23:36	24
25:23-38	184
26:10	65

Numbers
19:11-12	110

Deuteronomy
4:24	41
34:8	109

1 Kings
1	1
9:3	167
10:18	87

1 Chronicles
29:17-18	168

2 Chronicles
6:21	167

Nehemiah
9:27	52

Tobit
4:18	45

Job
7:12	65
7:16-21	119
38:32	61

Psalms

Reference	Page
1	22
6:4	135
8:5	152
10:1	69
17:3	83
19:1	129
19:1-5	68
19:4	146
19:4-5	14
21:3	151
21:5	151
23:4	124
24	165
26:8	3
33:1	52, 152
34:8	146
37:31-32	150
38	119
43	165
45	161
45:1	162
46	165
46:4	95
48	165
48:9-10, 1	38
64:2, 1	22, 152
64:10, 1	152
65	119
65:1-2	118
67:1	54
68:18	14
68:33	14
84	165
84:1-2	105, 167
85:8, 1	60
87	165
88	165
89:20-21	158
91	166
91:15	7
92:1	62, 137, 162
92:12-13	62
93:1	167
96:6	84
96:6, 1	82
103:20, 1	57, 58
103:20	59
107:32	44
110:1	14
110:46-47	162
112:1	155, 167
112:1-2	151
112:9, 1	82
115:17	118, 124
119:23, 86	135
119:23, 86, 23, 1	135
119: 95, 1	162
119:95-86, 1	30
132:1	158
138:1	58
139:1-2	68, 69
148	65
148:2	152
149:6	124

Proverbs

Reference	Page
3:13-23	152
8:22-24, 32-35	163
8:22-35	95
10:28-32	93, 154

11:10	157	8:1-2	163
15:2-7	153	10:10	160
18:4	146	10:10-14	159
31:10-31	70	10:12	160
31:17	162	10:17	154
		10:19-20	157
Ecclesiastes		17	42
7:2	119	18:14-15	8
Song of Songs		**Ecclesiasticus**	
1:2	86	14:1-11	153
1-5, 12, 15	161	14:22	156
2:6	150	15:1	137
2:12	61	15:1-6	136
4:15	147	15:3	137, 150
5:6	39	15:5	137, 150, 151
5:10	134		
6:12	147	15:6	150
8:6	40	22:13	109
8:13	58	24:1-4; 12-16	159
		24:1-6	162
Wisdom		24:11-13	86, 87
3:1-7	153	24:14-16	86
3:1-9	153	24:16	40
3:1-22	157	24:17	40
3:4-6	155	24:23	95
3:6	157	24:23-31	87, 95
3:7-8	155	31:8-11	153
3:8	152	31:8-9	156
4:7-10	153	31:10	157
5:1	52	39:6	160
5:1-5	52, 153	39:6-14	152, 159
5:16-17	157	39:12	160
5:16-20	154	44:10	154
5:4	52, 143	44:10-15	143
7:30	162, 163	44:14	143

44:15, 14	152	49:7	63
44:16	158, 160	56:7	167
44:20	160	59:1	1
44:25	160	59:21	167
44:25-27, 2-4, 6-9	143, 153	63:1	123
44:26	160	63:2	123
45:1	150	63:16	116
45:1-6	159	66:10-11	7
45:2	142		
45:3	160	**Jeremiah**	
45:4	143	1:5	63
45:8	142, 158	1:5, 9	62
45:9	157	31:15	139
47:9-13	159	31:18-20	140
45:19	160	33:15	48
51:1-3	69		
51:1-12	162	**Ezekiel**	
51:3	162	1:10-14	100, 151
51:11	162	1:16	147
51:13-17	162	29:3	65
Isaiah		**Daniel**	
1:15	114	3:84, 87	152
6:6	56	7:10	56
7:10-15	47	9:24	194
11:1-5	47		
25:8	156	**Amos**	
30:21	39	5:22	115
35:2	159		
38:1	139	**Zechariah**	
41:27	151	9:11	14
45:8	47		
46:13	40	**Malachi**	
49:1	63	2:7	160
49:1-2	62	3:1	36, 40
49:1-3, 5-7	62	3:1-4	39

SCRIPTURE INDEX

1 Maccabees
4:42-43	164

2 Maccabees
12:42-48	125

Matthew
1	95
1:1	148
2:13-18	140
2:18	139
3:7	62
3:13-14	63
4:18-19	129
4:18-22	129
4:19-20	129
5:1-12	107, 154
5:13-19	159
5:18	155
7:25	167
9:9-13	100
10:15	155
10:16-22	144
10:26-32	153
10:34-42	153
11:3	91
11:10	142
11:11	61, 62, 137
11:25-30	46, 155
11:28-30	144, 146
12:50	155
13:44-46	55
13:44-52	163
16:13-19	46, 68, 77
16:16-19	69
16:18	68
16:18-19	46
16:24-27	153
18:1-10	58
19 27-29	144
19:27-29	31
19:28	69, 144
19:28-29	144
20:20-23	73
21:13	166
23:34-39	135
24:3-13	154
24:25-35	99
24:42-47	159
24:45	159
25:1-13	163
25:4-6	163
25:14-30	159
25:20	159
26:12	120
26:29	80
26:7-12	120
27:37	157
28:3	123

Mark
3:3	148
6:17-29	93
13:1-13	154
13:33-37	159
16:14-20	68
16:15	146
16:17	155

Luke
1:1	147
1:5	149
1:14	61
1:26-38	47, 88
1:38	175
1:39-41	87
1:39-47	88
1:41	63
1:44	63
1:46	87
1:57-68	62
1:76	62
2:15	21
2:19	88
2:22-32	39
2:24	37
2:26	39
2:28	40
5:27-32	100
6:17-23	107, 154
6:19	155
7:36-50	70
10:1-9	144, 151
10:15-20	155
10:38-42	87
11:27-28	87, 88
11:33-36	159
11:47-51	154
12:1-8	154
12:32-34	159
12:35-40	159
14:26-33	153
15:7	1
18:12	10
19:1-10	167
19:12-26	159
21:9-19	154
22:10-11	21
22:24-30	144

John
1:1	149
1:12	2
1:35-51	130
1:41-42	130
1:9	65
3:1-15	55
3:14	99
3:30	66
4:24	3
5:21-23	125
5:25-20	125
5:35	65, 93
6:37-40	125
6:51-55	125
9:31	114
10:22-23	164
11:11	10
11:21-27	125
12:24-26	83, 153
12:26	84
12:31-36	99
14:1-13	52
14:9-10	52
15:1-7	22, 143, 144
15:12-16	69
15:12-17	144
15:15	2
15:16	142, 144
16:17-25	144

19:19	157	8:28-30	143
19:25-27	88	8:29	143
20:24-29	133	8:35-39	154
21:10-24	136	10:10-18	129
21:15-19	70		
21:18-19	69	**1 Corinthians**	
21:23	137	1:31	162
21:23, 19	137	3:6	147
21:24	137	3:8	166
		3:10	166
Acts		3:22-23	1
1:10-11	123	4:9-14	144
1:15-26	46	6:19	2
3:1-10	69	6:20	40
5:12-16	143	7:25-28	163
5:41	143	9:24	iv
6:8	136	9:27	iv
6:8-10	135	13:8	124
6:9	136	15:10	69
7:54-59	135	15:41-42	17
7:55	136	15:61-57	125
7:56	135		
9:1-22	31	**2 Corinthians**	
9:10	31	1:3-7	144, 153
9:15	69	9:6	84
12:1	68	9:6-10	82
12:1-11	68, 72, 77	10:17-19	162
		11:1-2	162
12:7	68	11:2	86, 162
12:11	68, 69	12:2	85
14:11-15	4	13:3	3
15:9	38		
		Galatians	
		1:11-20	69
Romans		2:8-9	69
8:16-17	2	6:14	53, 54, 55
8:17	143		

Ephesians
1:3	137
1:3-14	73
2:19	142
2:19-22	72, 143
2:20	143
4:7-13	100, 144
4:8	14
5:16	204

Philippians
2:5-11	55
2:8	99
2:8-9	99
2:24-30	54
3:12	iv

1 Thessalonians
4:13-14	10
4:13-18	125

2 Timothy
1:12	69
2:1-7	153
2:8-10	153
2:12	182
3:10-12	153
4:1-8	159
4:4-8	159
4:7	69

Hebrews
1:14	56
7:23-27	159
7:26	160
10:32-38	154
11:33	157
11:33-34	157
11:33-39	154
11:37	156
11:40	iv
12:1	iv
13:9-17	159

James
1:12	142, 156
1:17	230

1 Peter
1:1-7	46
1:3-7	153

1 John
4:9	12

Revelation
1:1	59
1:1-15	58
1:3	59, 151
1:4	59
4:1-2, 6, 9	150
4:1-9	151
5:6-12	107
7:2-12	107
7:9	107
7:9, 11	107
7:14	157
7:16	52, 143, 157
7:17	156
8:3	57, 58
8:4	58

11:4	154
12:7	56
12:9	56
12:10	107
12:19	161
14:1	140
14:1-5	140
14:4	140, 161
14:6	161
14:13	119, 125
19:10	4
19:6	107
21:2	166
21:2-5	154, 167
21:3	166
21:4	156
21:16	148

SUBJECT INDEX

A

abbot 34, 89, 112
Alcuin 134
allegorical sense 58, 86, 145
allegory 60, 155
alphabet192, 194, 198, 207, 208, 212, 213, 217, 223, 224
Ambrose 3, 17, 66, 108, 114, 146
Ambrosian Office 21
Anastasius 91
angel1, 3, 4, 10, 13, 15, 18, 20, 21, 24, 31, 32, 33, 46, 47, 55, 56, 57, 58, 60, 67, 75, 85, 86, 87, 94, 97, 101, 104, 105, 106, 109, 115, 122, 131, 135, 136, 139, 143, 151, 165, 175
Apostolic See 229
Augustine2, 3, 17, 26, 84, 108, 110, 111, 112, 113, 114, 115, 118, 119, 123, 134, 146, 150, 163, 171

B

bissextile 178, 179
bride 85, 146, 160
bridegroom 14, 41, 110, 133, 160

C

Caesar 73, 75, 137, 183, 187, 217
calends6, 15, 30, 31, 40, 46, 53, 71, 75, 76, 91, 93, 104, 144, 173, 176, 179, 180, 181, 182, 188, 189, 190, 191, 193, 196, 197, 200, 207, 209, 210, 211, 214, 215, 217, 222, 223, 224, 225, 227
Charlemagne 134
cherubim 146
Church Militant 5, 18, 43, 163, 164
Church Triumphant1, 5, 18, 43, 163, 164
Clement 181
Compostela 23, 49, 71
Constantine 15, 52, 66, 73, 128
Council
   of Africa 15
   of Ancyra 116
   of Antioch 189
   of Chalcedon 85
   of Chalons 111
   of Ephesus 85
   of Lyons 16
   of Orleans 16
   of Toledo 118, 119
Cyprian 3

D

Dionysius 17, 73, 117, 227

E

Egyptian days 173, 191, 204
equinox 173, 178, 182
eternal life 9, 24, 37, 86, 111, 118
Eusebius 15

SUBJECT INDEX

F

finger of God 14
five senses 154, 160

G

Gentiles 4, 5, 6, 11, 15, 20, 40, 41, 44, 45, 63, 64, 67, 91, 109, 121, 183, 186, 194

H

historical sense 58
Hours (Canonical) 47, 52, 67, 107, 136, 141, 149, 155, 159, 165
Hypante 34, 38, 42

I

ides 6, 66, 173, 188, 189, 190, 191, 192, 222, 223, 224, 225
indiction 172, 173, 175, 183, 201
Isidore 10, 11, 108, 179, 185, 186, 194, 202, 204, 223, 226

J

Jerome 15, 17, 84, 85, 101, 112, 114, 119, 146
jubilee 110, 175, 183, 184

L

Lamb of God 91
Lauds 26, 68, 116, 135, 149
litany 11, 15
literal sense 138
Lombards 59
lustral 175, 183

M

Master Guilbert 91
Matins 16, 21, 130, 141, 160, 164

N

Nero 66, 75, 99
Night Office 16, 21, 63, 68, 82, 134, 139, 140, 154
nones 7, 173, 180, 188, 189, 190, 191, 192, 222, 223, 224, 225, 226
nundines 188, 189

O

Octavio Augustus 187
Olympiad 172, 173, 175, 183

P

penance 31, 37, 95, 121, 146, 164
Pope
    Alexander 75, 76
    Boniface 104
    Celestine 85, 95
    Clement 181
    Eusebius 52, 98
    Eutychian 80
    Eutycian 122
    Gregory..12, 15, 17, 19, 40, 59, 67, 81, 90, 95, 104, 110, 115, 128, 146, 150, 166
    Hormisdas 123
    Innocent 95, 148
    John 127
    Leo 69
    Melchiades 125
    Nicholas 66
    Pelagius 66
    Sergius 41, 97
    Sixtus 79
    Sylvester 6, 16, 66
    Urban 181
Prime 149

Q

Quadragesima 63, 222

R

Rabanus 3

S

Septuagesima19, 184, 220, 221, 222, 224, 225
seraphim 55
Sexagesima 110
solstice 173, 174, 180, 182, 183
suffrages 11, 112, 113, 114, 115

T

Terce 61

V

Vespers 8, 16, 118, 140, 165
vigil12, 19, 25, 27, 61, 62, 68, 71, 81, 85, 95, 99, 106, 107, 118, 127, 128, 130, 135, 142, 151, 179
virgin3, 10, 16, 18, 22, 24, 27, 33, 34, 35, 37, 38, 39, 41, 42, 46, 52, 60, 84, 85, 86, 87, 88, 94, 95, 101, 104, 105, 106, 133, 135, 157, 160, 161, 162, 177

Z

zodiac173, 175, 176, 177, 178, 179, 185, 205

This translation of the
RATIONALE DIVINORUOM OFFICIORUM
Consists of the following volumes:

Volume 1
Author's Preface
Book 1 - The Church and its Parts

Volume 2
Book 2 - Ministers, Ecclesiastical Dignities and their Duties
Book 3 - The Sacred Vestments

Volume 3
Book 4 - The Mass and its Mysteries

Volume 4
Book 5 -The Divine Offices

Volume 5
Book 6 - The Liturgical Year

Volume 6
Book 7 - The Festivals of Saints
Book 8 - Computation and the Calendar

Volume 7 – The Indices

IN HIS PREFACE TO BOOK ONE DURANDUS WRITES:

1. All things belonging to the Offices, customs, or ornaments of the Church are full of divine figures and mysteries. Each of these, in particular, is overflowing with a celestial sweetness; when they encounter a man who examines them with attention and love, and who knows how 'to suck honey out of the rock, and oil out of the flinty rock.'[656] However, 'Knowest thou the ordinances of heaven? canst thou set the dominion thereof in the earth?'[657] Certainly, whoever wishes to scrutinize His majesty would be crushed by His glory; for it is a deep well. I have nothing with which to draw from it,[658] unless He who gives to all abundantly, and without admonishing them,[659] presents me with the necessary vessel. Then I may drink with joy, from the fountains of the Saviour, the water which flows from the midst of the mountains[660] But, we cannot give the reason for all that has been transmitted to us by our ancestors, since it is necessary to remove what has no foundation. That is why I, Guillaume Durandus, appointed bishop of the holy Church of Mende, by the sole permission of God, will knock and I will not cease from knocking at the door. Perhaps 'the key of David'[661] will consent to open it to me, so that the king may introduce me into the cellar where He keeps His wine.[662] There also the divine model which was shown to Moses on the mountain[663] will be revealed to me, until I can explain in clear and precise terms what is signified, and what is contained in all things which relate to the Offices, usages, or ornaments of the Church. Then I may fix their rules; after it has been revealed to me by Him who makes the children's tongues

---

[656] Deuteronomy 32:13
[657] Job 38:33
[658] See John 4:11
[659] See James 1:5
[660] See Psalm 104:10 and Isaiah 12:3
[661] Revelation 3:7
[662] See Song of Songs 2:4
[663] See Deuteronomy 5:4

speak,[664] and whose spirit 'bloweth where it listeth',[665] 'dividing to every man severally as he will,'[666] for the praise and glory of the Trinity.

---

[664] See Wisdom 10:21
[665] John 3:8
[666] 1 Corinthians 12:11

IN HIS PREFACE TO BOOK TWO DURANDUS WRITES:

1. In this second book we intend to treat of the ministers and dignities of the Church, and of their duties. In principle, we shall lay down that there are three principle sects,[667] namely, the Gentiles, the Hebrews, and the Christians. The first is a sect of error; the second, of truth; the third, of truth and salvation. In the first we are shipwrecked; in the second, we are torn from the peril; in the third, we are saved. The first sect (*secta*) derives its name from *sectare* (cut off), because it subtracts us, that is, separates us from God; the second and third sects, in a similar way, are called *secta*, from *sectare* (seek and possess), because they enlighten, save and deliver. Both the secular and the ecclesiastical among the Christians are taken from the two other sects, which are Hebrew and pagan. Now, just as there are two kinds of people among us, namely, the laity and the ecclesiastics, so it was with the Gentiles and the Hebrews.

2. Among the Gentiles, the secular people were the monarch or the Roman emperor; the patricians, who were also called senators, according to which everything was ordered; kings, dukes, counts, governors, prefects, suffrages, tribunes of soldiers, tribunes of the people, praetors, centurions, decurions, quarteniers, decemvirs, quaestors, aediles and ushers of the palace. Among the literary inventers were advocates, epic poets, historiographers in verse, comedians, tragedians and historiographers in prose.[668]

3. The word *vates*, which comes from *vi mentis* (the transport of the soul), sometimes means the priest, sometimes the prophet, sometimes the poet. According to St Isidore,[669] the Gentiles, in

---

[667] *Secta*, Durandus says; is to conform to the strict word for word that we translate *secta* by *sect*. Here, this word has the meaning of *part, portion*, and not of *sect* in the mystical sense of the branches separated from the nutrient trunk of the tree of life

[668] Praetors (moneylenders), centurions, decurions, and quarteniers, (army officers) decemvirs (law makers), quaestors (public investigators), aediles (responsible for public order and maintenance of public buildings).

[669] Saint Isidore of Seville, (c. 560–636), a scholar and, for over three decades, Archbishop of Seville, is widely regarded as the last of the Fathers of the Church

the order of the ceremonies of the temple, counted the archiflamines,[670] the protoflamines, the flamines, and the priests, as will soon be said. There were also religious convent communities of men and women.

4. Among the Hebrews there also existed the same diversity of people; for some were secular, and others consecrated to divine worship in the temple. In the temple there was the high priest, like Melchizedek; the priests of an inferior Orders, the Levites; the Nethinim,[671] those who extinguished the lights; the exorcists, the doorkeepers and the elect or cantors.

---

[670] In ancient Roman religion a *flamine* was a priest assigned to one of fifteen deities

[671] Mentioned in the books of Ezra, Nehemiah and Chronicles the Nethinim were the servants or slaves entrusted by the priests with subordinate labours in the Temple of Jerusalem

IN HIS PREFACE TO BOOK THREE DURANDUS WRITES:

1. We must not use sacred vestments as usual garments, because, as we change our clothes according to the letter, so we must act according to the spirit. Therefore, we will not enter the Holy of Holies with the dirty clothes of the common life; but we must touch the sacraments of God with a pure conscience and chaste and consecrated clothing. Regarding this Pope Stephen decided that sacred clothing should be used only in ecclesiastical ceremonies and at the Offices celebrated in honour of God. Also Ezekiel said that they should not bless the people by wearing their vestments outside of the temple.[672] There is therefore one set of clothes for divine religion, for the Offices of the Church, and another for the ordinary use of life. The purpose of this is to show to all Christian people the example of a good life, and how, after having first washed away their defilements, they become new men in the eyes of Christ. Indeed, the priest strips off the old man by his deeds, and then puts on the new one, which was created according to God.[673] By the clothes also, which we use only to celebrate the holy mysteries, we mean that we must not reveal them all to the people.[674] It should be observed that in the time of Louis, Emperor, son of Charles the Great,[675] the bishops and clerics laid down their belts of gold, their exquisite, and the other ornaments of the age.

2. The sacred clothes seem to have been taken from the old law; for the Lord commanded Moses to make holy garments for

---

[672] See Ezekiel 44:19
[673] See Colossians 3:9-10
[674] There have always been many mysteries in the Christianity that have only been revealed to those who are spiritually prepared and ready to receive them. The *Divine Rationale* opens the door to some of these and, as found in the writings of the Fathers, points to others for those who have eyes to see. Jesus Himself (Matt 13:11, Luke 8:10) indicated that this was ever the case. There is a teaching which says that all is open and revealed within Christianity but this is true only in the sense that all teachings are *available* to anyone. There are many things which are not properly understood but this does not mean that a sound understanding of them does not exist
[675] Louis the Pious, 778–840

Aaron the priest and for his sons, to glorify Him and to honour Him,[676] so that after washing and putting on their vestments they should perform their work in the ceremonies.[677] The Lord also instructed Moses, for forty days, to make the pontifical and sacerdotal vestments for his priests and Levites, and also adornments for the linen clothes. Miriam wove and did what was to be used for ministry in the tabernacle of the Covenant; and Ecclesiasticus says, 'to the festivals he added beauty, etc.'[678] There are, however, vestments borrowed from the Apostles but these are those which mark the virtues of the virtues of the mystery of the Incarnation.

---

[676] See Exodus 28:2
[677] See Exodus 40:12-13
[678] Ecclesiasticus 47:12

IN HIS PREFACE TO BOOK FOUR DURANDUS WRITES:

1. Of all the mysteries (*sacramenta*) of the Church, it is agreed that the one which is of the greatest importance is the Office of the Mass which is celebrated on the most holy altar. This mystery is the feast of the Church in which the father kills the fatted calf to celebrate the return of His Son,[679] and where He offers the bread of life and wine mixed with wisdom.[680]

2. However, it is Christ himself who instituted the Office, when He concluded the New Testament,[681] by sharing His kingdom with His heirs, as His father had arranged with Him, so they eat and drink on His table in His kingdom.[682] It is for this that the Church has been consecrated. For, as they ate supper, Jesus took bread and giving thanks, blessed and broke it, and gave it to His disciples, saying, 'This is my body which is given for you: this do in remembrance of me.'[683] So the Apostles, formed by this teaching, began to frequently offer the most holy mystery for the reasons that Christ had expressly indicated. They keep the same form in the words and the same material in species[684] and as the Apostle says to the Corinthians, 'For I have received of the Lord that which also I delivered unto you, That the Lord Jesus the same night in which he was betrayed took bread: And when he had given thanks, he brake it, and said, Take, eat: this is my body, etc.'[685] Therefore, the Office of the Mass is more dignified and solemn than the rest of the Divine Offices. That is why we must speak of it in this Fourth Book before the other Offices. We will

---

[679] See Luke 15:23
[680] See Proverbs 9:1-2
[681] The New Testament is normally considered to end with the book of Revelation. However the *new testimony* or *new testament* which Jesus presented ended at the Last Supper.
[682] See Luke 22:29-30
[683] Luke 22:19
[684] Or in kind.
[685] 1 Corinthians 11:23-25

also consult the *Speculum* of Pope Innocent III,[686] with regards to some mysteries and some points which have been attacked by heretics.

---

[686] In office from 1198-1216

IN HIS PREFACE TO BOOK FIVE DURANDUS WRITES:

1. It is written in Exodus that the Lord said to Moses, 'And look that thou make them after their pattern, which was shewed thee in the mount.'[687] That is why we must conform ourselves to that heavenly Jerusalem which was commanded to praise the Lord, and which, as the Apostle says to the Galatians, 'But Jerusalem which is above…is the mother of us all,'[688] but above all, at all times, in praising God, according to these words, 'I have set watchmen upon thy walls, O Jerusalem, which shall never hold their peace day nor night.'[689] And in the Apocalypse it is said that the animals, 'rest not day and night, saying, Holy, holy, holy, etc.'[690] However, the Church Militant cannot completely imitate the Church Triumphant; for as it is read in the book of Wisdom, 'For the corruptible body is a load upon the soul.'[691] Therefore precluded in advance by our infirmity, we cannot, at every hour of the day, continually celebrate the divine praises, because it is necessary for man, from time to time, to supply the needs of the body, according to these words of Genesis, 'In the sweat of thy face shalt thou eat bread.'[692] That is why we do what we can, by praising God at certain hours of the natural day.

2. Therefore on returning from the captivity of Babylon the prophet Ezra taught the people of Israel to praise God four times during the night and four times during the day, so that man offered himself and his work to the Creator for a number of hours equal to the number of the four elements that make up his body. In this way he could fittingly offer his allegiance to God at the appropriate hours, that is to say during the night at Vespers,

---

[687] Exodus 25:40
[688] Galatians 4:26
[689] Isaiah 62:6
[690] Revelation 4:8
[691] Wisdom 9:15
[692] Genesis 3:19

Compline, and the Night Office,[693] then at daybreak following with Lauds and Matins, and then during the day, the hours of Prime, Terce, Sext, and None. Now, it is proved that Vespers, which is the start of all the Offices, and which, according to St Isidore, gets its name from, *vespera stella*, or the, 'evening star,' which appears at the approach of night, belongs to the night. But David said, 'Seven times a day do I praise thee,'[694] and then, 'At midnight I will rise to give thanks unto thee, etc.'[695] This order was approved by the Council of Agde,[696] and is preserved by the Holy Church, since the Night Office is sung in the middle of the night. The other seven Canonical Hours are said to be of the day, namely, Lauds and Matins, which are linked and said at dawn, then, Prime, Terce, Sext, None,[697] Vespers, and Compline. These seven hours are called 'Canonical,' as if they are said to be, 'regular,' because the holy Fathers regularly observed them

---

[693] For clarity, 'Night Office,' will indicate the Office held in the middle of the night and, 'night Offices,' will be used to refer to Vespers, Compline, the Night office, Lauds and Matins
[694] Psalm 110:164
[695] Psalm 119:62
[696] A.D. 506
[697] Prime, Terce, Sext, None, are Latin words which, respectively, mean First, Third, Sixth and Ninth

IN HIS PREFACE TO BOOK SIX DURANDUS WRITES:

1. In the preceding part of this work, which we now leave, we have treated of the Divine Offices in general; now we will take them in particular and show them in their diversity throughout the course of the year. Thus, we will review the Sunday services, a few week days, the solemnities of the Lord, and the fasts of the ember days;[698] we will see the agreement of the same Offices,[699] both those of the night and those of the Mass. We will not speak only of those of one church but will endeavour to treat the Offices of various churches. For the better understanding of this work, we will begin by considering the distinctions of time. The solar year includes the succession of the four seasons, that is to say, the winter season when the fields are sown, then spring when the seeds grow and elongate into spikes. Next comes the summer when the crops bleach and fall under the edge of the scythe and finally autumn, when the grain, separated from its envelope by the winnower, is put in reserve in the attics. Now the great year of the present life, which extends from the beginning of the centuries to the end of the world, is also measured by four different ages.

2. The first is an age of degeneration in the human race. It extends from Adam to Moses. At that time men gave up the worship of God, who is the true light, and they became idolaters, no longer preserving the shadow of the light of true doctrine. Of that time we read that, 'They are corrupt, they have done abominable works, there is none that doeth good.'[700] Then man abandons his Creator, and, addressing a rough stone, he says to it, 'You are my god.' This time of ignorance and blindness goes well with winter, where darkness reigns.

3. The second age is that of recall or renovation. It extends from Moses to the Nativity of Christ. At that time men are instructed,

---

[698] Four separate sets of three days within the same week, (more precisely, the Wednesday, Friday, and Saturday) roughly equidistant in the circuit of the year, that are set aside for fasting and prayer
[699] Services
[700] Psalm 14:1

by the law and the prophets, of the coming of Christ, the forgiveness of sins, and the love of one God. Then the Lord said to Israel, 'Hear, O Israel: The Lord our God is one Lord: And thou shalt love the Lord thy God with all thine heart, and with all thy soul, and with all thy might.'[701] So man then knew his duties to himself, to God, and to his neighbour. God, afterwards and for the same reason, raised up the prophets, so that their preaching might bring man back increasingly from his errors. This time coincides with spring, which possesses some light mingled with much darkness.

---

[701] Deuteronomy 6:4-5

IN HIS PREFACE TO BOOK SEVEN DURANDUS WRITES:

1. Having first spoken of the Divine Offices in general, the Sunday services and the Lord's festivities in particular, it is useful for us to add something about the Offices of the saints' festivities in this seventh book. Certainly, the Church celebrates the feasts of the saints for many reasons. First, so that we may reciprocate; for they themselves celebrate feasts concerning us, since the angels of God and the souls of the saints experience great joy in heaven, 'over one sinner that repenteth.'[702] Secondly, because by honouring them we do our own proper actions, for their feast is ours too, hence the Apostle says, 'all are yours; And ye are Christ's.'[703] Thirdly, that they may intercede in our favour, which comes from reading in the third book of Kings[704] that Beersheba, which by interpretation means, 'the well of satiety,' that is to say, the Church Triumphant, obtained the kingdom for her son. Fourth, so that we may imitate them, for their examples excite us to imitate them. Fifth, to increase our security and raise our hope. For if men, mortals like us, could have been brought up so high by their merits, we could rise in the same way; because, 'the Lord's hand is not shortened.'[705] Sixthly, to honour the divine majesty whom we honour in the saints, when we honour them, and when we proclaim admirable the One who sanctified them. Seventhly, so that at the sight of their beauty and purity man remains confounded, looking back at his own sins, and disdains the goods of the earth, as they did themselves.

2. The eighth and principal reason is that we recall the memory of the saints on the anniversary of their honour, for our own benefit, because in them we honour God. For, as they are perfectly happy, they do not need our prayers, since they have every wish; moreover, it is an insult to a martyr when one prays for him.

---

[702] Luke 15:7
[703] 1 Corinthians 3:22-23
[704] 1 Kings 1 First and Second Samuel are also called first and second books of Kings, First and second Kings then become third and fourth
[705] Isaiah 59:1

3. St John Damascene[706] provides other reasons why we must honour the saints, and also their bodies or relics. Among the reasons he gives, some relate to the dignity of these saints, others relate to the inestimable price of their bodies themselves. They are worthy of our veneration for four reasons; for they are the friends of God and the children of God, the heirs of God and guides to us. Regarding the first reason St John says, 'I call you not servants, etc.'[707] Regarding the second the same saint says, 'to them gave he power to become the sons of God.'[708] Regarding the third, the Apostle says, 'we are the children of God: And if children, then heirs; etc.'[709] Regarding the fourth, it is said, 'If anyone goes out of his way to find a guide who leads him to some mortal king and pleads his cause before this king, how much more must we not honour the guides of the human race, who intercede for us with God, erecting temples and venerating their memory?'

---

[706] St John of Damascus (Book 4, chap. 7)
[707] John 15:15
[708] John 1:12
[709] Romans 8:16-17

IN HIS PREFACE TO BOOK EIGHT DURANDUS WRITES:

1. Priests, as the Blessed Augustine says, are obliged to know the compute, otherwise they would hardly deserve the name of priests. Under this word 'compute' we understand the knowledge of the course of time, the moon and the calendar.

2. Now the compute is a science whose object is to make time known according to the course and the march of the sun and the moon. That is why, in this eighth and last book we shall say, in a clear and concise abstract, a few words of the compute, as we know it is in use in the Church, for the instruction of those priests who are ignorant.

3. The word, 'compute,' comes from 'computations', 'calculating', 'counting', not that in the compute we learn the art of calculating and counting, but because in the compute we proceed by calculating, by the knowledge of arithmetic, which is then both useful and necessary. There are two kinds of computes, namely, the astronomical or philosophical compute, and the vulgar or ecclesiastical compute, but nothing is said now of the astronomical compute. The vulgar compute is the knowledge whose object is to distinguish, or to divide time in a fixed or certain way, or the knowledge which divides time according to the use of the Church.

4. Time here is taken, according to Cicero, for a certain portion or quantity of the year, the month, the day, or some other period. Or again, it is the time or interval that variable things take to execute their movement and to provide their course.

www.ingramcontent.com/pod-product-compliance
Lightning Source LLC
Chambersburg PA
CBHW021357290426
44108CB00010B/286